THE PROBLEM PLAYS
OF SHAKESPEARE

THE
PROBLEM PLAYS
OF SHAKESPEARE

A Study of
Julius Caesar, Measure for Measure,
Antony and Cleopatra

by
ERNEST SCHANZER

SCHOCKEN BOOKS · NEW YORK

TO THE MEMORY
OF MY PARENTS

CONTENTS

CONTENTS

PREFACE

THIS BOOK has been written out of a feeling of acute dissatisfaction—which I share with many students of Shakespeare—with the common grouping together of *All's Well*, *Measure for Measure*, *Troilus and Cressida*, and sometimes *Hamlet*, as Shakespeare's Problem Plays. It seeks to define the term 'problem play' more narrowly and precisely than has been done in the past and to apply it to a largely different group of plays, which it seems to fit more adequately. *Measure for Measure* remains, but to it are added *Julius Caesar* and *Antony and Cleopatra*, to which the term has not, to my knowledge, been previously applied.

Each of the three plays is discussed in a separate chapter, which has been written in such a way that it can be read and understood by itself, without knowledge of the chapters that precede it.

With each of the plays I have discussed all those elements which seemed to me of importance and about which I felt I had something new and not irrelevant to say. The 'problem play' aspect is only one of these elements, and by no means always the one to which I have given most space.

I am most grateful to a number of scholars, who have read one or all of the chapters in manuscript, and from whose advice and criticism I have profited: Professor Adrien Bonjour, Dr. Hermann Fischer, Mrs. Shelagh Hunter, Dr. J. W. Lever, Mr. J. C. Maxwell, Mr. Brian Morris, Professor Kenneth Muir, Dr. F. W. Sternfeld and, above all, Miss Inga-Stina Ekeblad (Mrs. R. Ewbank), and Dr. G. K. Hunter.

My specific obligations to works of Shakespeare criticism I have tried to acknowledge as fully as possible in the course of the discussion.

Preface

All Shakespeare quotations follow the text of the *Tudor Shakespeare* (1951), edited by Peter Alexander.

Parts of the chapter on *Julius Caesar* have appeared in *ELH* (1955), in *Shakespeare Quarterly* (1955), in *Œuvres Complètes de Shakespeare*, vol. 4 (1958), and in the Introduction to *Shakespeare's Appian* (1956); and parts of the chapter on *Measure for Measure* in *Œuvres Complètes de Shakespeare*, vol. 5 (1959), and in *Shakespeare Survey* (1960). I wish to thank those responsible for permission to reprint this material in a revised form.

E. S.

INTRODUCTION

IT SEEMS that the first to have thought of grouping together *All's Well*, *Measure for Measure*, *Troilus and Cressida*, and *Hamlet*, and of calling them 'Shakespeare's Problem Plays', was F. S. Boas. In *Shakspere and his Predecessors* (1896) he wrote:

> All these dramas introduce us into highly artificial societies, whose civilization is ripe unto rottenness. Amidst such media abnormal conditions of brain and emotion are generated, and intricate cases of conscience demand a solution by unprecedented methods. Thus throughout these plays we move along dim untrodden paths, and at the close our feeling is neither of simple joy nor pain; we are excited, fascinated, perplexed, for the issues raised preclude a completely satisfactory outcome, even when, as in *All's Well* and *Measure for Measure*, the complications are outwardly adjusted in the fifth act. In *Troilus and Cressida* and *Hamlet* no such partial settlement of difficulties takes place, and we are left to interpret their enigmas as best we may. Dramas so singular in theme and temper cannot be strictly called comedies or tragedies. We may therefore borrow a convenient phrase from the theatre of to-day and class them together as Shakspere's problem-plays.
>
> (p. 345)

It is already implicit in this passage, and his subsequent discussion of each of the four plays makes abundantly clear, that the problems he finds in them are of the most diverse sorts. In *All's Well* and *Measure for Measure* they are moral problems: he speaks of their 'perplexing moral entanglements' (p. 409)—though it is difficult to see how this accords with his detailed discussion of the two plays, in which, on the contrary, he insists that the presentation of their moral issues is quite unequivocal and devoid of perplexity.[1] The problem he finds in *Hamlet* is psychological. Its protagonist 'remains a mystery, eternally

---

[1] For example, he declares that in *Measure for Measure* Shakespeare deliberately abstained from 'blurring the line between right and wrong' by not depicting Isabel as 'torn by the conflict between sisterly love and her ideal of duty' (p. 366).

fascinating, eternally inscrutable' (p. 389). The problem that he sees in *Troilus and Cressida*, on the other hand, is neither moral nor psychological, but rather one of interpreting so complex a play, above all of discovering the relation of the war-plot to the love-story (p. 370). It presents the reader with a problem in the sense of 'a difficulty' of understanding what Shakespeare was up to. And a further kind of problem which he finds in the four plays is one of classification. 'Dramas so singular in theme and temper cannot be strictly called comedies or tragedies.' But although he gives the most diverse meanings to the term 'problem play', he nowhere gives it the meaning it had in the theatre of his own time, from which he declares to have borrowed this 'convenient phrase': namely, a play dealing with problems confronting not a single and unique individual but contemporary society as a whole, as is the case with some of the drama of Ibsen and the early Shaw.

What chiefly unites the four plays for Boas is 'the atmosphere of obscurity which wraps' them and which 'closes most thickly round *Hamlet*' (p. 384). And he compares the change from this group to what he calls 'the tragedies in the stricter sense' to 'the passage from a valley swathed in folds of mist into a bare, storm-swept upland' (p. 409). On this upland one is surprised to encounter not only Macbeth and Lear, Othello and Coriolanus, but also the Queen of Egypt, though we are told that 'in *Antony and Cleopatra* and *Coriolanus* the dead-weight of historical material hampered the free movement of the tragic spirit' (pp. 409-10).

Although Boas's notion of what constitutes the Shakespearian problem play is, to borrow a convenient phrase from him, 'swathed in folds of mist', although it is undefined and muddled —or, dare one suggest, just because of these qualities—both his grouping and his label found very general acceptance in the decades that followed.

Thirty-five years later W. W. Lawrence published his *Shakespeare's Problem Comedies* (1931). He decided to exclude *Hamlet* from his discussion and to confine it to the other three plays in Boas's group, largely because he felt that the term 'problem play' is most usefully applied 'to those productions which clearly do not fall into the category of tragedy, and yet are too serious and analytic to fit the commonly accepted conception of comedy' (p. 5). 'Problem comedy', he declared, 'is a kind of bastard brother of tragedy' (p. 233). Lawrence's discussion has the great merit of containing a precise, clear, and, above all, an acceptable definition of what constitutes a problem play. 'The essential characteristic of a problem play, I take it, is that a perplexing and distressing complication in human life is presented in a spirit of high seriousness. This special treatment distinguishes such a play from other kinds of drama, in that the theme is handled so as to arouse not merely interest or excitement, or pity or amusement, but to probe the complicated interrelations of character and action, in a situation admitting of different ethical interpretations.' And he adds: 'The "problem" is not like one in mathematics, to which there is a single true solution, but is one of conduct, as to which there are no fixed and immutable laws. Often it cannot be reduced to any formula, any one question, since human life is too complex to be so neatly simplified' (p. 4).

Lawrence thus, very properly to my mind, confines the problem in these plays to the sphere of ethics. The crucial words in his definition I take to be 'in a situation admitting of different ethical interpretations'. But I am unable to see how this definition can be made to fit the three plays as Lawrence interprets them. For the main thesis of his book is that what may seem morally perplexing or ambiguous in these plays to our age would not have seemed so to an Elizabethan audience, that the situations in which their protagonists are placed do not, in fact, admit of 'different ethical interpretations'. This is especially true of his discussion of *All's Well*, with its insistence that Helena's actions conform to the common folk-tale motif of the Clever Wench fulfilling her seemingly impossible tasks, that an Elizabethan audience would have felt undivided sympathy and admiration for her, and that Shakespeare wanted us to respond in this simple and single way. I happen to agree with this view of *All's Well*. But I do not see how it can be made to square with Lawrence's definition of the Shakespearian problem play. And the same holds true, if less blatantly, of his discussion of *Measure for Measure* and *Troilus and Cressida*. His concept of the Problem Play and his view of the proper interpretation of the three plays he discusses under this label are irreconcilable, because they point in opposite directions.

Twenty years after Lawrence's book appeared E. M. W. Tillyard's *Shakespeare's Problem Plays* (1951). Tillyard followed Boas, not only in restoring *Hamlet* to the group but also in using the term Problem Play much more broadly and ambiguously than Lawrence had done. But, unlike Boas, Tillyard is very much aware of the vague and varied way in which he uses the term. For only by failing to define it, by making it mean different things for different plays, does he find himself able to use it at all as a descriptive label for the four plays he wishes to consider as a group. With engaging frankness he remarks:

> It is anything but a satisfactory term, and I wish I knew a better. All I can do now is to warn the reader that I use it vaguely and equivocally; as a matter of convenience. . . . To achieve the necessary elasticity and inclusiveness, consider the connotations of the parallel term 'problem child'.
>
> There are at least two kinds of problem child: first the genuinely abnormal child, whom no efforts will ever bring back to normality; and second the child who is interesting and complex rather than abnormal: apt indeed to be a problem for parents and teachers but destined to fulfilment in the larger scope of adult life. Now *All's Well* and *Measure for Measure* are like the first problem child: there is something radically schizophrenic about them. *Hamlet* and *Troilus and Cressida* are like the second problem child, full of interest and complexity but divided within themselves only in the eyes of those who have misjudged them. To put the difference in another way, *Hamlet* and *Troilus and Cressida* are problem plays because they deal with and display interesting problems; *All's Well* and *Measure for Measure* because they *are* problems.
>
> (pp. 1-2)

It is scarcely a very satisfactory state of affairs: on the one hand we have a descriptive label that is consciously equivocal (Tillyard) or that is misty and protean, changing its meaning with each of the plays to which it is applied (Boas); on the other a label which is clearly defined and usefully limited but does not accord with the critic's own interpretation of the plays to which it is fitted (Lawrence). Ought we, then, to get rid of the term altogether when talking of Shakespeare? I do not think so. For even if it were possible to do this—and it is notoriously difficult to kill off a term which has become generally current—I think it is too useful to be lightly given up. I propose, therefore, to follow the opposite procedure from that of Boas, Lawrence, and Tillyard: I shall look first for a satisfactory definition of the term and shall then consider which, if any, of Shakespeare's plays this definition fits.

I shall follow Lawrence in restricting it to moral problems, and exclude plays—if such there be—which primarily concern themselves with problems that are psychological, metaphysical, social, or political. For the usefulness of any grouping will be in direct proportion to its exclusiveness. The broader the definition, the more plays we include in the group, the less significant and illuminating will be the points of kinship between its members.

I shall begin by quoting an observation made by L. C. Knights. 'In *Macbeth*', he remarks, 'we are never in any doubt of our moral bearings. *Antony and Cleopatra*, on the other hand, embodies different and apparently irreconcilable evaluations of the central experience.'[1] It is a vital distinction and takes us a good part of the way towards our definition. In watching a problem play our predominant state of mind during at least part of the action is one of doubt of our moral bearings. But such doubt is not in itself enough to make it a problem play. For in watching the opposition between Patricians and Plebeians in *Coriolanus*, or the opposition between Eastcheap and Westminster in *Henry IV*, or the opposition between Shylock and his enemies in *The Merchant of Venice*, we frequently find ourselves in doubt of our moral bearings. What seems needed as well in a problem play is a concern with a central moral problem, which will inevitably take the form of an act of choice confronting the protagonist, and in relation to which we are in doubt of our moral bearings. In Hal's choice between Falstaff and the Lord Chief Justice,[2] in Coriolanus's choice between destroying and saving Rome, in Shylock's choice between taking and sparing Antonio's life, we experience no such doubts.

It is essential that this moral problem should be central to the play. In *King John*, for example, from Faulconbridge's light-hearted choice between Wealth and Honour at the play's

---

[1] *Some Shakespearean Themes* (1959), p. 144.
[2] This is elaborated in ch. 3, pp. 166-7.

opening to the rebellious nobles' tragic dilemma at its end, character after character is presented with a moral choice. It is, indeed, this series of confrontations with moral problems of varying degrees of perplexity—rather than the concern with Commodity, of which some critics have made far too much as the supposed unifying theme of *King John*—that seems to me above all to lend the play coherence and unity. Sometimes, as in the French King's need to choose which of two solemn oaths he should break (3.1.195-320), or in the need of the nobles to choose between the evil of making war upon their country, to 'march / Upon her gentle bosom, and fill up / Her enemies' ranks' (5.2.27-9) and the evil of enduring the rule of a wicked king, the act of choice takes the form of an intolerable moral dilemma. But even if the audience, in these and other cases, should feel in doubt of their moral bearings, none of these problems seems sufficiently central to *King John* to make one feel tempted to call it a problem play.

The moral issue must not only be central to the play but it must appear problematic to the audience rather than to any of the characters. The fact that Macbeth and Coriolanus both find themselves confronted with what appears to them a difficult and painful moral choice, and one which is central to the plays in which they appear, does not turn these into problem plays. For, however great our imaginative identification with the protagonists, *we* are never in doubt whether Macbeth should murder Duncan or whether Coriolanus should destroy Rome. There may, of course, be problem plays in which the moral issue appears problematic to both audience and protagonist. *Julius Caesar* is one of these. But there are others—*Measure for Measure*, as we shall see, is an instance—in which it is only the audience and not the protagonist who are in doubt of their moral bearings.

The definition of the Shakespearian problem play which I therefore suggest is: 'A play in which we find a concern with a moral problem which is central to it, presented in such a manner that we are unsure of our moral bearings, so that uncertain and divided responses to it in the minds of the audience are possible or even probable.'

It will be seen that my definition does not conflict with that of Lawrence, is, indeed, in essential agreement with it. It will also be noted that, in opposition to Boas, Lawrence, and Till-yard, I do not mark off the problem play from the comedies and tragedies as a separate type. What, to my mind, distinguishes the problem play is a particular mode of presenting moral problems and this can be found in Shakespeare's tragedies and comedies alike. As it happens, two of the dramas which I class as problem plays are tragedies, while one is a comedy.

Of the four plays that Boas and Tillyard have labelled problem plays, which can be accepted as coming under my definition?

Certainly not *All's Well*. For Helen's problem of fulfilling Bertram's tasks is not presented by Shakespeare as a moral problem (though he could easily have done so had he wished).[1] Neither is Helen anywhere shown to be uncertain of her moral bearings, nor are we, the audience, ever made to be so.[2] Helen's 'problem' can only be called such if we mean by it 'difficulty' rather than 'moral perplexity'.

In *Troilus and Cressida* I can find only one moral problem which is reasonably central to the play, that concerned with the return of Helen to the Greeks, as discussed in the Trojan council-scene (2.2.). And I do not think that we are made to experience here any real uncertainty in our moral bearings. Reason, common sense, compassion, the Law of Nature and of

[1] I do not share Lawrence's view that, writing for a public reared on traditional medieval tales, Shakespeare had his hands tied, that he 'was not free, as is a dramatist or novelist of today, to make such sweeping changes in the meaning of traditional stories' (pp. 68-9). At least one of Shakespeare's audiences—the young lawyers at the Inns of Court—would have 'delighted in clever perversions of familiar tales' as much as any audience of today. But even the audience at the Public Theatre must have displayed a far greater diversity of education, taste, and moral sensibility than Lawrence allows for.

[2] I am, of course, aware that many critics—though, ironically, neither Boas, nor Lawrence, nor Tillyard, who are chiefly responsible for the appearance of *All's Well* among the Problem Plays—have responded to Helena's actions throughout the play and especially to the 'bed-trick' in a divided or hostile manner. This is not the place to argue the matter, so that I can only express my conviction (which I share with Lawrence, though it is not gained by the same means) that Shakespeare wanted us to feel undivided sympathy and admiration for her and her actions throughout the play.

Nations, all of which call for the return of Helen and an end to the war, are opposed by Honour, i.e. the prestige and the military glory that is gained in keeping her and continuing the fighting. But even if we did not have all the rest of the play reinforcing and pressing home Hector's point of view against that of Troilus and Paris, even if the scene is considered in isolation, I do not think that Shakespeare leaves us confused or doubtful or divided in our response. He makes Troilus continually shift his ground, advance arguments that are muddled, bolstered up by analogies that are false. The only problem raised in this scene that may leave us in a state of doubt is not a moral but a metaphysical problem: What is value? Is it inherent in the object, as Hector maintains, or does it reside in the estimation put upon the object by the observer, as Troilus would have it? It is a problem that is ironically relevant to Troilus's relations with Cressida and his final tragic disillusion with her. And it is again taken up in Ulysses' speech to Achilles (3.3.95 ff.), where the imaginary 'strange fellow' is made to express Troilus's point of view, while Ulysses, for strategic reasons, adopts the position of Hector. But with whatever doubt or perplexity this problem may fill us, it is, I repeat, not a moral but a metaphysical problem and so does not help to bring *Troilus and Cressida* within our definition of the problem play.

And now, what of *Hamlet*? It puts before us, in the behaviour of its protagonist, a variety of psychological problems, but I find no evidence in it of a central moral problem. Indeed, it is the very absence of such a problem, of any suggestion that Hamlet's delay is prompted by moral scruples or that Shakespeare wished us to feel unsure or divided about the righteousness of the act of revenge, which is one of the most remarkable things about the play. It is true that critics have recurrently claimed that Hamlet's delay is to be explained by such moral scruples, whether these are thought to be conscious (as has recently again been argued by D. G. James[1]) or whether, more persuasively, it is maintained that Hamlet is himself unconscious of them but that Shakespeare's audience would have been aware of their hidden presence (as has recently been

---

[1] *The Dream of Learning* (1951), ch. 2.

argued by John Lawlor).[1] As both these versions of what he calls 'the conscience theory' have been very cogently refuted by A. C. Bradley,[2] I need not here repeat what seem to me the overwhelming arguments against them.

Of the four dramas that have been repeatedly classed together as problem plays it is only *Measure for Measure* which seems to fit our definition.[3] And it is joined by two other plays to which the term has not up to now been applied: *Julius Caesar* and *Antony and Cleopatra*. It is to a consideration of each of these three plays, grouped in their chronological order, that we must now turn.

We shall be concerned not only with what makes them problem plays but also with such questions as: what are their dominant themes and preoccupations? What gives unity and coherence to their diverse elements? How far are *Julius Caesar* and *Antony and Cleopatra* typical Shakespearian tragedies? In an attempt to answer these and other questions, discussions of a variety of matters, such as a play's character-problems, its structural pattern, its imagery, its relation to its sources and analogues as well as to other plays in the canon, will be introduced as the occasion demands.

---

[1] 'The Tragic Conflict in *Hamlet*', *R.E.S.*, N.S., vol. 1 (1950), pp. 97ff. Reprinted in *The Tragic Sense in Shakespeare* (1960), ch. 2.

[2] *Shakespearean Tragedy* (1904), pp. 97-100.

[3] But if we abandon the notion that *All's Well*, *Measure for Measure*, and *Troilus and Cressida* can be classed together as Problem Plays, is there anything to be said for treating them any longer as a separate group? It is a question which is not strictly relevant to the concerns of this book. Yet as it badly needs putting, it is discussed in an appendix (pp. 187-91).

I

JULIUS CAESAR

I

JULIUS CAESAR is one of Shakespeare's most controversial plays. Commentators have been quite unable to agree on who is its principal character or whether it has one; on whether it is a tragedy and, if so, of what kind; on whether Shakespeare wants us to consider the assassination as damnable or praiseworthy; while of all the chief characters in the play contradictory interpretations have been given. To illustrate this polarity of views it will be enough to quote two of its editors. Professor Dover Wilson tells us that in this play Shakespeare adopted what he claims to be the traditional Renaissance view of Caesar, derived from Lucan, which regarded him as 'a Roman Tamburlaine of illimitable ambition and ruthless irresistible genius; a monstrous tyrant who destroyed his country and ruined "the mightiest and most flourishing commonwealth that the world will ever see" '. The play's theme 'is the single one, liberty *versus* Tyranny'. The assassination is depicted as wholly laudable, the conspirators as unselfish champions of freedom, while Brutus's tragedy consists in his vain struggle against the destiny of Rome which lies in the establishment of Caesarism.[1]

When we turn to Sir Mark Hunter's interpretation of the play, we find that 'there can be no doubt that to Shakespeare's way of thinking, however much he extends sympathy to the perpetrators of the deed, the murder of Julius was the foulest crime in secular history'. Of Caesar we learn, 'when put to the test of the stage the personality of Julius "moves before us as something right royal", a character sufficiently great to render the impassioned eulogy of Antony and the calm tribute of Brutus not inconsistent with what we have actually heard and

[1] *Julius Caesar, New Shakespeare* edition (1949), pp. xx ff.

seen of the object of their praise'. Of the conspirators we are told, 'Brutus excepted, there is no sign anywhere that the enemies of the Dictator, though they have all the political catchwords at command—Liberty, Enfranchisement, etc.—care one jot for the welfare of any one outside their own order'. And of Brutus, 'Noble-hearted and sincere beyond question, Brutus is intellectually dishonest', he is self-righteous, pathetically inconsistent, a 'befogged and wholly mischievous politician'.[1] Thus, while Dover Wilson roots the play in the republican tradition of the Renaissance, which is overwhelmingly hostile to Caesar, Hunter, with equal confidence, places it in the popular medieval and Renaissance tradition, which is wholly eulogistic.

The reader of Shakespeare's play is consequently faced with a difficult choice. Is he to throw in his lot with Dover Wilson and Cassius, and regard Shakespeare's Caesar as a boastful tyrant, strutting blindly to his well-merited doom, and the assassination as a glorious act of liberation? Or is he to follow Mark Hunter and Mark Antony, and look at him as 'the noblest man / That ever lived in the tide of times', and at the assassination as a hideous crime? Fortunately for the irresolute there is a third way in which the play may be viewed and a third tradition in which it may be placed.

Perhaps more than any other figure in history, Julius Caesar has evoked a divided response in the minds of those who have written about him. Indeed, it would not be an exaggeration to say that such a response, made up of attraction and repulsion, admiration and hostility, was the prevailing one among informed and educated men throughout Antiquity, the Middle Ages, and the Renaissance, so that we can speak of it as forming a tradition extending from Caesar's own day down to that of Shakespeare. A brief outline of this tradition, with a closer look at those of its representatives with whom Shakespeare was certainly or probably acquainted, will help to place his own presentation of the Caesar story in its proper setting.[2]

---

[1] *Trans. Royal Soc. Lit.*, vol. 10 (1931), pp. 136 ff.

[2] For what follows I owe much to Friedrich Gundolf's *Caesar: Geschichte seines Ruhms* (1924), which traces the shifting images of Caesar throughout the ages. However erratic in parts, this is a work of great brilliance and penetration.

It begins with Cicero, in whom admiration for Caesar's splendid endowments and great achievements is joined with an abhorrence of his political aims and methods. The divided response resulting from this had the greatest influence on later writers, especially during the Renaissance.

Caesar's two ancient biographers, Plutarch and Suetonius, and the two ancient historians who dealt most extensively with the events of his life, Appian and Dio Cassius, all four preeminently exhibit a divided attitude towards him. And with all these except Dio Shakespeare seems to have been acquainted, though of his knowledge of Suetonius's *Divus Iulius* there is no conclusive evidence.

In Plutarch's attitude towards Caesar dislike and admiration mingle, much as with Cicero. The dislike comes out strongly already in the opening pages of his *Caesar*, when he tells us that 'Cicero, like a wise shipmaster that feareth the calmness of the sea, was the first man that, mistrusting his manner of dealing in the commonwealth, found out his craft and malice, which he cunningly cloaked under the habit of outward courtesy and familiarity' (pp. 5-6).[1] He makes it clear that for him Caesar's chief fault lay in his devouring ambition. In the *Marcus Antonius* he comments: 'But to say truly, nothing else moved him to make war with all the world as he did, but one self cause, which first procured Alexander and Cyrus also before him: to wit, an insatiable desire to reign, with a senseless covetousness to be the best man in the world' (pp. 9-10). And in the *Caesar* he tells us: 'But the chiefest cause that made him mortally hated was the covetous desire he had to be called king: which first gave the people just cause and next his secret enemies honest colour, to bear him ill will' (p. 90). He appears undecided whether Caesar's rule at any time deserved the name of tyranny, but his prevailing opinion is that it did not. In the 'Comparison of Dion with Brutus' he declares his belief that Caesar 'rather had the name and opinion only of a tyranne, than otherwise that he was so indeed. For there never followed any tyrannical or cruel act, but contrarily, it seemed that he was a merciful Physician, whom God had ordained of special grace to be Governor of the Empire of Rome, and to set all things again at

[1] All page references are to *Shakespeare's Plutarch*, ed. Tucker Brooke, 2 vols. (1909).

quiet stay, the which required the counsel and authority of an absolute Prince. And therefore the Romans were marvellous sorry for Caesar after he was slain, and afterwards would never pardon them that had slain him.'[1] This passage also gives fullest expression to Plutarch's view of Caesar as the Man of Destiny, and of the whole drama of his rise to power, his establishment of absolute rule, and of the defeat of his assassins at Philippi, as the work of Providence. It is voiced again in his *Brutus*, where, after pointing out how Brutus's cause was destroyed by his failing to receive in time the news of an important victory by sea, Plutarch comments: 'Howbeit the state of Rome (in my opinion) being now brought to that pass, that it could no more abide to be governed by many lords, but required one only absolute Governor, God, to prevent Brutus that it should not come to his government, kept this victory from his knowledge, though indeed it came but a little too late' (p. 182). He repeatedly emphasizes that it was Caesar's flatterers who were mainly responsible for making him hated, and he lays the blame above all at the door of his *bête noire*, Mark Antony. 'To conclude, Caesar's friends that governed under him were cause why they hated Caesar's government (which indeed in respect of himself was no less than a tyranny), by reason of the great insolencies and outrageous parts that were committed: amongst whom Antonius, that was of greatest power, and that also committed greatest faults, deserved most blame' (*Antonius*, pp. 10-11). This ill agrees with the picture of Caesar as the merciful physician. Yet, however divided in his attitude towards Caesar, Plutarch's prevailing opinion seems to have been that his offences were committed under the influence of bad friends and against his better nature and that, although his motives were unworthy, his influence upon the state of Rome was largely beneficial.

But all wavering, all contradictions cease when Plutarch turns to 'his angel', Brutus. Nothing can impair his admiration for him, not his repeated political and military blunders, nor his opposition to the will of God as Plutarch interprets it, nor the murder of his benefactor. This last charge he takes up in his 'Comparison of Dion with Brutus': 'Furthermore, the greatest reproach they could object against Brutus was that Julius

[1] *Tudor Translations*, ed. W. E. Henley, vol. 12, p. 237.

Caesar having saved his life, and pardoned all the prisoners also taken in battle, as many as he had made request for, taking him for his friend, and honouring him above all his other friends: Brutus notwithstanding had imbrued his hands in his blood.'[1] Yet even this is for him only a more signal demonstration of Brutus's virtue, a proof that he set the public good above the bonds of friendship. Even the greatness of the man he murdered is to Plutarch only a further sign of Brutus's courage and his 'marvelous noble mind' in killing a man of such great power and wisdom as Caesar.

His view of the other conspirators seems largely determined by a desire to show Brutus as the only just man among the wicked, coupled with a reluctance to accept the conclusion that he chose other than honest men for his associates. He is thus driven to alternate between blackening and whitewashing their character and motives. The assassination he calls 'this treason', 'their traitorous enterprise', and 'a devilish attempt'.[2]

In Suetonius we find an even less integrated agglomeration of eulogistic and opprobrious comments on Caesar. As a Swiss scholar puts it, 'Sueton moechte der historischen Wahrheit naeher kommen, indem er aus beiden Traditionen, der caesarischen und der republikanischen, die Nachrichten auswaehlt, ohne eine von ihnen zu bevorzugen, wie er glaubt'.[3] Thus, side by side with an account of Caesar as a consummate Machiavel, for ever secretly plotting to acquire greater power, filled with *hubris*, infamous as a sodomite and adulterer ('a woman for all men, and a man for all women'), plundering cities 'more often for bootie sake and pillage, than for any trespasse committed', we hear of his great eloquence, his painstaking administration of justice, his 'courtesie and tender respect' towards his friends, his gratitude towards his supporters, his sobriety in food and drink, and his great clemency towards his enemies. 'Howbeit', Suetonius comments, 'the rest of his deedes and words overweigh and depress his good parts downe: so as he might be thought both to have abused his soveraintie, and worthily to have been murthered.'[4]

[1] *Tudor Translations, op. cit.*, p. 238.   [2] *Caesar, op. cit.*, pp. 100, 101.

[3] Cordula Brutscher, *Analysen zu Suetons 'Divus Iulius'* (1958), p. 100.

[4] Suetonius, *History of Twelve Caesars*, transl. Holland, *Tudor Translations* (1899), vol. 1, p. 69.

Appian is more single-minded in his admiration of Caesar than either Plutarch or Suetonius. His divided attitude to the events which he reports seems to stem principally from a mingling of esteem for Brutus and Cassius, 'most noble and worthy *Romanes*, and but for one facte, euer folowed vertue' (p. 66),[1] and his abhorrence of this 'one facte', the murder of Caesar. After describing the estimation in which they were held, and listing their virtues, Appian comments: 'Yet by these men, the acte agaynst *Caesar* was done, contrary in all thyng, beyng no simple worke, nor in no small matter, for it was agaynst their freende, contrary to reason, and agaynst their well doer, vnthankfully, whom hee had saued in the warre, and agaynst the chiefe ruler, iniustly in the Senate house, and agaynst an holy man, hauying on an holy vesture: and suche an officer, as neuer was the lyke, so profitable to all menne and to his countrie and Empire. The whiche God did punishe in them, and many times gaue tokens of it' (pp. 67-8). About the motives of the conspirators Appian refuses to commit himself. He remarks that '*Brutus* and *Cassius*, eyther for enuye of his greatnesse, or for zeale of their countrey, kylled him in the Senate house, being most accepted to the people, and most expert in gouernement' (p. 8). With true scholarly caution he offers a long string of alternative motives for Brutus's part in the conspiracy. After describing Caesar's great affection for him and mentioning that he was thought by some to have been his son, he continues: 'But *Brutus* either as an ingrate man, or ignorant of his mothers faulte, or distrustfull, or ashamed, or very desirous of his countrys libertie, preferring it before all other things, or that he was descended of the auntient *Brutus*, that droue out the Kings: or that he was incensed and rebuked of the people . . .' (p. 16). He makes no mention anywhere of Cassius's cruelty and malpractices, nor does he follow Plutarch in contrasting his character with that of Brutus. To him both were equally 'noble and worthy *Romanes*'.

Like Plutarch, Appian sees the hand of God in the defeat and suicide of Brutus and Cassius, but for a different reason: Not in pursuit of the providential plan for the establishment of imperial

---

[1] Page references are throughout to *Shakespeare's Appian*, ed. Ernest Schanzer (1956), which reprints selections of the 1578 translation of the *Bella Civilia*.

rule, but in punishment of the multiple crime which they committed in slaying Caesar. It was this direct intervention of God, Appian declares, that made Cassius give way to despair without cause and kill himself, and that forced Brutus against his better judgement into a foolish and fatal battle (pp. 68-9).

The most perfect balance between Caesar's vices and virtues, above all between his *hubris* and his *clementia*, is kept, among the ancients, in Dio Cassius's account. Caesar's good and evil actions are carefully juxtaposed. He is shown to be gradually corrupted by the flatteries of his friends and enemies, who bear most of the blame. Of the assassination Dio writes: 'but a baleful frenzy which fell upon certain men through jealousy of his advancement and hatred of his preferment to themselves caused his death unlawfully, while it added a new name to the annals of infamy.'[1]

In considering medieval and Renaissance attitudes to Caesar, one must distinguish between the popular tradition, in which he figures as an image rather than a person, the first of the Emperors, the Mirror of Knighthood, one of the Nine Worthies, the World Conqueror[2]; and the response of educated men who had access to some of the ancient historians, biographers, and poets. Where in the popular tradition Caesar was extolled and his assassins execrated, educated men, both in the Middle Ages and the Renaissance, derived from their reading of the ancients a predominantly divided response. This is already notable in John of Salisbury's Mirror for Magistrates, the *Polycraticus* (1160), where a knowledge of Cicero, Lucan, and Suetonius, coupled with that of early Christian and medieval writers, has resulted in a wavering and mixed response, not dissimilar to Cicero's. In the *De Regimine Principum* (1270) of Thomas Aquinas we find, side by side, much as in Suetonius and Dio, the two opposed views of Caesar as the virtuous, just, and merciful Emperor and as the tyrannical usurper who richly deserved his death. As I have argued elsewhere,[3] even in Dante, who is commonly taken as a typical exponent of the medieval apotheosis of Caesar, we get glimpses of an essentially divided attitude, in spite of the fate allotted in the *Inferno* to Brutus and

[1] *Roman History*, transl. Cary (1916), Bk. 44.1.
[2] See Gundolf, *op. cit.*, ch. 2.
[3] 'Dante and Julius Caesar', *Medium Aevum*, vol. 24 (1955), pp. 20-2.

Cassius. Dante's divided attitude towards Caesar, as far as it can be inferred from the scant references to him in his works, seems to have been the reverse of Cicero's, stemming from an apparent lack of esteem for his personal qualities and an approval of his historic rôle in founding the Empire. His attitude seems closest to that of Plutarch, for with both writers what appears to be scant liking for Caesar as a man is coupled with a belief in him as the agent of Destiny, and with an enthusiastic admiration for the virtues of Cato of Utica.

The young Petrarch's divided response to Caesar is very similar to Cicero's and partly derived from it, resulting from admiration for Caesar's personal qualities and achievements and hatred of him as the destroyer of the Republic. But in addition to this we find a radical change of attitude in the course of the poet's life. As Dr. Hans Baron puts it, 'In the years when he had first conceived his *Africa*, and had been associated with Rienzo, he had given enthusiastic praise to the *Respublica Romana*, at the expense of the Emperors. In his old age, profound admiration for Caesar reigned once more supreme. . . . His growing interest in Caesar—whom in his youth he had considered the destroyer of Roman liberty—sprang largely from his conviction that Caesar was the prototype of those enlightened tyrants at whose courts Petrarch spent the second half of his life.'[1] In this opposition of attitudes towards Caesar between the young republican and the old courtier, Petrarch provides in his own person an epitome of the Caesar controversy that divided the humanists of the early Italian Renaissance. Dr. Baron has well brought out how closely this division between Caesar's detractors and admirers reflected that between civic humanists, mostly Florentine, and those attached to the courts of Princes. Thus, much as in Caesar's own day, the polemics concerned with him and his assassins formed part of the political struggle between republican and anti-republican forces. These polemics reached a climax in the prolonged controversy, beginning in 1435, between the Florentine Poggio Bracciolini and the Veronese humanist at the court at Ferrara, Guarino. But while this partisan controversy banished for a time any mixed response to the Caesar story among its most vocal participants, it inevitably reasserted itself among readers

[1] *The Crisis of the Early Italian Renaissance* (1955), vol. I, pp. 95-6.

of Plutarch and Suetonius, of Cicero, Appian, and Petrarch—
in other words, among all educated men. It makes its most
surprising appearance in Orlando Pescetti's *Cesare* (1594), for
this play was dedicated to Alfonso d'Este, whom, in his dedication, Pescetti compares to Caesar and claims as one of his
descendants. Yet it is Brutus who is treated, throughout the
play, with the greatest sympathy, while of Caesar we are given
a divided, though predominantly unsympathetic, picture, based
in the main on Lucan, Plutarch, Appian, and Muret.[1]

In France the tradition of a divided response is continued in
the Caesar plays of Muret (first publ. 1553) and Grévin (1558),
where, as H. M. Ayres has shown,[2] Plutarchian narrative and
Lucanic sentiments are presented in a Senecan mould, with
Caesar transformed into a Hercules-like braggart, but with his
Plutarchian stoicism and other noble qualities unimpaired.
MacCallum thus can speak of Muret's 'divided admiration for
Brutus and Caesar'.[3] And the same holds true of Garnier's
Cornélie (1574), which Shakespeare may have known in Thomas
Kyd's translation (1594).[4] Garnier, much as Plutarch, Sue-
tonius, and Dio, presents two antithetical images of Caesar.

[1] A strong case for Pescetti's *Cesare* as a source of Shakespeare's play has
been made by Alexander Boecker, *A Probable Source of Shakespeare's 'Julius
Caesar'* (1913). Some of the verbal echoes seem too close for coincidence.
For instance, the notion, put forward in both plays by Brutus, that Antony
should not be killed, for, once the head is off, the limbs are powerless

> (Col troncar della testa all'altre membra
> Troncasi ogni valore, ogni possanza . . .
>
> For he can do no more than Caesar's arm
> When Caesar's head is off . . .)

is too unusual to be accepted as a plausible coincidence. Therefore, unless
one assumes an English intermediary play that closely echoed Pescetti's,
I think we have to accept the notion that Shakespeare had looked at *Il
Cesare* in the Italian original. As Boecker points out, *Il Cesare* also provides
an interesting parallel to Shakespeare's play in that it is named after
Caesar, who, though constantly discussed, plays a subordinate part in the
action and only appears in two of the five acts, while Brutus is the central,
as well as the most sympathetic, character throughout.

[2] 'Shakespeare's *Julius Caesar* in the Light of some other Versions',
P.M.L.A., vol. 25 (1910), pp. 203 ff.

[3] *Shakespeare's Roman Plays* (1910), p. 27.

[4] See Joan Rees, '*Julius Caesar*—an Earlier Play, and an Interpretation',
M.L.R., vol. 50 (1955), pp. 135 ff.

Cassius (iv.1) depicts him as a usurping tyrant, who 'hath vnpeopled most part of the earth' by his 'bloody jarres'. This is followed by the Chorus of Caesar's friends, who see him as the great conqueror who brings peace to Rome, the merciful victor who '(abhorring blood) at last / Pardon'd all offences past.'[1] When Caesar appears on the stage (iv.2), he begins his speech as the vainglorious, boastful victor, but in conversation with Antony reveals his clemency, his trust in his friends, his Stoic contempt of death.

Montaigne's divided attitude is very similar to Cicero's, stemming from the keenest admiration for Caesar's personal qualities and the strongest abhorrence of his political pursuits. One sentence brings this out most pointedly: 'When I consider the incomparable greatnesse and unvaluable worth of his minde, I excuse Victorie, in that shee could not well give him over, in this most unjust and unnatural cause.' He speaks enthusiastically of Caesar's mildness and extraordinary clemency towards his enemies, and continues: 'Never was man, that shewed more moderation in his victorie, or more resolution in his adverse fortune. But all these noble inclinations, rich gifts, worthy qualities, were altered, smothered and eclipsed by this furious passion of ambition; by which he suffered himselfe to be so farre mis-led, that it may be well affirmed, she onely ruled the Sterne of all his actions. . . . To conclude, this only vice (in mine opinion) lost, and overthrew in him the fairest naturall and richest ingenuitie that ever was; and hath made his memorie abhominable to all honest mindes, insomuch as by the ruine of his countrey, and subversion of the mightiest state and most flourishing Common-wealth, that ever the world shall see, he went about to procure his glorie.'[2]

All the evidence suggests that in England, too, such a divided response was the prevailing one among educated men. It is found already in Sir Thomas Elyot's *Governour* (1531), a work which, as Mr. J. C. Maxwell has shown,[3] Shakespeare seems to have drawn on for at least one passage in *Julius Caesar*. Elyot speaks of 'this moste noble Cesar, unto whom in eloquence, doctrine, martiall prowesse, and gentilnesse, no prince may be

[1] I quote from Kyd's translation, *Works*, ed. Boas (1901).
[2] *Essays*, transl. Florio (1603), Bk. II, ch. 33.
[3] '*Julius Caesar* and Elyot's *Governour*', *N. & Q.*, vol. 201 (1956), p. 147.

comparid', 'the perfecte paterne of Industrie', 'nat so much honoured for his lernynge as he is for his diligence'. But 'beinge radicate in pride', he 'abandoned his naturall disposition, and as it were, being dronke with ouer moche welth, sought newe wayes howe to be aduaunced aboue the astate of mortall princes. Wherfore litle and litle he withdrewe from men his accustomed gentilnesse, becomyng more sturdy in langage, and straunge in countenance, than euer before had ben his usage ... wherby he so dyd alienate from hym the hartis of his most wise and assured adherentis, that, from that tyme forwarde, his life was to them tedious, and abhorring him as a monstre or commune enemie, they beinge knitte in a confederacy slewe hym sitting in the Senate'.[1]

In the account of his death by Caesar's ghost in the 1587 additions to *The Mirror for Magistrates* he sees himself successively as overthrown by cruel Fortune (ll. 319-20), as the victim of the envious conspirators 'that sude aloft to clime' (l. 329), and as killed in just revenge for his savage slaughter of his enemies.

> But sith my whole pretence was glory vayne,
> To haue renowne and rule aboue the rest,
> Without remorce of many thousands slayne,
> Which, for their owne defence, their warres addrest:
> I deeme therefore my stony harte and brest
> Receiu'd so many wounds for iust reuenge, they stood
> By iustice right of *Ioue*, the sacred sentence good,
> That who so slayes, hee payes the price, i[n] bloud for bloud.
>
> (ll. 401-8)

He alternates between praise and condemnation of his deeds. No wonder D. S. Brewer is moved to speak of 'the equivocal, not to say contradictory attitude to Caesar expressed by the writer in the *Mirror for Magistrates*'.[2]

Finally, the divided response at its most blatant is found in the anonymous play commonly called *Caesar's Revenge* (published in 1606 but, on stylistic evidence, placed by general

---

[1] *The Governour*, Everyman edition, pp. 101, 105, 133, 134.
[2] 'Brutus' Crime: A Footnote to *Julius Caesar*', *R.E.S.*, N.S., vol. 3 (1952), pp. 52-3.

consent in the nineties).[1] It seems based mainly on Appian, but, in its depiction of Caesar in its second half, clearly draws also a good deal on Lucan and on the Muret-Grévin tradition. In the early scenes Caesar is portrayed in a wholly sympathetic manner. On his first entry after Pharsalia he does not boast of his victory but weeps for the destruction caused by the civil broils, blaming his own ambition, which led him to inflict wounds on his mother, Rome. We next see him enamoured of Cleopatra, and weeping for Pompey's death. Brutus points to the dram of evil that douts Caesar's noble substance:

> To what a pitch would this mans vertues sore,
> Did not ambition clog his mounting fame.

> (ll. 210-11)[2]

And Cicero, who in this play is one of Caesar's sturdiest admirers and later one of his chief mourners, exclaims (much like the historical Cicero):

> *Caesar* although of high aspiring thoughtes,
> And vncontrould ambitious Maiesty,
> Yet is of nature faire and courteous.

> (ll. 1028-30)

Having given us in the first part of the play the fair, courteous Caesar, in its remainder we are shown Caesar's uncontrolled, ambitious Majesty, the Caesar of Muret and Grévin. He now

---

[1] In a note in *N. & Q.*, vol. 199 (1954), pp. 196-7, I have argued that this play was one of the sources of *Julius Caesar*. I feel no longer so confident of Shakespeare's knowledge of it. The fact that in both plays Brutus's evil spirit is turned into Caesar's ghost, which is sometimes mentioned as if it were the chief point of identity between the two plays, does not suggest indebtedness. For in North's translation of the *Caesar* we read of 'the ghost that appeared unto Brutus' and declared himself to be his 'ill angel' (*op. cit.*, pp. 106-7). A ghost and Brutus's ill angel? Most Elizabethans would have identified it as Caesar's ghost, come to seek revenge for his murder. But the appearance on the battle-field of Caesar's ghost in the company of Discord, who has come from the Underworld, so strikingly parallels Antony's prophecy about 'Caesar's spirit, ranging for revenge, / With Até by his side come hot from hell' that, joined with the other points of resemblance, it makes Shakespeare's knowledge of the play still seem probable to me. And the style of *Caesar's Revenge* to my mind rules out the possibility that it was the later play.

[2] Line references are to the Malone Society reprint of the play.

declares that he will 'leaue Heauen blind, my greatnes to admire' (l. 1216), that Alexander 'Must to my glory vayle his conquering crest' (l. 1267), and caps it all with the announcement,

> Of *Ioue* in Heauen, shall ruled bee the skie,
> The Earth of *Caesar*, with like Maiesty.

(ll. 1510-11)

In the eyes of his friends Caesar is 'faire vertues flowre / Crowned with eternall honor and renowne' (ll. 1841-2), while to the conspirators, who are shown to be inspired by genuine devotion to the commonwealth, he is a tyrant and the great enemy of Rome.

After the assassination we find Brutus stricken with guilt at having murdered his friend and benefactor. To put an end to his mental torments he implores Caesar's ghost to kill him (ll. 2316 ff.). And, oddly reversing the parental relationship, he compares himself to Althea, who murdered her son:

> *Althea* raueth for her murthered Sonne,
> And weepes the deed that she her-selfe hath done:
> And *Meleager* would thou liuedst againe,
> But death must expiate *Altheas* come [?staine].
> I, death the guerdon that my deeds deserue . . .

(ll. 2321-5)

And he slays himself, anticipating, much in the manner of Othello, an eternity of tortures in Hell (ll. 2516-25). Caesar's ghost, on the other hand, now glutted with the blood of his enemies, looks forward to his blissful abode in the Elysian fields.

> There with the mighty champions of old time,
> And great *Heroes* of the Goulden age,
> My dateless houres Ile spend in lasting ioy.

With these words the play ends. Dante's divine punishment has been combined with a divided attitude to Caesar and his assassins which is much like that of Appian and Dio.

I have traced this tradition of a complex and divided response to the Caesar story at such length in order to make clear that in all ages well-informed men have belonged to it and that it includes, with very few exceptions,[1] all writers on Caesar whom

[1] Lucan and Sallust are among these, the one wholly hostile towards Caesar, the other wholly laudatory.

Shakespeare is known or suspected to have read. A simple, undivided response, like that claimed by Dover Wilson, or, conversely, by Sir Mark Hunter, would thus constitute a surprising deviation by Shakespeare from almost all his known reading. But I do not wish to argue that the complex and divided attitude to the Caesar story found in Shakespeare's play is merely an accidental inheritance from his 'sources'. On the contrary, I believe, and hope to show, that, however much it may also be a reflection of what he had read and felt about the matter, it is used by him as a deliberate dramatic device.

II

It may well be that Shakespeare's own attitude to the Caesar story underwent a radical change as the result of his preparatory reading for *Julius Caesar*.[1] For the references to it in his earliest plays, above all the *Henry VI* trilogy, are wholly in accord with the popular medieval and Renaissance attitude.

> A far more glorious star thy soul will make
> Than Julius Caesar or bright—,

Bedford says of the dead Henry V (1 *Henry VI*, 1.1.55-6).

> They that stabb'd Caesar shed no blood at all,
> Did not offend, nor were not worthy blame,
> If this foul deed were by to equal it,

Queen Margaret exclaims at the murder of her son (3 *Henry VI*, 5.5.53-5).

> Great men oft die by vile bezonians:
> A Roman sworder and banditto slave
> Murder'd sweet Tully; Brutus' bastard hand
> Stabb'd Julius Caesar,

Suffolk tells his assassins (2 *Henry VI*, 4.1.134-7). Added to this we find the knowledge of Caesar as the writer of commentaries (2 *Henry VI*, 4.7.56-7), a man of learning and wit. In *Richard III* Prince Edward exclaims:

> That Julius Caesar was a famous man;
> With what his valour did enrich his wit,

---

[1] This has also been tentatively suggested by D. S. Brewer, *op. cit.*, p. 54.

His wit set down to make his valour live.
Death makes no conquest of this conqueror;
For now he lives in fame, though not in life.

(3.1.84-8)

After this the tone of the Caesar references becomes frequently
mocking and critical. Rosalind speaks of 'Caesar's thrasonical
brag of "I came, saw, and overcame" ' (*As You Like It*, 5.2.29);
Falstaff alludes to the same dictum by 'the hook-nos'd fellow
of Rome' (2 *Henry IV*, 4.3.41); and the Queen in *Cymbeline* also
calls it 'his brag' (3.1.23). And Cloten speaks of

Caesar's ambition—
Which swell'd so much that it did almost stretch
The sides o' th' world

(3.1.47-9).

But the references to Caesar and Brutus in the *Henry VI* plays
are chiefly of value in indicating what must have been the
attitude to the Caesar story of at least a considerable part of the
audience. If the majority of spectators had in fact felt that
the murderers of Caesar 'did not offend, nor were not worthy
blame', Queen Margaret's analogy would have been unhappily
chosen. In the same way Bedford's comparison would have
failed in its purpose unless a large part of the audience were in
sympathy with the apotheosis of Caesar. But there must have
been others present, readers of Plutarch and Lucan, who, a few
years later, could respond sympathetically to Shakespeare's
presentation of Brutus without the interference of preconceptions about his bastard hand that stabbed his friend and benefactor. And there must have been many others, those that knew
their Cicero and Suetonius, Petrarch and Montaigne, who were
divided and uncertain in their attitude. It is this variety and
division of views among his audience which, as it seems to me,
Shakespeare played upon.

With these points in mind, let us look, then, at his presentation of Caesar in this play. Its true nature will be most clearly
perceived if we follow it rapidly, scene by scene, from the play's
opening until Antony's funeral oration.

In Flavius and Marullus we get our first glimpse of the
Republican opposition to Caesar's rule. The metaphor which

Flavius uses to justify their 'disrobing' of Caesar's images strikes an ominous note.

> These growing feathers pluck'd from Caesar's wing
> Will make him fly an ordinary pitch,
> Who else would soar above the view of men,
> And keep us all in servile fearfulness.

It points forward to the image of the serpent's egg applied to Caesar in Brutus's soliloquy. There a more drastic operation is advocated, but in both cases the action is thought of as preventive, directed not against what Caesar is but what he may become if not checked in time. Both images probably have their genesis in a passage in Plutarch's *Caesar*, where his favourite equestrian metaphor is used to convey the same thought: 'But in fine, when they had thus given him the bridle to grow to this greatness, and that they could not then pull him back, though indeed in sight it would turn one day to the destruction of the whole state and commonwealth of Rome: too late they found, that there is not so little a beginning of anything, but continuance of time will soon make it strong, when through contempt there is no impediment to hinder the greatness.'[1]

Immediately upon Flavius's words Caesar makes his first appearance, and the imaginative impact of this short scene tends to bear out rather than to discredit Flavius's fears. With the utmost economy Shakespeare creates the atmosphere of an oriental court, with its cringing attendants and fawning favourites. 'Peace, ho! Caesar speaks.' 'When Caesar says "Do this", it is perform'd.' And into this atmosphere intrudes the first of many warnings that come ever thicker as the moment of the murder approaches, and like all the others it is contemptuously brushed aside by Caesar. 'He is a dreamer; let us leave him. Pass.'

From this slow-moving and portentous scene we pass at once to the rapid, feverish, and impassioned utterances of Cassius in his great seduction-scene. The contrast which he draws between Caesar's physical defects, which make him succumb in a swimming-match and shake when suffering from a fever-fit, and the greatness of the position he has come to occupy, is part of a general contrast, pervading the whole play, between

[1] *Op. cit.*, p. 5.

Caesar's frailties of body and the strength of his spirit, which has enabled him to become 'the foremost man of all the world'. Cassius is genuinely perplexed by this contrast. He is like a schoolboy who is puzzled and angry that someone whom he has always beaten at games should have become prefect and exact obedience from his physical equals and superiors.

> Now, in the names of all the gods at once,
> Upon what meat doth this our Caesar feed,
> That he is grown so great?

Contrary to his intention, he does not throw doubt on Caesar's courage but unwittingly testifies to it. It is the fever-fit that makes him shake, not the prospect of jumping into 'the troubled Tiber chafing with her shores'. The story of the swimming-match epitomizes the triumph of Caesar's 'spirit' over his physical frailties.

It is significant that in this crucial scene, where Cassius can be relied upon to make the most of the opposition's case against Caesar, he does not mention any specific acts of tyrannical behaviour. There is only the general assertion that Rome is 'groaning underneath this age's yoke'. But the yoke to Cassius lies in one man's usurpation of the honours and powers that previously belonged to many. To him it is therefore very much an existing reality, whereas to Brutus the threat lies not in present but in impending conditions.

> Brutus had rather be a villager
> Than to repute himself a son of Rome
> Under these hard conditions as this time
> Is like to lay upon us,

he tells Cassius (1.2.172-5). And in his soliloquy it is again not what Caesar *is* but what he may *become* that causes his fears.

What, then, is the effect of this scene upon our mental picture of Caesar? It heightens, rather than alters, our previous impression of him as an oriental monarch, a Colossus with clay feet, and begins the process, continuing through much of the play, of disjoining and contrasting the human and the super-human Caesar, the man with his physical and moral frailties and the God who is beyond all frailties. Caesar, by constantly putting himself outside the pale of humanity, collaborating, as

John Palmer so well puts it,[1] in his own deification, yet remind-
ing us of his weaknesses on each of his appearances, underlines
this dissociation. In the very next episode we find him angry at
the mob's opposition to his acceptance of the crown, afraid of
Cassius, yet assuring Antony,

> I rather tell thee what is to be fear'd
> Than what I fear; for always I am Caesar.

And at once follows the body-spirit contrast:

> Come on my right hand, for this ear is deaf,
> And tell me truly what thou think's of him.

> (1.2.213-14)

As Dover Wilson remarks,[2] the atmosphere is again that of an
oriental court. When Caesar is angry, 'all the rest look like a
chidden train'. In his remarks about Cassius we get our chief
glimpse of the Caesar we know from Plutarch, the shrewd
politician, the keen observer of men, the writer of the Commentaries.

In Casca's narration of the day's events a new Caesar is
revealed to us, again with Plutarchian traits; Caesar the play-
actor, skilfully exploiting the passions of the common people.
While his fall in the market-place is a kind of preview of his
later fall in the Capitol, his adroit play upon the feelings of the
plebs adumbrates Antony's manipulation of them in his funeral
oration. Casca's report ends on an ominous note, which for the
moment makes the worst fears of the enemies of Caesar seem
justified: 'Marullus and Flavius, for pulling scarfs off Caesars'
images, are put to silence.' Not deprived of their tribuneship,
as in Plutarch. Just the sinister 'put to silence'.

Up to this point Shakespeare has tipped the balance in favour
of the conspirators' views of Caesar and has made us share
Brutus's apprehensions. Now, by making Cassius, in his soliloquy, so frankly impugn the integrity of his own motives
and show so clearly the personal nature of his opposition,[3]
Shakespeare brings us to question the truth of our impressions
of Caesar, so many of which we have received through Cassius.
And our doubts are strengthened by the play's next image of

---

[1] *Political Characters of Shakespeare* (1945), p. 37.
[2] *Op. cit.*, p. 113.
[3] For a defence of this view of the soliloquy see pp. 40-41.

him, again drawn by Cassius, this time for the terror-stricken Casca. For Cassius's picture of Caesar and his explanation of the portents are clearly part of an *argumentum ad hominem*. Cassius himself is an Epicurean and does not, at least not yet, 'credit things that do presage'. But to convince Casca, who *does* credit them, of the monstrosity of Caesar's rule, he is quite ready to put them to use to prop up his arguments. Against Cassius's explanation of the omens we have been indirectly warned just before by Cicero:

> But men may construe things after their fashion,
> Clean from the purpose of the things themselves.

The groundwork of Cassius's indictment of Caesar here is much the same as in his scene with Brutus. There is again the contrast between what Caesar really is and what he has become, but what he has become is something rather different, fitting the altered circumstances. It is no longer a God or a Colossus who dwarfs his fellow-men and blocks the road to glory. This image of Caesar had seemed appropriate for Brutus, in whom Cassius is trying to awaken a feeling of thwarted ambition. But upon the terrified Casca it is above all a sense of the fearfulness of Caesar that he is trying to impress.

> Now could I, Casca, name to thee a man
> Most like this dreadful night;
> That thunders, lightens, opens graves, and roars
> As doth the lion in the Capitol;
> A man no mightier than thyself or me
> In personal action, yet prodigious grown,
> And fearful, as these strange eruptions are.
>
> (1.3.72-8)

(This is the Lucanic Caesar. Indeed memories of Book I of the *Pharsalia*, where Caesar is compared successively to thunder and lightning and to a roaring lion,[1] appear to have been active

---

[1] In Marlowe's translation of Book I (publ. 1600) the two passages read:
> So thunder which the wind teares from the cloudes,
> With cracke of riuen ayre and hideous sound
> Filling the world, leapes out and throwes forth fire,
> Affrights poore fearfull men, and blasts their eyes
> With ouerthwarting flames, and raging shoots

here, a point that seems to have been overlooked by commentators.) But while the picture of Caesar as a God and Colossus bore some resemblance to the reality of which we have been allowed a few glimpses, the Caesar that 'thunders, lightens, opens graves, and roars' is too obviously a fabrication of the moment to affect our conceptions of him. (The ironic fact that Caesar later seems to bear out this description by referring to himself as a lion, and Danger's elder twin-brother, does not alter this impression. For it is Caesar's most ludicrous utterance, and no more affrights us than Snug the joiner's impersonation of that 'fearful wildfowl'.)

Our image of Caesar receives its next modification in Brutus's soliloquy. His Caesar bears no resemblance either to Cassius's God and Colossus or to his roaring lion. He appears to Brutus in the image of a serpent's egg, someone yet harmless, but potentially mischievous. At the very moment when it is most in his interest to incriminate Caesar, his honesty forces him to declare,

> and to speak truth of Caesar,
> I have not known when his affections sway'd
> More than his reason.

But are we to take this as a valid view of Caesar? Or is it as mistaken as Brutus's view of Antony? His reference to Caesar's 'lowliness' suggests this, for it is absurdly out of accord with what we see of him in this play. Thus Shakespeare calls in doubt the validity of Brutus's image of Caesar, just as he calls in doubt that of Cassius's and Antony's image, so that the nature of the real Caesar remains an enigma.

Nor is this enigma dispelled by what we see of Caesar in the following scenes. Even in the privacy of his home he is strenuously engaged in the creation of the legendary figure. There is

---

Alongst the ayre and nought resisting it
Falls, and returnes, and shiuers where it lights.

(ll. 152-8)

Like to a Lyon of scortcht desart *Affricke*,
Who seeing hunters pauseth till fell wrath
And kingly rage increase, then hauing whiskt
His taile athwart his backe, and crest heau'd vp,
With iawes wide open ghastly roaring out . . .

(ll. 208-12)

never any real intimacy in his scene with Calpurnia, no momentary lifting of the mask in soliloquy or aside. Here and in the Capitol Shakespeare gives us above all the thrasonical Caesar, who sees himself as outside and above humanity. Only upon the arrival of the conspirators does he unbend a little, for the first and last time in the play. For his bearing here Shakespeare was, no doubt, drawing on Plutarch's description of the youthful Caesar. 'And the people loved him marvellously also, because of the courteous manner he had to speak to every man, and to use them gently, being more ceremonious therein than was looked for in one of his years. Furthermore, he ever kept a good board, and fared well at his table, and was very liberal besides.'[1] Plutarch's coupling of Caesar's hospitality with his courtesy probably suggested to Shakespeare his

> Good friends, go in and taste some wine with me;
> And we, like friends, will straightway go together.

But these lines also call up memories of the ceremonial sharing of wine before another betrayal, memories which are strengthened by the kiss which Brutus gives to Caesar in the Capitol ('I kiss thy hand, but not in flattery, Caesar'), and later by Antony's reproach of Brutus at Philippi:

> In your bad strokes, Brutus, you give good words;
> Witness the hole you made in Caesar's heart,
> Crying 'Long live! Hail, Caesar!'
>
> (5.1.30-32)

('And forthwith he came to Jesus, and said, Hail master; and kissed him.' *Matthew* xxvi, 49.)

We are next given another view of Caesar and the conspiracy in Artemidorus's

> My heart laments that virtue cannot live
> Out of the teeth of emulation.
> If thou read this, O Caesar, thou mayest live;
> If not, the fates with traitors do contrive.

Having engaged our sympathies for Caesar more fully than at any previous point in the play, Shakespeare loses little time to alienate them again, so that by the moment of the assassination

---

[1] *Caesar, op. cit.*, p. 5.

our antipathies are more strongly aroused than ever before. In his two short speeches in the Capitol Shakespeare gives us a compendium of his Caesar's most unamiable traits. He here speaks with the voice of the Angelo of *Measure for Measure*, rejecting, like him, a plea for the pardon of a brother by insisting on the rigour of the law and on his own separateness from common humanity.

> I must prevent thee, Cimber.
> These couchings and these lowly courtesies
> Might fire the blood of ordinary men,
> And turn pre-ordinance and first decree
> Into the law of children . . .
> Thy brother by decree is banished;
> If thou dost bend, and pray, and fawn for him,
> I spurn thee like a cur out of my way.

His next speech, like Othello's comparison of himself to the Pontic sea, is full of irony, both in view of the vacillation we have witnessed in his scene with Calpurnia, and of his impending fall.

> I could be well mov'd, if I were as you;
> If I could pray to move, prayers would move me;
> But I am constant as the northern star,
> Of whose true-fix'd and resting quality
> There is no fellow in the firmament.

A final ironic touch is added in his 'Hence! Wilt thou lift up Olympus?', which, juxtaposed with the immediately succeeding spectacle of his lifeless body lying at the foot of Pompey's statue, crystallizes the contrast between the corporeal and spiritual Caesar, which is summed up a little later by Antony's

> O mighty Caesar! dost thou lie so low?
> Are all thy conquests, glories, triumphs, spoils,
> Shrunk to this little measure?
>
> (3.1.149-51)

From Antony we now receive our last image of Caesar. His is the Caesar of popular tradition, the mighty conqueror, the Mirror of Knighthood, the noble Emperor. There is Caesar's nobility,

> Thou art the ruins of the noblest man
> That ever lived in the tide of times;

his fidelity,

> He was my friend, faithful and just to me;

his largesse,

> To every Roman citizen he gives,
> To every several man, seventy-five drachmas;

his military prowess,

> He hath brought many captives home to Rome;

his compassion,

> When that the poor have cried, Caesar hath wept.

Yet though we are not made to doubt the sincerity of Antony's tribute to Caesar in his soliloquy, the image of him created in the funeral oration is called into question by its forming part of his carefully contrived play upon the emotions of the *plebs*. Nor are we encouraged to put much trust in the judgement of the man who assures Caesar that Cassius is not dangerous but 'a noble Roman, and well given' (1.2.196-7).

Throughout the first half of the play, then, we are given a series of images of Caesar, none of which bear much mutual resemblance, though some of them are not irreconcilable. But doubt is thrown in one way or another on the validity of most of them. And to these Shakespeare adds his own presentation of Caesar, a presentation so enigmatic and unrevealing that none of the other images are really dispelled by it. It is a dramatic treatment of Caesar in the manner of Pirandello. 'Which of all these is the real Caesar?', Shakespeare seems to ask. And he takes care not to provide an answer. But does not Shakespeare further anticipate Pirandello by making us feel that perhaps there *is* no real Caesar, that he merely exists as a set of images in other men's minds and his own? For his Caesar is continuously engaged in what Pirandello calls *costruirsi*, 'building himself up', creating his own image of himself, until we are left to wonder whether a lifting of the mask would reveal any face at all.

In a sense, all that Shakespeare does is to dramatize the

views of Caesar and the conspirators which he found in his 'sources', and especially Plutarch, distributing what are the divided and contradictory responses of a single writer among several characters who take different sides, so that what is a mental conflict in Plutarch and others becomes a dramatic conflict in his play (Brutus alone exhibits a divided response to Caesar). Except for the much greater variety of views and the more enigmatic portrayal of Caesar himself, Shakespeare's procedure is not so very different from that found in *Cornélie* and *Caesar's Revenge*. What seems fundamentally different is the use to which this procedure is put by Shakespeare. So far from creating a fortuitous medley of attitudes to the Caesar story through the process of drawing on a number of divergent sources (as would seem to be the case with *Caesar's Revenge*), or merely endowing Caesar with certain characteristics in order to satisfy the anticipations of Elizabethan playgoers, as H. M. Ayres suggested,[1] Shakespeare seems to me to be playing on his audience's varied and divided views of Caesar, encouraging and discouraging in turn each man's preconceptions. And since on our view of Caesar depends, very largely, our judgement of the justifiability of the entire conspiracy, the whole drama is thus kept within the area of the problem play. For though, as it seems to me, Shakespeare makes abundantly clear the folly and the catastrophic consequences of the murder, he does not, I think, make clear its moral indefensibility. His enigmatic presentation of Caesar's character and motives allows responses like that of Dover Wilson to be formed. And I see no reason to doubt that there were people who shared these responses in Shakespeare's audience. In fact, the diversity of critical opinion on the main characters and on Shakespeare's

[1] His argument (*op. cit.*, pp. 225-6) that Shakespeare turned his Caesar into the vainglorious, hubristic figure of the French Senecan Caesar-plays, because that was what Elizabethan playgoers had come to expect, seems to me to have little foundation. Even if one were to accept this view of Shakespeare as a purveyor of the expected, we simply do not know what the stage-Caesar in the public theatres before Shakespeare's play was like. The French Senecan Caesar-plays and their imitations, like Pescetti's *Cesare*, were severely academic, and even *Caesar's Revenge*, written in the much more popular manner of Marlowe and Kyd, probably never reached the public stage, for on its title-page it is stated to have been 'Priuately acted by the Studentes of Trinity Colledge in Oxford'.

attitude to the conspiracy[1] bears witness to his success in making *Julius Caesar* a problem play. It is a problem play in much the same way as Ibsen's *Wild Duck*, which has a very similar theme: the tragic mischief created by the actions of a young idealist in fulfilment of the highest principles, partly through his utter blindness to what people really are like. In both cases the question is put to the audience: 'Was he morally justified in doing what he did?' And in both cases the dramatist's answer seems to me to be an insistent but not a compulsive 'No'.

The main purpose of Shakespeare's persistent dissociation of Caesar's body and spirit is, no doubt, to show up the foolishness and futility of the assassination. The whole second part of the play is an ironic comment on Brutus's

> We all stand up against the spirit of Caesar,
> And in the spirit of men there is no blood.
> O that we then could come by Caesar's spirit,
> And not dismember Caesar!
>
> (2.1.167-70)

What is involved in the last two acts is something more than a grim pun, which makes the conspirators find that, while they have dismembered Caesar's body, his spirit, i.e. his ghost, still walks abroad, and exacts his revenge. For the spirit of Caesar is also that legendary figure, that God and Colossus, whom

[1] Apart from the diametrically opposed views quoted at the beginning of the chapter, almost every intermediary shade of opinion has been expressed by commentators. The *via media* is trodden by those who hold, with Kittredge, that 'Shakespeare is no partisan in this tragedy. He sides neither with Caesar and his avengers nor with the party of Brutus and Cassius. The verdict, if there must be a verdict, he leaves to history' (ed. *Julius Caesar*, 1939, p. xix); and by those who claim that Shakespeare keeps our sympathy divided: e.g. by MacMillan, 'The poet's aim was to produce in the first part of the play an even balance in our sympathies, so that they should waver to and fro, inclining alternately to Caesar and the conspirators' (Arden ed. of *Julius Caesar*, 1902, p. xxv); by Wilson Knight, 'For the poet and the reader, like Brutus, see both sides of the question, and suffer a division of sympathy' (*The Wheel of Fire*, 1930, p. 151); and by Adrien Bonjour, 'It looks indeed as if Shakespeare wanted "to prove the moral value of suspended judgment". And before it is suspended, our judgment has been constantly questioned, shifted and revised; in fact, Shakespeare made of *Julius Caesar* the drama of divided sympathies. (*The Structure of 'Julius Caesar'*, 1958, p. 3.)

Cassius deplores, and whom Caesar seeks to impose upon the imagination of his countrymen. In this he is handicapped by frailties of body and character from which the murder frees him and allows the legendary Caesar to come into his own, assisted by Antony's rhetoric, just as Antony's military skill later assists that other 'spirit' of Caesar, his ghost, in executing his revenge.

That the spirit of Caesar in the sense of 'Caesarism', the absolute rule of a single man, informs the second part of the play, as many critics maintain, seems to me unsupported by anything in the text. Dover Wilson, for instance, writes: 'When Brutus exclaims

> We all stand up against the spirit of Caesar,

he sums up the play in one line. For the spirit of Caesar, which was the destiny of Rome, is the fate against which Brutus struggles in vain.'[1] And MacCallum, from a rather different standpoint, tells us that 'Shakespeare makes it abundantly clear that the rule of the single master-mind is the only admissible solution for the problems of the time.'[2] Both these critics seem to me to be reading Plutarch's view into Shakespeare's play. Nothing there suggests to me that Caesar is to be thought of as the Man of Destiny, or that the establishment of one man's rule is the inevitable outcome of the Civil Wars. As in Plutarch, who declares that the people 'could not abide the name of a king, detesting it as the utter destruction of their liberty', they are shown to be strongly opposed to Caesar's acceptance of the crown (1.2.241 ff.). Against this can only be set the people's shouts after Brutus's oration, 'Let him be Caesar', 'Caesar's better parts shall be crown'd in Brutus', but to take this as evidence of strong monarchic feelings in the *plebs* seems rather naïve. At Philippi it is not Caesarism or the providential scheme of Plutarch and Dante which defeats Brutus and Cassius, but their human flaws, which make Brutus give the word for attack too early, and make Cassius slay himself rashly, in premature despair. As far as the supernatural interferes in the affairs of men, it is Caesar's ghost rather than Destiny or the hand of

---

[1] *Op. cit.,* p. xxii.
[2] *Op. cit.,* p. 214.

God that contributes to the defeat of the conspirators.[1] Nor are we made to feel anywhere, as we are in Appian, that the Roman Republic has sunk into a state of disorder and corruption which only the establishment of one man's rule can cure.

III

Let us turn next to Shakespeare's treatment of the other main characters, Cassius, Antony, and, lastly, Brutus.

The first and fullest comment on Cassius is found in Caesar's description of him, which owes nothing to Plutarch.

> He reads much,
> He is a great observer, and he looks
> Quite through the deeds of men. He loves no plays,
> As thou dost, Antony; he hears no music.
> Seldom he smiles, and smiles in such a sort
> As if he mock'd himself, and scorn'd his spirit
> That could be mov'd to smile at anything.
> Such men as he be never at heart's ease
> While they behold a greater than themselves,
> And therefore are they very dangerous.
>
> (1.2.201-10)

It is a highly unattractive picture, and there seems no reason for questioning its truth. Fondness or dislike of music is always with Shakespeare a touchstone of character, and the comment that Cassius hears no music reminds one of Lorenzo's

> The man that hath no music in himself,
> Nor is not mov'd with concord of sweet sounds,
> Is fit for treasons, stratagems, and spoils;
> The motions of his spirit are dull as night,
> And his affections dark as Erebus.
> Let no such man be trusted
>
> (*Merchant of Venice*, 5.1.83-8)

[1] J. E. Phillips quite unjustifiably identifies Caesar's ghost with the spirit of Caesarism when he writes: 'The reaffirmation of the monarchic principle ... is substantiated by evidence in the play itself, particularly by that 'spirit of Caesarism' which, as many critics have observed, permeates the action of the whole play and is represented in dramatically concrete form by the ghost of Caesar. . . . This spirit which is "Thy evil spirit, Brutus", and which "walks abroad, and turns our swords In our own proper entrails" is the concept of unitary sovereignty.' (*The State in Shakespeare's Greek and Roman Plays*, 1940, pp. 187-8.)

and heightens the contrast between him and the 'well-tempered' Brutus with his love of music (4.3.254 ff.). Caesar's suggestions of the Machiavel in Cassius are borne out by his philosophy of self-dependence.

> Men at some time are masters of their fates:
> The fault, dear Brutus, is not in our stars,
> But in ourselves, that we are underlings.

Shakespeare's noblest characters generally affirm their belief in man's dependence on an ulterior power, while it is his villains, such as Iago and Edmund (*Othello*, 1.3.318 ff.; *Lear*, 1.2.112 ff.) who insist on men's mastery of their fates.

For Cassius's great seduction-scene Shakespeare had little in Plutarch to go on apart from the following passage: 'But Cassius being a choleric man, and hating Caesar privately, more than he did the tyranny openly, he incensed Brutus against him. It is also reported that Brutus could evil away with the tyranny, and that Cassius hated the tyrant, making many complaints for the injuries he had done him.'[1] And though Plutarch proceeds to discredit this distinction by telling us that 'Cassius even from his cradle could not abide any manner of tyrants', Shakespeare fastens upon it, and, by extending it, makes it the basis of his contrast of the two men throughout the play. Cassius is depicted as a person to whom abstractions, principles, generalities, mean little or nothing. Personal relations alone concern him; personal loves and enmities lie behind all his actions.[2] In his relations with Brutus he is swayed by a craving for affection which comes out in his first words in the play:

> Brutus, I do observe you now of late;
> I have not from your eyes that gentleness
> And show of love as I was wont to have.
> You bear too stubborn and too strange a hand
> Over your friend that loves you.

(1.2.32-36)

It is largely because of this that, in spite of his assumed rôle of the Machiavel, we never feel towards him as we do towards

---

[1] *Brutus*, *op. cit.*, p. 119.
[2] This is also emphasized by Wilson Knight in *The Imperial Theme* (1931), ch. 3.

Iago or Edmund. His attitude to Caesar is equally personal. 'Caesar doth bear me hard'. That is the core of his motivation. Added to this is the feeling that Caesar's greatness dwarfs his own achievements, and makes it impossible for him to gain glory and renown.

> Why, man, he doth bestride the narrow world
> Like a Colossus, and we petty men
> Walk under his huge legs, and peep about
> To find ourselves dishonourable graves.
>
> (1.2.135-8)

'Honour', a word which occupies the same central position in this play as does 'honesty' in *Othello*, means to him 'personal renown', whereas to Brutus 'honour' is gained by actions in accord with his high principles and of benefit to his fellow-men. It is of this kind of honour that Brutus speaks when he declares,

> If it be aught toward the general good,
> Set honour in one eye and death i' th' other,
> And I will look on both indifferently;
> For let the gods so speed me as I love
> The name of honour more than I fear death.
>
> (1.2.85-9)

'Well, honour is the subject of my story', Cassius replies. But it is his own kind of honour, that of personal renown, that is the subject of his story. Cassius, in fact, is not at all well fitted for the rôle of guileful seducer. In spite of Caesar's remark that 'He is a great observer, and he looks / Quite through the deeds of men', he suffers from the egoist's limitation of vision. He can understand people sufficiently like himself, such as Casca, and perceive the 'shrewd contriver' in Antony. But with a man whose mental landscape is so remote from his own as that of Brutus he is entirely adrift. Throughout this scene he tries to arouse in Brutus emotions towards Caesar identical with his own, feelings compounded of envy and resentment of Caesar's greatness, of thwarted ambition and neglected merit. He has clearly much in common with Milton's Satan. Both resent the dominion of one above them in authority, assert their equality with him, mask as a campaign for liberation what is essentially one for self-aggrandisement, and try in their seduction-scenes to arouse in their victims the same feelings that motivated their own rebellion. The various steps in Satan's temptation of Eve, his flattery of her to foster her sense of equality with 'the gods', to make her feel herself kept down, oppressed by a jealous tyrant, the doubts thrown on God's power, are all paralleled in Cassius's temptation of Brutus. Satan's temptation is, however, a much more subtly contrived affair. Cassius is genuinely perplexed about the causes of Caesar's rise to power, and guile is mixed throughout with passionate indignation and bewildered resentment. Most of his arguments seem misdirected, while he leaves unsaid all the things that could have moved Brutus. No reference is made to the welfare of the people. From first to last he treats Brutus as if he were another Cassius. In his pseudonymous letters he uses the same method to win over Brutus.

> I will this night,
> In several hands, in at his windows throw,
> As if they came from several citizens,
> Writings, all tending to the great opinion
> That Rome holds of his name; wherein obscurely
> Caesar's ambition shall be glanced at.
>
> (1.2.314-19)

In Plutarch we are told: 'But for Brutus, his friends and countrymen, both by divers procurements, and sundry rumours of the city, and by many bills also, did openly call and procure him to do that he did.'[1] By making Cassius the sole author of these 'divers procurements', and by showing him first plying Brutus and later enlisting the support of Casca, Shakespeare makes the conspiracy seem largely the work of a single man.

Our image of Cassius will be greatly affected by the way in which we interpret his soliloquy, since it is his only direct self-revelation in the play.

> Well, Brutus, thou art noble; yet, I see,
> Thy honourable metal may be wrought
> From that it is dispos'd. Therefore it is meet
> That noble minds keep ever with their likes;
> For who so firm that cannot be seduc'd?
> Caesar doth bear me hard; but he loves Brutus.
> If I were Brutus now and he were Cassius,
> He should not humour me.
>
> (1.2.307-14)

---

[1] *Brutus, op. cit.*, p. 120.

It is a pity that this all-important utterance should have been so ambiguously phrased that for two centuries commentators have been divided over its meaning. The chief crux is to be found in the last three lines. Johnson, Capell, Hunter, Mac-Millan, Furness, Dover Wilson, and others, all take 'He should not humour me' to refer back to Caesar, and consequently believe that

> yet, I see,
> Thy honourable metal may be wrought
> From that it is dispos'd

refers to Caesar's attempts to humour Brutus. Hunter and Wilson find their chief support for this view in a passage in Plutarch in which we are told that Cassius's friends dissuaded Brutus from becoming intimate with Caesar, 'and prayed him to beware of Caesar's sweet enticements, and to fly his tyrannical favours: the which they said Caesar gave him, not to honour his virtue but to weaken his constant mind, framing it to the bent of his bow'.[1]

The ambiguity of the lines makes it impossible to prove conclusively that this reading of the soliloquy is wrong. But the evidence against it seems to me overwhelming. On purely stylistic grounds there is the extreme awkwardness of the retrospective 'he', which Dover Wilson admits by suggesting to change 'Cassius' to 'Caesar'. But this only makes matters worse, for Brutus's hypothetical transformation into Caesar would be even more gratuitous and clumsy than his redundant transformation into Cassius, for which at least a parallel can be found in the similarly unnecessary, though less awkward, double exchange of identity in Antony's

> But were I Brutus,
> And Brutus Antony, there were an Antony . . .
>
> (3.2.226-7)

But there are much more serious objections to this reading than merely stylistic ones. The Cassius in Plutarch may have seen Brutus's honourable metal wrought by Caesar, but Shakespeare's Cassius has seen no such thing. But he *has* seen the at least partial success of his own labours (cf. Brutus's 'What you

---

[1] *Brutus, op. cit.,* p. 118.

would work me to, I have some aim'). The Plutarch passage, in which Caesar figures as the seducer, carries little weight. Shakespeare not infrequently picks up hints from Plutarch and applies them to a different character. For instance, Plutarch speaks of Antony's 'outrageous manner of railing he commonly used, mocking and flouting of every man'[1]. Shakespeare, it seems, took this over and made it characteristic not of Antony but of Casca. Again, Plutarch tells us of Brutus that 'by flattering of him a man could never obtain anything at his hands, nor make him do that which was unjust. Further, he thought it not meet for a man of calling and estimation to yield unto the requests and entreaties of a shameless and importunate suitor, requesting things unmeet: the which not withstanding some men do for shame, because they dare deny nothing.'[2] This seems to have suggested to Shakespeare Caesar's behaviour over Metellus Cimber's suit.

But what weighs most heavily against Johnson's exegesis is the evidence from character. Cassius's remark that if he were loved by Caesar he would not allow himself to be cajoled into plotting his death, that personal relations, not general principles, motivate him, is in full accord with all that we see of him in the play, whereas the reading of Johnson and his followers would involve him in an uncharacteristic piece of self-deception. And, as MacCallum points out,[3] the gibe at himself in 'therefore it is meet / That noble minds keep ever with their likes' is just in that vein of self-mockery and scorn which Caesar had observed to be characteristic of Cassius.

Plutarch could not quite make up his mind about Cassius's motives, sometimes declaring them to have been wholly selfish, at others discrediting that view. Shakespeare depicts him throughout as swayed by purely personal feelings. His presentation of the character really owes very little to Plutarch. Both the Machiavel and the loving friend in Cassius are his own inventions. Wanting to show Brutus as the victim of Cassius's machinations, he had to subordinate the loving friend to the Machiavel in the first part of the play. But in the last two acts Shakespeare could afford to dismiss the Machiavel altogether and to play up to the full the loving friend with his craving for

[1] *Antonius, op. cit.*, p. 36. [2] *Brutus, op. cit.*, p. 116.
[3] *Op. cit.*, p. 278.

affection, so that we become emotionally attuned to the final tributes paid over his dead body, by Titinius,

> The sun of Rome is set. Our day is gone
>
> (5.3.63)

and Brutus (closely following Plutarch):

> The last of all the Romans, fare thee well!
> It is impossible that ever Rome
> Should breed thy fellow.
>
> (5.3.99-101)

That, in spite of what we have seen of Cassius in the first part of the play, we should feel these tributes to be something other than ironic mockery is proof of Shakespeare's great skill in manipulating our emotions. He needs Cassius as a wily seducer and as a man guilty of malpractices (though he omits all mention of his cruelty, which Plutarch makes much of) in order to bring out Brutus's tragedy. But he also wants him as a loyal friend, who can inspire such love in his subordinates that they kill themselves in despair at his death. And he manages to combine the two into a single and consistent portrait by showing how personal passions, which inspire his love and hatred alike, underlie all that he does and says. Shakespeare wins our affections for him chiefly in the quarrel scene, the very scene in which he had to be shown guilty of malpractices. Here he reveals most fully Cassius's simple, essentially guileless, passionate nature, which makes him so little suited to the rôle of Machiavel, and shows his real genius to lie in friendship. He understands Brutus as little as ever. He cannot comprehend why there should be all this talk about justice and ideals, above all why their personal relations should be sacrificed to abstractions. He merely realizes that he is no longer loved by Brutus,

> Hated by one he loves; brav'd by his brother;
> Check'd like a bondman; all his faults observ'd,
> Set in a notebook, learn'd, and conn'd by rote,
> To cast into my teeth. O, I could weep
> My spirit from mine eyes!
>
> (4.3.95-9)

It is by such means that we are being prepared for the final tributes to Cassius on the battlefield.

Little needs be said about Mark Antony, since his character
and the superb skill and cunning of his funeral oration have
been well analysed by John Palmer in his perceptive discussion
of the play.[1] Unlike the Antony of *Antony and Cleopatra*,[2] who is
an entirely separate dramatic creation, the Antony of *Julius
Caesar* is not based on Plutarch's portrayal of him. Indeed, he
has scarcely a trait in common with Plutarch's, except a fondness for revelry, which is repeatedly alluded to (2.1.188-9;
2.2.116; 5.1.62). For all his most characteristic qualities, his
consummate histrionic powers, his great skill in manœuvring,
the mixture of emotionalism with Machiavellism, of loyalty
and devotion with ruthlessness and treachery, Shakespeare
could have got no hints from Plutarch's narrative. For these
qualities he seems to have received suggestions from the portrayal of Antony in Appian's *Roman History*, which, as I have
tried to show elsewhere,[3] he drew on for the writing of both
Julius Caesar and *Antony and Cleopatra*. Appian's Antony has just
the qualities which Shakespeare gives him. Again and again we
are told of his subtlety and guile, e.g. '*Antony* markyng all
thyngs deceytefully' (p. 29); '*Antonyes* sutteltie' (gloss, p. 29);
'Thus wrought *Antony* artificially' (p. 32). In his speech to his
military tribunes, in which he justifies his course of action since
the assassination, he reveals the great dexterity and cunning
with which he has ordered matters, commenting: 'for on the
one side, was neede of boldnesse vehemente, and on the other
dissimulation extreame' (p. 54). It is the rare combination of
these two qualities which marks the Antony of both Appian and
Julius Caesar. And both exhibit the same masterful showman-
ship. The funeral oration by Appian's Antony is above all a
great theatrical, almost an operatic, performance, and this is
precisely its quality in our play. Comparing the matter of the
two orations, MacCallum could find little to suggest indebtedness.[4] But it is in their manner that the kinship lies. 'When he
had saide thus, he pulled vp his gowne lyke a man beside hym-
selfe, and gyrded it, that he might the better stirre his handes:
he stoode ouer the Litter, as from a Tabernacle, looking into it,
and opening it, and firste sang his Himne, as to a God in
heauen. . . . And when he had made these and many other

---

[1] *Op. cit.*, pp. 16 ff.   [2] See pp. 141-2.
[3] *Shakespeare's Appian*, pp. xix-xxviii.   [4] *Op. cit.*, p. 647.

inuocations, he tourned hys voice from triumphe to mourning matter, and began to lament and mone him as a friend that had bin vniustly vsed, and did desire that he might giue hys soule for *Caesars'* (pp. 43-4). It is not only of the funeral oration in Shakespeare's play that these passages remind us in their emotional colouring, but also of Antony's first speeches to the conspirators after the assassination.

Plutarch notes that Antony 'used a manner of phrase in his speech, called Asiatic, which carried the best grace and estimation at that time, and was much like to his manners and life: for it was full of ostentation, foolish bravery, and vain ambition.'[1] Shakespeare does not altogether ignore this, but endows his Antony with an extreme simplicity of speech, which, especially in the funeral oration, has about it a strong Counter-reformation flavour, with its loving and detailed dwelling on wounds and tears, and the sensuous naïveté of the conceits:

> Over thy wounds now do I prophesy—
> Which like dumb mouths do ope their ruby lips
> To beg the voice and utterance of my tongue . . .

> I tell you that which you yourselves do know;
> Show you sweet Caesar's wounds, poor, poor dumb mouths,
> And bid them speak for me . . .

> Through this the well-beloved Brutus stabb'd,
> And as he pluck'd his cursed steel away,
> Mark how the blood of Caesar follow'd it,
> As rushing out of doors, to be resolv'd
> If Brutus so unkindly knock'd or no . . .

Antony exhibits that same polarity, that combination of opposite qualities, which marks Brutus and Cassius. The Antony who sheds tears over Caesar's body is as far removed from the Antony of the proscription-scene as is the Cassius of the soliloquy (1.2.307 ff.) from the Cassius of the quarrel-scene, or the Brutus in the scenes with Lucius from the Brutus who upbraids Cassius. There is in all three that same combination of almost feminine tenderness with hardness which, in spite of the great differences of character that make them such good

---

[1] *Antonius, op. cit.*, p. 3.

foils of each other, provides a link between them, and helps to bring out the special flavour of the play. For although, as J. I. M. Stewart says, 'primarily, this is a direct and manly play; and one filled with straight talk,'[1] it is also a rather feminine play,[2] full of indirection, and filled with talk which is anything but straight.

The opposition between the two Cascas found in the play, on the other hand, cannot be explained as another example of such polarity. Antony, Brutus, and Cassius remain coherent and persuasive dramatic creations, while no psychologizing, however ingenious, can make a single stage-character out of the two Cascas. For not only are the Casca of the Lupercal-scene (1.2.215 ff.) and the Casca of the storm-scene (1.3) wholly opposed in character and outlook, but, what is even more fatal to their dramatic unity, they are also wholly opposed in idiom. It seems to me quite inconceivable that Shakespeare could have created the highly idiosyncratic, vital prose-idiom of the Casca of the Lupercal-scene and at none of his subsequent appearances have allowed him to utter a sentence that recalled it. Coleridge's attempt to explain the puzzle by suggesting that 'for want of actors the part of some other conspirator was thrown into Casca's',[3] is very implausible, since only extreme incompetence could have made anyone assign the part of the unknown conspirator to the highly individualized Casca, rather than to any of the several conspirators who are mere shadows. More persuasive is Dover Wilson's suggestion that 1.2.215-93 is 'a piece of re-writing or a later addition'.[4] I think, however, that a more probable explanation can be found in the assumption that Shakespeare wrote the Lupercal-scene after he had already written the other scenes in which Casca appears (there are no good grounds for thinking that Shakespeare always began by writing the opening scene, and so went on through the play). When he came to Casca's description of the offer of the crown

---

[1] *Character and Motive in Shakespeare* (1949), p. 50. This is one of the best discussions of the play known to me.

[2] 'The whole', declares Wilson Knight, 'is suffused with a soft emotionalism.' 'No play of Shakespeare concentrates more on "emotion", "heart", "love" ' (*The Imperial Theme*, pp. 44, 61).

[3] *Coleridge's Shakespeare Criticism*, ed. T. M. Raysor (1930), vol. 1, p. 15.

[4] *Op. cit.*, p. 97.

he realized the effectiveness of turning him into a blunt, mocking fellow, and did not trouble to bring his speeches that he had already written into conformity with the new conception. This hypothesis would also explain why in the storm-scene Cassius approaches Casca so cautiously, though in the previous scene the latter had made no secret of his loathing for Caesar. The process of character-creation here would then parallel that found in the case of Mercutio, where again the blunt, coarse jester and railer, whose natural medium of speech is prose, only gradually emerges in the course of creation, while there are few hints of him on Mercutio's first appearance. It is thus that I would account for the divergence between his earliest speeches and his later utterances. In this connection it is significant that for the characterization of none of his outspoken, blunt railers, his Mercutio, Casca, Enobarbus, Kent (none, in fact, except Faulconbridge), did Shakespeare receive any hints from his sources, a circumstance which lends support to the notion that in the case of Mercutio and Casca the outlines of their character only suggested themselves to the playwright in the course of composition, through the requirements of a particular dramatic situation.[1]

IV

Finally, let us take a look at Brutus and the nature of his tragedy. While Shakespeare's Caesar, Cassius, and Antony owe little to their prototypes in Plutarch, his Brutus is substantially Plutarch's Brutus. Yet, even here, for all that makes him a dramatic character as distinct from a copy-book hero, his divided mind, his self-deception, his final tragic disillusion, Shakespeare received no hints from Plutarch.

It is a mistake to see Brutus as the unwordly scholar, blind to political realities, devoid of a knowledge of life, called from his books to assume a task for which he was not fitted. This view was dear to Romantic critics, who liked to present this phantom Brutus as Shakespeare's first sketch in preparation for their phantom Hamlet. Shakespeare depicts Brutus as a bad judge of character, but as by no means devoid of political

---

[1] A similar claim has been made for Shakespeare's creation of Ancient Pistol. See S. Musgrove, 'The Birth of Pistol', *R.E.S.*, N.S., vol. 10, p. 56.

shrewdness and practical wisdom.[1] For instance, in Plutarch it is Antony who suggests that Caesar's 'body should be honourably buried, and not in hugger mugger, lest the people might thereby take occasion to be worse offended if they did otherwise'.[2] Shakespeare transfers the argument to Brutus, making him declare:

> What Antony shall speak, I will protest
> He speaks by leave and by permission;
> And that we are contented Caesar shall
> Have all true rites and lawful ceremonies.
> It shall advantage more than do us wrong.
>
> (3.1.239-43)

That Shakespeare regarded the argument as by no means 'fatuous', as one commentator calls it, but as shrewd, practical politics is shown by his putting a variation of it a year or two later into the mouth of his arch-politician Claudius:

> the people muddied,
> Thick and unwholesome in their thoughts and whispers
> For good Polonius' death; and we have done but greenly
> In hugger-mugger to inter him.
>
> (*Hamlet*, 4.5.78-81)

(The 'hugger-mugger' suggests that Shakespeare had that very passage from Plutarch at the back of his mind when writing these lines, a striking example of how North's more vivid idioms were garnered up in the poet's memory, to be brought out when some similarity of situation recalled them.) Brutus's advice is in itself sound enough and would have justified itself with anyone but Antony, whom he so fatally misjudges.

Again, I cannot agree with commentators who speak of Brutus's oration as an example of his political naïveté, of the scholar's inability to understand the common people or to present his case effectually. It seems to me, on the contrary, an extremely shrewd and highly effective piece of oratory. In his soliloquy Brutus could find nothing with which to reproach Caesar except his desire for the crown. The murder is in his eyes

---

[1] This combination is not unique in the play. It is found again in Antony: witness his remark about Cassius (1. 2.196-7).

[2] *Brutus, op. cit.*, pp. 136-7.

purely preventive, designed to protect the commonwealth from the kind of person Caesar is likely to become upon the acquisition of greater power. To win the support of a mob clamouring for satisfaction with no better arguments to justify the murder of their hero is clearly no simple matter. How does Brutus achieve it? He begins by subtly, unobtrusively, flattering his audience. The very fact that he does not talk down to them, will not speak their language, as Antony does, is a compliment to their intelligence. And even if they cannot quite follow him in his clipped, carefully patterned sentences, they can at least make out that the noble Brutus asks them to respect his honour, to censure him in their wisdom, to be his judges. Nothing could be more flattering except his next suggestion, that among them there may be a dear friend of Caesar's. Then comes the assertion, true as we know it to be, but therefore none the less effective, that only a superior love of his country made him slay his dearest friend. Still no charge has been brought against Caesar. Then suddenly the question is sprung on them: 'Had you rather Caesar were living, and die all slaves, than that Caesar were dead, to live all free men?' That the alternative may be quite unreal will not occur to the people under the influence of Brutus's oratory. At last an accusation is made, but one of the vaguest kind: Caesar was ambitious. And at once, before they have time to ask for evidence, there follows the series of rhetorical questions which so ingeniously forestall any objections from his audience:

> Who is here so base that would be a bondman? If any, speak; for him have I offended. Who is here so rude that would not be a Roman? If any, speak; for him have I offended. Who is here so vile that will not love his country? If any, speak; for him have I offended. I pause for a reply.

Nothing could be more skilful. He has brought only the vaguest charge against Caesar and yet effectively blocked all further questions from the crowd, shown himself the saviour of his country, and gained the love and admiration of the people. The speech is kept as short as possible, so that detailed accusations would seem out of place, and, in closing, he hurriedly refers the people for facts to the records in the Capitol, with a final display of fairmindedness:

The question of his death is enroll'd in the Capitol; his glory not extenuated wherein he was worthy; nor his offences enforc'd, for which he suffered death.

Brutus ends with a parting glance at the benefits the people will derive from Caesar's death, and with an expression of his willingness to die for his country. The whole speech is as shrewdly contrived and, as the response of the people shows, quite as effective as Antony's. And Brutus has the far more difficult task: that of defending the murder of 'the foremost man of all this world' on a charge which he cannot substantiate. All that Antony needs to do is to discredit the allegation of Caesar's ambition in order to nullify Brutus's entire argument. The fact that all that Brutus says no doubt appears to him strictly true and is sincerely felt in no way lessens the great skill of the speech.

At other times, too, in the play Brutus does not show himself devoid of practical wisdom. The reasons he gives for marching to Philippi may be mistaken, but they certainly show no lack of an eye for the expedient and politic. Altogether, I think we must banish the myth of the unpractical dreamer from our image of Shakespeare's Brutus.[1]

It would seem that just as in Hamlet Shakespeare wished to represent the Renaissance ideal of the encyclopaedic man, the 'uomo universale', in Brutus he wished to represent the ideal of the harmonious man, whose gentleness, courtesy, and love of music all bear witness to his 'well-tempered' nature. It is to this quality in him that Antony pays his final tribute:

> His life was gentle; and the elements
> So mix'd in him that Nature might stand up
> And say to all the world 'This was a man!'

Yet both Hamlet and Brutus are depicted from their first appearance as wrenched from their ordinary selves, steeped in melancholy, so that their normal nature is largely veiled from

---

[1] In this view of Brutus I am supported by Brents Stirling (*Unity in Shakespearian Tragedy*, 1956, p. 47); by Adrien Bonjour (*op. cit.*, p. 20); and above all by Maria Wickert, who, in a valuable article, provides further evidence against the view that Shakespeare wanted us to regard Brutus's oration as deficient in skill ('Antikes Gedankengut in Shakespeares *Julius Caesar*', *Shakespeare-Jahrbuch*, vol. 82/83, 1948, pp. 10-24).

us, and is glimpsed chiefly through the tribute of others, an Antony or an Ophelia. Brutus, the harmonious man, is ironically shown to us throughout the first half of the play as rent by discordant emotions, and later, in the quarrel-scene, 'like sweet bells jangled, out of tune and harsh'. Of the civil war in Brutus, resulting from the conflict between personal and public loyalties, we learn upon his first appearance, when he speaks to Cassius of 'poor Brutus with himself at war', and of his being vexed of late 'with passions of some difference' (i.e. with conflicting emotions). It is echoed and amplified by the tempests that precede the assassination and which appear to Casca to spring from 'civil strife in heaven' (1.3.11). And finally, in fulfilment of Antony's terrible prophecy, the civil war spreads from microcosm and macrocosm to the body politic, finding its culmination at Philippi and its reflection even in the quarrel-scene. Brutus's inner struggle continues until the assassination, taking on a nightmare quality, and somewhat altering its nature. For while the earlier struggle seems caused mainly by rival loyalties, by warring principles, after Brutus's decision to murder Caesar is reached it is the deed itself, now revealed to his imagination in all its stark horror, that causes his feelings to rebel against the decision which his intellect has made. This, I take it, is the meaning of the much disputed

> Between the acting of a dreadful thing
> And the first motion, all the interim is
> Like a phantasma or a hideous dream.
> The Genius and the mortal instruments
> Are then in council; and the state of man,
> Like to a little kingdom, suffers then
> The nature of an insurrection.

(2.1.63-9)

While his mind considers the various possible ways of carrying out the murder (pictured as a council meeting between man's presiding genius, his intellect, and the mortal instruments, the means of bringing about the death), his instincts and passions are in revolt against the decision of their ruler. Insurrection has taken the place of Civil War within him. His gentle, frank, and generous nature is in revolt not only against the deed itself, but against the whole conspiracy, with all the secrecy and deceitfulness it entails. This is how he greets the announcement of the arrival of his fellow-conspirators:

> They are the faction. O conspiracy,
> Sham'st thou to show thy dang'rous brow by night,
> When evils are most free? O, then by day
> Where wilt thou find a cavern dark enough
> To mask thy monstrous visage? Seek none, conspiracy;
> Hide it in smiles and affability!
> For if thou path, thy native semblance on,
> Not Erebus itself were dim enough
> To hide thee from prevention.

To save himself from these nightmare realizations he plunges headlong into self-delusion. In his soliloquy he had acquitted Caesar of any kind of tyrannical behaviour:

> and to speak truth of Caesar,
> I have not known when his affections sway'd
> More than his reason.

A little later, in the company of the conspirators, he tries to persuade himself that Caesar is already a full-blown tryant.[1]

> No, not an oath. If not the face of men,
> The sufferance of our souls, the time's abuse,
> If these be motives weak, break off betimes,
> And every man hence to his idle bed.
> So let high-sighted tyranny range on,
> Till each man drop by lottery.

(2.1.114-19)

Caesar here is no longer the serpent's egg of Brutus's soliloquy, nor Flavius's young hawk whose growing feathers must be plucked betimes (1.1.73-6), but a full-grown falcon, scouring for prey. Plutarch, as we saw, could not make up his mind whether Caesar at the end of his life was a tyrant or not, asserting now the one and then the other. Shakespeare embodies these self-contradictions in Brutus, but gives them a psychological basis in his need for the comforts of self-delusion.

Like Othello, Brutus tries to free himself both from the

---

[1] This element of self-delusion has already been pointed out by Sir Mark Hunter, *op. cit.*, pp. 136 ff., and by J. I. M. Stewart, *op. cit.*, pp. 51 ff.

burden of guilt and from the physical horror of the murder by
adopting a ritualistic and aesthetic attitude towards it.[1]

> Let's kill him boldly, but not wrathfully;
> Let's carve him as a dish fit for the gods,
> Not hew him as a carcase fit for hounds.
>
> (2.1.172-4)

Both these 'honourable murderers' picture the deed as an act
of sacrifice. 'Let us be sacrificers, but not butchers, Caius.' It
is not a husband murdering his wife, not a friend murdering
his 'best lover' and benefactor; they are 'purgers, not murderers'. 'It is the cause, it is the cause, my soul.' Caesar must be
killed beautifully, ceremonially.

The ritualistic bathing of their hands in Caesar's blood,
suggested by Brutus after the murder, carries this further, and,
incidentally, fulfils Calpurnia's prophetic dream.

> Stoop, Romans, stoop,
> And let us bathe our hands in Caesar's blood
> Up to the elbows, and besmear our swords.
>
> (3.1.106-8)

But, ironically, the action suggests another ritual, far removed
from that which Brutus has in mind, the custom of huntsmen
at the kill to steep their hands in the blood of their victim. It
is to this bloody rite that Antony refers.

> Here wast thou bay'd, brave hart;
> Here didst thou fall; and here thy hunters stand,
> Sign'd in thy spoil, and crimson'd in thy Lethe.[2]

Whereas Brutus pictures to himself the murder as a ceremonial
slaying of the sacrificial beast on the altar of the commonweal,
Antony sees it as the bloody slaughter of the noble stag, the
King of the Forest, for the sake of the spoil. For under cover

---

[1] This point has also been made by Brents Stirling, who brings out the
pervasive presence of elements of ritual and ceremony throughout the play
(*op. cit.*, ch. 4).

[2] Whether we accept Capell's explanation of 'lethe' as 'a term used by
hunters to signify the blood shed by a deer at its fall'—and I can find no
evidence to support it—or take it to mean 'stream of death' and hence
'life-blood', does not much affect the force of the image.

of his metaphor Antony can dare to accuse the conspirators to their faces of killing Caesar for the sake of booty, the basic meaning of 'spoil'.[1] But fearing he has gone too far he at once insinuates a piece of flattery, as is his practice throughout this scene:

> How like a deer strucken by many princes
> Dost thou here lie!

From Antony's soliloquy we realize that even the hunting-metaphor was a form of flattery.

> O, pardon me, thou bleeding piece of earth,
> That I am meek and gentle with these butchers!

It is an ironic comment on Brutus's illusions and his 'Let us be sacrificers, but not butchers, Caius'. The assassination turns into something very different from a ritual slaying. Plutarch mentions that 'divers of the conspirators did hurt themselves striking one body with so many blows'.[2] Shakespeare makes Antony allude to this during the 'flyting' on the battle-field, when he speaks of how the conspirators' 'vile daggers / Hack'd one another in the sides of Caesar' (5.1.39-40). It is not a very pretty picture. Nor does the reality of Caesar's body 'marr'd with traitors' bear much relation to Brutus's aesthetic vision. Disconcerting to it is also the conspirators' flattery of Caesar, which makes him speak of Metellus' 'spaniel-fawning' and threaten to spurn him like a cur out of his way. It is not as priests officiating at a sacrifice that the conspirators are here seen, not even as huntsmen, but as hounds that fawn upon their victim before tearing it to pieces. It is to this image that Antony returns on the battle-field, when he accuses them of having 'fawned like hounds',

> Whilst damned Casca, like a cur, behind
> Struck Caesar on the neck.

On one other occasion Antony uses a metaphor from the hunt. In his soliloquy he envisages the war of revenge as a savage

---

[1] According to Onions (*A Shakespeare Glossary*), 'spoil' means '(in hunting) capture of the quarry and division of rewards to the hounds, (hence) slaughter, massacre'.

[2] *Caesar, op. cit.*, p. 102.

hunting-scene in which this time the conspirators are the quarry, no quarter is given, and Caesar's ghost acts as the chief huntsman:

> And Caesar's spirit, ranging for revenge,
> With Até by his side come hot from hell,
> Shall in these confines with a monarch's voice
> Cry "Havoc!" and let slip the dogs of war.
>
> (3.1.271-4)

This whole complex of hunting-metaphors was presumably set off in the poet's mind by Plutarch's description of Caesar as 'hacked and mangled among them, as a wild beast taken of hunters'.[1]

The need for self-delusion, which drives Brutus to depict Caesar as a dangerous tyrant and to visualize his murder as a sacrificial rite, makes him afterwards try to persuade himself that they have done a benefit not only to their country but to Caesar himself. He eagerly takes up Casca's

> Why, he that cuts off twenty years of life
> Cuts off so many years of fearing death,

exclaiming,

> Grant that, and then is death a benefit.
> So are we Caesar's friends, that have abridg'd
> His time of fearing death.
>
> (3.1.104-6)

In his soliloquy we find Brutus engaged in a more subtle form of self-deception in the attempt to still his inner conflict. We are not here watching an act of choice. The choice has already been made, as the opening line makes us realize: 'It must be by his death'. How Brutus arrived at this absolute 'must' we are never shown. It would seem that Shakespeare wishes us to feel that the decision had nothing to do with reason and logic, that he has somehow fallen victim to Cassius's rhetoric without being able to accept his arguments or share his motives. What we are watching in the soliloquy is Brutus's attempt to defend his

---

[1] *Caesar, op. cit.*, pp. 101-2.

decision before the court of his conscience. The rhythm of the verse, the disjointed sentences, the wording in such lines as

> And since the quarrel
> Will bear no colour for the thing he is,
> Fashion it thus—
>
> (2.1.28-30)

all bring out the anxious groping for some plausible justification of the deed. Caesar's desire for the crown does not in itself appear sufficient cause to Brutus. Shakespeare's Brutus is by no means a doctrinaire republican, in contrast to Plutarch's Brutus, who reproaches Cicero for favouring Octavius, declaring, 'For our predecessors would never abide to be subject to any Master, how gentle or mild soever they were'[1]. Brutus's opposition to kingship rests on his fears of the corrupting effect of the power it bestows, not on the nature of its office. 'Th' abuse of greatness is, when it disjoins / Remorse from power' (2.1.18-19). It is startling to find Brutus in the remainder of the soliloquy speak of Caesar as if he were still at the beginning of his career, to hear him talk of 'the bright day that brings forth the adder', of 'young ambition's ladder', of Caesar as a serpent's egg. Like the reference to his 'lowliness' it is absurdly out of keeping with the picture of Caesar as the aging Colossus that we are given in the course of the play. It would seem that, finding nothing in the mere fact of kingship, nor anything in Caesar's past behaviour to justify the assassination, Brutus deludes himself by vastly exaggerating the gap that separates the present from the future Caesar, the dictator from the king. Once this position is taken up, Brutus has no difficulty in advancing a logical argument for the assassination, and in this he is aided by his metaphor. It suggests the justification for the preventive murder, since it implies that, just as the adder, once hatched, is a menace that can no longer be controlled, so Caesar, once crowned, would be out of reach of the assassins' daggers. He must therefore be destroyed while he is still accessible, even though there is the possibility that the egg may hatch not a serpent but a dove. The argument is quite cogent and contains no confusion, as some commentators have claimed. But it is founded on self-deception.

[1] *Brutus, op. cit.*, p. 141.

By thus putting the justification for the murder on a pragmatic basis Brutus lays the foundation for his later tragedy. Had he been a doctrinaire republican and murdered Caesar to save the republic from kingship he would have been safe, if not from inner conflict, at least from tragic disillusion. For his purpose would have been accomplished. But by justifying the deed to himself and others on the grounds of 'pity to the general wrong of Rome' (3.1.171), the wrong that Caesar may have committed in the future, he puts himself at the mercy of events. For it is only by establishing a government under which the people suffer less wrong than they would have done under Caesar's rule that the murder can, to Brutus, be justified. And what are the consequences as they are depicted in the play? They are adumbrated in Antony's prophecy: 'Domestic fury and fierce civil strife / Shall cumber all the parts of Italy. . . . All pity chok'd with custom of fell deeds . . .' (3.1.264 ff.). It is a grim, ironic comment on Brutus's words in the same scene:

> And pity to the general wrong of Rome,
> As fire drives out fire, so pity pity,
> Hath done this deed on Caesar.
>
> (3.1.171-3)

In the succeeding scenes we find Antony translating his prophecy into fact. We see the domestic fury unchained by him tearing the harmless Cinna to pieces, and in the following scene observe, in all its cold-blooded ruthlessness, the régime that has been set up in Rome in the place of Caesar's. The blood-bath of the triumvirs contrasts with Caesar's scrupulous and unselfish administration of justice of which we had glimpses in his 'What touches us ourself shall be last serv'd' (3.1.8), and his behaviour over the repeal of Cimber's banishment. News reaches Brutus that seventy senators have been put to death. His wife has committed suicide. And, to cap it all, his cause has been tarnished by Cassius's malpractices. Instead of benefiting his country, Brutus has, from the best of motives and the highest of principles, plunged it into ruin. The two elements which Aristotle thought necessary for the profoundest tragedy, *peripeteia* and *anagnorisis*, an ironic turn of events which makes an action have the very opposite effect of that intended, and the realization of this by the agent, are thus seen to be fundamental to our play. They are found, in varying degrees of prominence, in all of Shakespeare's mature tragedies.

V

Before looking more closely at the nature of Brutus's tragedy, a brief excursus of a more general nature on the subject of Shakespearian Tragedy seems necessary. It appears to me that there are three basic ways of looking at Tragedy: (1) we can consider the play's plot and find the tragedy inherent in its events; (2) we can consider the nature of the tragic suffering of the protagonists; (3) we can consider the impact of all this upon the audience's minds and emotions. For the sake of convenience and for want of better names I shall call the first of these the 'formal', the second the 'experiential', and the third the 'affective' aspect of Tragedy.

The ancient grammarians and medieval writers who theorized on the subject of Tragedy paid attention to little except its 'formal' aspect. Their basic conception of Tragedy is conveniently summarized by Chaucer's Monk:

> Tragedie is to seyn a certeyn storie,
> As olde bookes maken us memorie,
> Of hym that stood in greet prosperitee,
> And is yfallen out of heigh degree
> Into myserie, and endeth wrecchedly.[1]

While retaining this concept of Tragedy as a *De Casibus* story (all Shakespeare's uses of the words 'tragedy' and 'tragic' are based on it, as J. V. Cunningham has shown[2]), the Elizabethans added to it other 'formal' types of Tragedy: the tragedy of Revenge (such as *Hamlet*); the tragedy of Italianate intrigue (such as *Othello*). But to this 'formal' view of Tragedy Renaissance theorists added a concern with its 'affective' aspect,

---

[1] *Canterbury Tales*, VII, ll. 1973-7.

[2] ' "Tragedy" in Shakespeare', *ELH*, vol. 17 (1950), pp. 36 ff. However, his inference that Shakespeare's views on the nature of Tragedy can be equated with this concept is wholly unwarranted. What Shakespeare thought about Tragedy as a literary form can only be inferred from his practice. That where he uses the word he does so in the popular sense, still current today, of 'violent, unexpected death', proves absolutely nothing.

partly through the renewed influence of Aristotle's concept of *catharsis*, and partly through their preoccupation with the moral and doctrinal effects of all literature. Sidney, for instance, in a famous passage in the *Apologie for Poetry*, speaks of Tragedy entirely in 'affective' terms, combining its doctrinal and cathartic functions, but substituting 'wonder' ('Admiration') for the Aristotelian 'fear'. Tragedy, he says, 'openeth the greatest woundes, and sheweth forth the *Ulcers* that are covered with *Tissue*, that maketh Kings fear to be Tyrants, and Tyrants manifest their tyrannicall humours, that with sturring the affects of *Admiration* and *Comiseration*, teacheth the uncertaintie of this world, and uppon how weak foundations guilden roofes are builded'.[1] Several decades later Chapman still speaks of tragedy in much the same terms: 'the soul, limbs, and limits of an authentical tragedy', he claims, are 'material instruction, elegant and sententious excitation to virtue, and deflection from her contrary'.[2] Renaissance theorists thus confined their attention to the 'formal' and 'affective' aspects of tragedy. What they never considered was the nature, or even the presence, of the protagonist's tragic suffering.

Nor has the criticism of later centuries done much to fill this gap. For instance, A. C. Bradley's chapter on 'The Substance of Shakespearean Tragedy' concerns itself with the 'formal' aspect of Shakespeare's tragedies, the tragic events and their causes in the character and actions of the hero as well as in the mysterious workings of 'the ultimate power' (conceived as a kind of cosmic Robespierre, who extirpates all that do not come up to its exalted standard of perfection). And above all—and this is the most admirable part of the chapter—it concerns itself with their 'affective' aspect, adding to the Aristotelian pity and fear 'a sense of waste' as the central feeling aroused in us. The nature of the protagonist's tragic suffering Bradley does not consider at all, beyond telling us that it is exceptional, unexpected, and 'of some striking kind' (p. 8). And yet it seems to me that it is this 'experiential' aspect which is all-important in any consideration of Shakespearian tragedy. For it is when we look at the nature of the tragic suffering that the specifically

[1] *Works*, ed. A. Feuillerat, vol. 3, p. 23.
[2] Dedication of *The Revenge of Bussy D'Ambois*, ed. T. M. Parrot (1910), p. 77.

Shakespearian qualities, which set his tragedies apart from those of his contemporaries, can be most fully perceived.

The evidence of his plays suggests that there were two such experiences which Shakespeare felt to be tragic above all others: one is the realization of having irrevocably lost, through one's own blind deed, the person or object on which all one's happiness on earth depends. The other is the experience of disillusion, whether justifiable or not, with such a person or object, of desertion and betrayal by it. Of the two the first, which depends upon *peripeteia* and *anagnorisis*, is the more tormenting. For nothing is more terrible than the realization of having, through one's own blind folly, cut oneself off for ever from all that makes for joy. It is this recognition which makes the Hell in the mind of Milton's Satan burn so fiercely, which makes him, in his soliloquy on Mount Niphates, seek so desperately to lay the burden of blame on God. The experience is undergone by Othello when he realizes that he has, with his own hands, killed the woman on whom all his happiness depended; by Lear when he realizes that he has given away his kingdom and driven away Cordelia, to put himself into the hands of his 'Pelican' daughters; by Macbeth when he realizes that evil isolates and that by his deeds he has cut himself off from all that he treasures, 'as honour, love, obedience, troops of friends', a condition epitomized in the banquet-scene. And all three characters also undergo the experience of tragic disillusion, which in the case of Othello precedes the realization of his self-induced loss, in that of Lear and Macbeth partly precedes and partly accompanies it. With Othello its object is Desdemona; with Lear it is first Cordelia and then Goneril and Regan (and this is echoed and amplified by Gloucester's parallel experience, with Edgar and later Edmund as the objects of his tragic disillusion); with Macbeth its object is the throne of Scotland, for the sake of which he has murdered Duncan.

In the case of *Hamlet*, the protagonist's experience of tragic disillusion is central to the play. Its object is his mother, and through her Ophelia and all womankind. But the other experience, the realization of having lost, through one's own blind deed, the person above all dear to one, and of thus having cut oneself off for ever from all hope of happiness, also seems to me

to play an important part in Hamlet's tragic suffering. As it
has not, I think, been ever discussed by critics, I shall have to
say a few more words about it here: it occurs, I believe, at
Ophelia's burial when Hamlet suddenly realizes, upon hearing
Laertes' words about him,

> O, treble woe
> Fall ten times treble on that cursed head
> Whose wicked deed thy most ingenious sense
> Depriv'd thee of!
>
> (5.1.240-43)

that his blind deed of killing Polonius has led to the madness
and death of the woman he loves. It is this sudden and therefore
all the more tormenting recognition, coupled with the shock of
finding himself hated and cursed by a man of whom he had
always been fond, which seems to me above all responsible for
his behaviour at the grave. Its explanation which he gives
afterwards to Horatio,

> But sure the bravery of his grief did put me
> Into a tow'ring passion
>
> (5.2.79-80)

appears to be based on self-deceit. Hamlet cannot bear to
acknowledge the truth to himself and to Horatio, and so an
explanation is devised which seems quite inadequate and un-
convincing. And the same need for self-deceit seems to me to
underlie his much debated apology to Laertes (5.2.218-36). By
trying to persuade himself as well as others that he killed Polonius
in a fit of madness, and that he was therefore not responsible
for the deed, Hamlet seeks to free himself from the tormenting
awareness of its consequences.

If we look for other plays by Shakespeare in which both these
tragic experiences are undergone by one of the protagonists, we
have to turn to two of the late comedies, *The Winter's Tale* and
Cymbeline. In *The Winter's Tale* the pattern is the same as in
Othello. Leontes' experience of tragic disillusion with Hermione
is followed by his experience of self-induced loss of all that is
dearest to him, his wife, his son, his daughter, his best friend.
In *Cymbeline* this pattern is again repeated, Posthumus's disillusion with Imogen being succeeded by the recognition of his
self-induced loss, even while he still believes in her guilt. But

Cymbeline is unique in providing a counterpart to Posthumus's tragic experience of disillusion with Imogen by fully displaying the same experience as undergone by Imogen with regard to Posthumus (3.4.44-94), whereas with Desdemona and Hermione this reciprocal experience is not developed.

When we focus our attention predominantly on the 'formal' aspect of Shakespeare's plays, an excessive division between the tragedies and comedies is created. In accordance with Donatan tradition, we tend to see them as antithetical forms (the tragedies begining in joy and ending in sorrow, the comedies beginning in sorrow and ending in joy, etc.). By attending to the 'experiential' aspect of the plays, this excessive and therefore misleading division is broken down and the close kinship between many of the tragedies and comedies brought out. It is, of course, true that an exclusive preoccupation with the 'experiential' aspect would lead to the opposite defect and not enable us to distinguish at all between many of the comedies and tragedies. The two ways of regarding the plays must supplement and correct each other.

Next to the group of plays in which the protagonist undergoes both types of tragic experience, there are some tragedies in which the experience of disillusion is found but not that of self-induced loss. These are *Julius Caesar, Troilus and Cressida,*[1]

[1] I deliberately list *Troilus and Cressida* among the tragedies, where the compilers of the First Folio placed it, and where it seems to me to belong. In its 'formal' aspect the play is a *De Casibus* tragedy, culminating in the death of Hector, which, as we are repeatedly made to feel (see esp. 5.3.59-62; 5.9.9-10) carries with it the ultimate destruction of the whole of Troy. In its 'experiential' aspect the play culminates in Troilus's tragic disillusion in 5.2. Its closest analogue among Shakespeare's tragedies is *Julius Caesar*. In both plays the tragedy of disillusion, experienced by its protagonist (Brutus, Troilus), is joined to a *De Casibus* tragedy, the assassination of the play's great warrior-hero (Caesar, Hector), who is shown driven to his doom by *ate*, the blind infatuation which makes him disregard all portents of his impending death, including the prophetic dream of his wife (*J.C.*, 2.2. 76 ff.; *T. & C.*, 5.3. 10 ff). Where the pattern of *Troilus and Cressida* differs chiefly from that of *Julius Caesar* is in the survival of its protagonist—not, to my mind, an important point, for Troilus, like all the Trojans, is left doomed to 'sure destruction' at the end of the play (see esp. 5.10.8-9)—and in the high incidence of scenes of satiric comedy. In this respect its closest analogue is *Hamlet*, where their incidence is nearly as great.

I presume—though I have not seen this argued—that the compilers' decision to put the play among the tragedies was also influenced by the

Timon of Athens. The object of Troilus's tragic disillusion is Cressida; with Timon, whose experience of disillusion is treated at greatest length, it is the whole of mankind.

Coriolanus seems unique among Shakespeare's tragedies in possessing a protagonist who undergoes neither of these experiences. The play also serves as a good example of how the 'formal' aspect of tragedy may be found unaccompanied by the 'experiential', and how the absence of the latter also often leads to the lack of the 'affective'.

In its 'formal' aspect *Coriolanus* is a *De Casibus* tragedy on the familiar *hubris-nemesis* pattern. What is here unique is that the pattern repeats itself, that we are twice shown Coriolanus's rise and his subsequent fall, brought about by his pride and choler, which deliver him into the hands of his enemies. (This pattern of repetition, with its ironic contrasts and parallels between the two phases, is, in fact, the play's dominant structural device.) But above all it is in its 'experiential' aspect that *Coriolanus* is unique among Shakespeare's tragedies. For alone among his tragic heroes its protagonist undergoes no experience to which the name 'tragic' can be applied—for a passionate sense of having been wronged and a burning desire for revenge are not tragic experiences, neither are the inner conflicts he undergoes in 3.2 and 5.3. This circumstance, coupled with the fact that Shakespeare scarcely lets us see into his mind in soliloquy or aside—another way in which Coriolanus differs from all of Shakespeare's other tragic heroes—results in a peculiar absence of a feeling of pity and fear at each of his falls. Our dominant emotions at the end of the play are awe and wonder rather than pity and fear, so that some critics have been doubtful whether *Coriolanus* is properly to be called a tragedy at all.

---

notion, widely held in the Renaissance and derived from the ancient grammarians, that the material of comedy is fiction, that of tragedy historical fact. (For a valuable discussion of this see G. Giovannini's 'Historical realism and the tragic emotions in Renaissance criticism', *P.Q.*, vol. 32 (1953), pp. 304 ff.) To the Folio compilers the matter of Troy would be historical fact. Their inclusion of *Cymbeline* among the tragedies may be due to the same consideration, for it is the only one of Shakespeare's comedies in which what would have been regarded as historical events play an important part, as well as the only one named, in the manner of the Histories, after its reigning monarch.

Macbeth, on the other hand, may serve as an example of how the 'experiential' may be found quite divorced from the 'formal' aspect of tragedy. For Macbeth's tragic disillusion, his sense of self-induced loss, are at their height at a point in the play where he is also at the pinnacle of his worldly fortunes.

One can say, by way of summing up, that while the 'formal' and 'experiential' aspects of tragedy will often occur together, they are not infrequently found without each other, while in the absence of the 'experiential' the 'affective' will also often be greatly diminished, if not entirely lacking.

VI

We can now return to Brutus's tragedy. There is no indication that the experience of self-induced loss forms part of his suffering. Unlike the Brutus of *Caesar's Revenge*, Shakespeare's Brutus is nowhere shown to be tormented by the thought of having murdered his friend and benefactor. Nor does he experience a realization similar to Macbeth's, that through the murder he has cut himself off for ever from the way of life he cherishes. His torments, as far as one can judge, stem not so much from the realization of what he has lost as of what he has gained, of the kind of world which he has helped to bring into existence. His 'best lover' is not really Caesar, or Portia, still less Cassius, but the Roman republic. It is her image which has become for him 'begrim'd and black' since she has gone a whoring with Antony and been besmirched by Cassius's malpractices. It is this tragic disillusion which seems to me implicit in the quarrel-scene, which vents itself in Brutus's passionate outbursts and in the harshness and bitterness of his recriminations. For it is Cassius who, as his associate and friend, has above all sullied for Brutus the image of his ideal republic, and so contributed most to his tragic disillusion. Hence the virulence of the accusations, the talk of chastisement, the repeated dwelling upon his own honesty. The mood finds at once expression upon Brutus's first stage-appearance since his oration to the people.

> Your master, Pindarus,
> In his own change, or by ill officers,
> Hath given me some worthy cause to wish
> Things done undone.

(4.2.6-9)

And it becomes most explicit in his passionate reminder to Cassius of the high ideals for which Caesar was murdered and which alone can make the assassination for him defensible:

> Remember March, the ides of March remember:
> Did not great Julius bleed for justice sake?
> What villain touch'd his body, that did stab,
> And not for justice? What, shall one of us,
> That struck the foremost man of all this world
> But for supporting robbers, shall we now
> Contaminate our fingers with base bribes
> And sell the mighty space of our large honours
> For so much trash as may be grasped thus?
> I had rather be a dog and bay the moon
> Than such a Roman.
>
> (4.3.18-28)

In the quarrel-scene, as elsewhere in the play, Brutus and Cassius talk an entirely different language. To Cassius the quarrel is a lover's quarrel. He cannot conceive why Brutus should be so passionately angry over such trivial offences, cannot understand that for him they are bound up with the justifiability of the entire conspiracy. He can merely see that Brutus loves him not, and that under such conditions life to him is valueless, so that with all sincerity he can exclaim:

> There is my dagger,
> And here my naked breast; within a heart
> Dearer than Plutus' mine, richer than gold;
> If that thou be'st a Roman, take it forth.
> I, that denied thee gold, will give my heart.
> Strike as thou didst at Caesar; for I know,
> When thou didst hate him worst, thou lov'dst him better
> Than ever thou lov'dst Cassius.
>
> (4.3.99-106)

The image of the heart and gold echoes a very similar one used earlier in the scene by Brutus:

> By heaven, I had rather coin my heart,
> And drop my blood for drachmas, than to wring
> From the hard hands of peasants their vile trash
> By any indirection.
>
> (4.3.72-5)

The two images epitomize the nature of the speakers. Brutus would rather die than injure his country; Cassius would rather die than live without the love of his friend. The conflict, fundamental to *Julius Caesar*, between private and public loyalties, which is waged in Brutus's mind in the earlier part of the play, has in the quarrel-scene become externalized, and is now fought out between the representatives of the two opposed ways of life.

We see, then, that the quarrel-scene, so far from being episodic and dramatically dispensable, as Bradley thought,[1] is in many ways the most important scene in the play.[2] Not only is it here that Brutus's tragic disillusion is most fully revealed to us, but the scene also crystallises the play's main moral issue, the rival claims of personal relations and the *res publica*.

An understanding of the nature of Brutus's tragedy also helps us to comprehend why Shakespeare depicted Caesar as he did. Had he made him a full-blown tyrant, there would have been no tragedy awaiting Brutus. Had he made him a wholly admirable figure, his tragedy would have been more like that of Othello, with Brutus murdering his 'best lover', misled by Cassius's Iago-like machinations, and the later terrible realization of what he has done. By depicting Caesar as he does, Shakespeare makes possible Brutus's experience of tragic disillusion without involving him in the accompanying experience of self-induced loss, an experience which would have been incompatible with the problematic presentation of the conspiracy.

Of all Shakespeare's tragedies it is *Macbeth* which shows the closest kinship to *Julius Caesar*. After much inner conflict and a nightmarish period of anticipation, which is described in closely similar terms in the soliloquies of Brutus (2.1.63-9) and Macbeth (1.3.137-42)[3], each, about half way through the play,

---

[1] *Shakespearean Tragedy* (1904), p. 60.

[2] This is also affirmed by MacCallum: 'More than any other single episode, more than all the rest together, it lays bare the significance of the story in its tragic pathos and its tragic irony' (*op. cit.*, p. 256).

[3] For a comparison of these speeches and a discussion of many other points of kinship between the two plays, see Wilson Knight's chapter on 'Brutus and Macbeth' in *The Wheel of Fire*. Allardyce Nicoll also briefly compares the two plays, declaring that 'the central theme of both is the same' (*Shakespeare*, 1952, p. 134). Minor parallels, such as the closely similar responses by Brutus (4.3.188-90) and Macbeth (5.5.17-18) to the news of their wife's suicide, suggest how much *Julius Caesar* was in Shakespeare's mind throughout the writing of *Macbeth*.

murders the ruler of his state, who had loved and favoured him. This violation in the body politic of the multiple bonds which tied the murderer to his ruler, friend and benefactor[1] is accompanied in both plays by unnatural and prodigious happenings in the macrocosm. The remainder of each play traces the consequences of the murder, including the experience of tragic disillusion in the hero. And this disillusion, in both cases, is not with a person but with the hoped for benefits of the murder.

So much for the 'experiential' aspect of *Julius Caesar* considered as a tragedy. In its 'formal' aspect it contains the framework of an Elizabethan Revenge-play, and within this framework a series of *De Casibus* tragedies, beginning with that of Caesar and ending with that of Brutus. In contrast to the tragedy of Brutus, where, as we have seen, the 'experiential' element is all-important, Shakespeare presents Caesar's tragedy almost entirely in 'formal' terms: as a *De Casibus* tragedy in which, in the manner of the Greeks,[2] Caesar's *hubris* and *ate* play an important rôle in his downfall. The 'experiential' element in Caesar's tragedy makes only a momentary appearance when, at the point of death, he realizes that Brutus is one of the assassins. In his 'Et tu, Brute?—Then fall, Caesar!' this experience of tragic disillusion in the man he dearly loved (as both Cassius and Antony testify, 1.2.310; 3.2.183-4), finds expression. But in spite of this solitary flicker of tragic experience in Caesar, I do not think that many playgoers are deeply moved by his death, or that Shakespeare wished them to be so. His alienation of our affections for Caesar just before the murder argues that Shakespeare wished to keep us emotionally detached, to reserve the tragic impact of the play until the last acts. And this 'distancing' of the assassination is greatly increased by Shakespeare's presentation of it almost as if it were a play within a play, so that we feel towards it more as we do towards 'The Murder of Gonzago' than the murder of Duncan.

[1] Cf. Macbeth's words, beginning, 'He's here in double trust' (1.7. 12-20), with Appian's description of the murder, quoted on p. 15, which Shakespeare may have remembered in writing that passage.

[2] J. A. K. Thomson has insisted on the close kinship between *Julius Caesar* and the spirit of Greek tragedy (*Shakespeare and the Classics*, 1952, pp. 242-50). Both H. M. Ayres (*op. cit.*, pp. 194 ff.) and Kittredge (*op. cit.*, p. xvi) have emphasized the elements of *hubris* and *ate* in Caesar's fall.

The careful assignment of rôles among the conspirators (3.1.25-30), Brutus's desire to enact a drama of ritual sacrifice (2.1.171 ff.; 3.1.106-11), his admonition of his fellow-conspirators,

> But bear it as our Roman actors do,
> With untir'd spirits and formal constancy
>
> (2.1.226-7)

and, above all, Cassius's description of the murder as if it were merely its world-*première*,

> How many ages hence
> Shall this our lofty scene be acted over
> In states unborn and accents yet unknown!
>
> (3.1.112-14)

all contribute to this effect. And it is heightened by the depiction of Caesar, too, as an actor, explicitly in Casca's comments on his bearing at the Lupercal, 'If the tag-rag people did not clap him and hiss him, according as he pleas'd and displeas'd them, as they use to do the players in the theatre, I am no true man' (1.2.257-9), and implicitly through his enactment of a self-imposed rôle on each of his appearances.

So much, then, for *Julius Caesar* considered as a tragedy. The play's unity, which has so often been impugned, is chiefly brought about in a twofold manner: By Shakespeare's adoption of the framework of an Elizabethan Revenge-play, which makes the last two acts, with the ghost's pursuit of the murderers and his final revenge on the battlefield, an integral part of the play's structure. And, more importantly, by Shakespeare's choice of Brutus for his tragic hero. This last fact has frequently been denied by commentators. Professor Charlton, for instance, has gone so far as to declare that 'Brutus is no more significant in the play than is Hotspur in *Henry IV*', and that 'it is impossible to fit *Julius Caesar* into Shakespeare's mode of tragedy'. To him, it is 'a history play in exactly the same sense as are *Henry IV* and *Henry V*: i.e. it is a political play'.[1] And to Dover Wilson 'the main issue of the play is not the conspirators' fate but the future of Rome, of liberty, of the human race, to which their fate is incidental'.[2] Both these views seem to me wholly at odds

---

[1] *Shakespeare, Politics and Politicians*, English Association Pamphlet No. 72, pp. 19 ff.

[2] *Op. cit.*, p. xx.

with the imaginative impact of the play. The main issue of *Julius Caesar*, as I see it, is not a political but a moral issue, consisting in the conflicting claims of the realm of personal relations and that of politics.[1] This issue is never for long lost sight of. In Brutus's murder of Caesar and in his quarrel with Cassius personal loyalties are sacrificed to political ideals.[2] In Antony's feigned league of friendship with the conspirators and in his treatment of Lepidus personal relations are made the dupe of political expediency. The same is true of Decius Brutus's relations with Caesar. And the conflicting claims of the two realms are again fought out in the two scenes that resemble each other in several ways, that between Caesar and Calpurnia and that between Brutus and Portia. Political issues, such as the choice between a republican and a monarchic form of government for Rome, enter the play only in so far as they impinge upon the moral issue. They are, in other words, not a concern of the play itself but merely of some of the play's characters.

Its central character is Brutus, in whom the moral issue is fought out, and whose tragedy, as we have seen, is very much of the Shakespearian kind. It is on Brutus, the only person in the play who experiences any inner conflict, that our main interest is focussed from the first, and it is with an eye on him that much of the play's material is presented. Had Shakespeare's chief concern been with Caesar or with political issues, he would hardly have denied himself the stage-presentation of Antony's offer of the crown at the Lupercal. But it is its effect on Brutus that chiefly concerns him, so that all he needs to give us are the shouts of the populace, Brutus's anxious surmises, and Casca's taunting report. Shakespeare's presentation of the character of Caesar itself seems partly determined, as we have seen, by its bearing upon Brutus's tragedy. And the play ends with the tribute to the tragic hero, as we find it in *Romeo and*

[1] The importance of this issue is well brought out by L. C. Knights in his admirable article on 'Shakespeare and Political Wisdom', *Sewanee Review*, vol. 61 (1953).

[2] Explaining Brutus's decision to side with Pompey against Caesar in the Civil War, Plutarch comments: 'But Brutus preferring the respect of his country and commonwealth before private affection . . .' (*Brutus*, p. 113). Shakespeare made this the basis of his portrayal of Brutus, and one of the main themes of the play.

Juliet, Hamlet, Antony and Cleopatra, and *Coriolanus* (Othello and Timon provide their own epitaphs).

But there is another, subtler, way in which the unity of *Julius Caesar* is achieved. Like all Shakespeare's mature tragedies, it is a highly integrated play. John Palmer has pointed out that 'there is something almost symphonic in its movement and structure' and that 'there is scarcely a line in this play which does not create echoes in the mind of something past or arouse anticipations of something which is yet to come'.[1] Maria Wickert has remarked how certain concepts, such as 'honour', 'nobility', 'constancy', 'redress', and 'fall', pervade *Julius Caesar,* and seem to play a part similar to that played by iterative imagery in other Shakespeare plays.[2] And Adrien Bonjour has pointed to certain iterative words which 'harp upon the very keynotes in the central theme of the play'.[3] The ironic function of some of the verbal echoes I have tried to indicate in the course of this chapter. The echoes of actions are also sometimes deeply ironic. There is, for instance, the scene in which, with superb impudence and only lightly veiled sarcasm, Antony solemnly shakes the hands of each of the conspirators. 'Let each man render me his bloody hand' (3.1.185). It recalls Brutus's ceremonial handshaking with the conspirators in his garden a few hours earlier. 'Give me your hands all over, one by one' (2.1.112). Other echoes are found in the voluntary offer of their life, made, with varying degrees of sincerity, by Caesar to the *plebs,* by Antony to the conspirators, and by Cassius to Brutus (1.2.264; 3.1.152-64; 4.3.99-104); in the two still night-scenes with Brutus and his drowsy page, first in his garden and later in his tent; in Caesar's fall in the market-place and in the Capitol. *Antony and Cleopatra* is also full of echoes, both of words and actions. But there, as we shall see, their function seems above all that of suggesting the close kinship of the two lovers. In *Julius Caesar* the echo, whether of words or actions, seems

---

[1] *Op. cit.,* pp. 62-3. For an interesting analysis of parallels in the action of the two halves of the play, see Mgr. Kolbe's *Shakespeare's Way* (1930), p. 157, which contains many perceptive comments. For a discussion of recurring motifs see R. A. Foakes, 'An Approach to *Julius Caesar*', *Sh. Q.,* vol. 5 (1954), pp. 259 ff.; Max Luethi, *Shakespeares Dramen* (1957), pp. 25-7; and Adrien Bonjour, *op. cit.,* ch. 2.

[2] *Op. cit.,* p. 15 n. 8.

[3] *Op. cit.,* ch. 3.

used either as a comment, often grimly ironic, on what has gone before, or to make us feel obscurely, as we occasionally do in life or in dreams, that we have been through all this, or something very like it before.

To conclude. In the course of this chapter I have tried, above all, to make two points: first, that as a tragedy *Julius Caesar* belongs with Shakespeare's mature tragedies in its emphasis on Brutus's tragic experience and in the form which this experience takes; that it is, indeed, the first of the tragedies to exhibit this characteristically Shakespearian pattern, and that it especially points forward to *Macbeth*. Secondly, that in this play Shakespeare put a twofold problem before his audience: the psychological problem of the nature of the 'real' Caesar; and, hinging upon this, the moral problem of the justifiability of the murder; that by the orientation of his material Shakespeare deliberately avoided giving a plain and clear-cut answer to either of these problems, and that *Julius Caesar* is therefore one of Shakespeare's few genuine problem plays. One of the marks of these plays— though it is by no means confined to them—is the playwright's procedure of manipulating our response to the principal characters, playing fast and loose with our affections for them, engaging and alienating them in turn. (For the sake of convenience, the term 'dramatic coquetry' may be coined to describe this procedure.) In *Julius Caesar* our response to all four main characters, Caesar, Cassius, Antony, and even Brutus, is thus manipulated.

Considered in this light *Julius Caesar* exhibits, as we shall see, a hitherto unobserved kinship with *Measure for Measure*, the next of Shakespeare's Problem Plays, to which we must now turn.

II

MEASURE FOR MEASURE

I

THERE IS probably no other play by Shakespeare which has
so much perplexed critics as *Measure for Measure*, nor one which
has aroused such violent, eccentric, and mutually opposed
responses. On perusing the not inconsiderable body of commentary on the play written over the last hundred and fifty
years, the astonished reader is again and again made to rub his
eyes and exclaim (adapting the words of Banquo),

> Are such things here as they do speak about?
> Or have they eaten on the insane root
> That takes the reason prisoner?

These violent and contradictory responses go back at least to
the beginnings of Romantic criticism. 'This play,' writes
Coleridge, 'which is Shakespeare's throughout, is to me the
most painful—say rather, the only painful—part of his genuine
works. The comic and tragic parts equally border on the
μισητόν, the one disgusting, the other horrible. . . .' 'It is a
hateful work', he repeats in his *Table Talk* (June 24, 1827).
'Our feelings of justice are grossly wounded in Angelo's escape.
Isabella herself contrives to be unamiable, and Claudio is
detestable.'[1] 'This play is as full of genius as it is of wisdom',
writes Hazlitt, though he goes on to complain of its want of
passion.[2] The prevailing attitude of Victorian critics is well
summed up by Walter Raleigh, writing at the beginning of this
century: 'In criticism of *Measure for Measure*', he remarks, 'we
are commonly presented with a picture of Vienna as a black
pit of seething wickedness; and against this background there

[1] *Coleridge's Shakespeare Criticism*, ed. T. M. Raysor (1930), vol. 1, p. 113;
vol 2, p. 352.
[2] *Characters of Shakespeare's Plays* (1817-18), Everyman edition, p. 245.

rises the dazzling, white, and saintly figure of Isabella.'[1] All
that remained in order to arrive at a picture of unrelieved
gloom was to blacken Isabella without whitening her surround-
ings. This was done most forcefully by Una Ellis-Fermor, who
expressed in extreme form what seems to have been the pre-
dominant critical view of the play between the two wars, when
she wrote that in *Measure for Measure* 'the lowest depths of
Jacobean negation are touched. Cynicism has taken on a kind
of diabolic vigilance; with the exception of the kindly, timid
Provost, there is no character who is not suspect, and those
whose claims to goodness or decency seem most vigorous are
precisely those in whom meanness, self-regard, and hypocrisy
root deepest.'[2] This 'cynical' view was strongly repudiated by
R. W. Chambers in his influential British Academy Lecture on
'The Jacobean Shakespeare and *Measure for Measure*' (1937),[3]
in which he insisted on the Christian spirit which informs the
play. Another important 'Christian' interpretation had been
given a few years earlier by Wilson Knight, who found *Measure
for Measure* filled with the spirit of the Gospels, a parable
exemplifying Christ's dictum in the Sermon on the Mount:
'Judge not, that ye be not judged. For with what judgement
ye judge, ye shall be judged: and with what measure ye mete,
it shall be measured to you again.'[4] Such readings of the play
were new in England. The first statement by an English critic
that *Measure for Measure* is an expression of a fundamentally
Christian ethos is found, as far as I know, in Raleigh's pages,[5]
which, incidentally, contain some of the sanest and most
balanced comments on the play that we possess. But it is found
much earlier in Germany, going back at least to Ulrici in the
mid-nineteenth century,[6] and being expressed most fully and
forcibly by Albrecht in his important but neglected study of
the play.[7] Since R. W. Chambers's essay, 'Christian' interpretations have proliferated (notable among these are the discussions

---

[1] *Shakespeare* (1907), pp. 165-6.
[2] *The Jacobean Drama* (1936), p. 260.
[3] Reprinted with minor alterations in *Man's Unconquerable Mind* (1939),
pp. 277 ff.
[4] *The Wheel of Fire* (1930), pp. 80 ff.   [5] *Op. cit.*, p. 173.
[6] *Shakespeare's Dramatische Kunst* (1847), vol. 2, pp. 576 ff.
[7] *Neue Untersuchungen zu Shakespeares Mass für Mass* (1914), pp. 281 ff.

of Roy Battenhouse,[1] E. T. Sehrt,[2] and Nevill Coghill[3]) and may be said to form the now dominant view of the play, the new orthodoxy.

There have, however, been others, notably, in the last century, such unlikely yoke-fellows as Gervinus in Germany[4] and Walter Pater in England,[5] who have seen the play neither as expressive of cynicism and disgust nor as filled with the spirit of the Gospels, and yet believe it to be no 'meaningless' entertainment but a serious and coherent exploration of certain moral issues. It is in support of this view that the following pages are written.

It seems wisest to approach the question of Shakespeare's concerns and attitudes in this play by way of a discussion of its five main characters, Claudio, Lucio, Angelo, Isabel, and the Duke, in that order. In *Measure for Measure* Shakespeare has created a greater number of complex characters which are apt to perplex the modern reader than perhaps in any other of his plays. And an understanding of Elizabethan tenets and feelings on certain matters seems particularly necessary in order to dispel or diminish some of these perplexities.

Claudio is not the least puzzling of the five. In a valuable essay on the play, published in 1942, L. C. Knights, discussing the presentation of Claudio, expressed his belief that 'it is the slight uncertainty of attitude in Shakespeare's handling of him that explains some part, at least, of the play's disturbing effect'. The source of this uncertainty he found in 'feelings at war with themselves' in the poet, the result of a temporary 'emotional bias' that 'seems to blur some of the natural positive values which in *Macbeth* and *Lear* are as vividly realized as the vision of evil'.[6] Apparently alone among commentators, he pointed to 'something odd and inappropriate' in Claudio's attitude towards the offence for which he has been sentenced to death.

---

[1] '*Measure for Measure* and the Christian Doctrine of the Atonement', *P.M.L.A.*, vol. 61 (1946), pp. 1029 ff.

[2] *Vergebung und Gnade bei Shakespeare* (1952), *passim*.

[3] 'Comic Form in *Measure for Measure*', *Shakespeare Survey*, vol. 8 (1955), pp. 14 ff.

[4] *Shakespeare* (1849), vol. 3, pp. 157 ff.

[5] '*Measure for Measure*', in *Appreciations* (1889), pp. 176 ff.

[6] 'The Ambiguity of *Measure for Measure*', *Scrutiny*, vol. 10 (1942), pp. 225, 228.

Upon his first appearance on the stage the following conversation takes place between him and Lucio:

> *Lucio:* Why, how now, Claudio, whence comes this restraint?
> *Claudio:* From too much liberty, my Lucio, liberty;
>   As surfeit is the father of much fast,
>   So every scope by the immoderate use
>   Turns to restraint. Our natures do pursue,
>   Like rats that ravin down their proper bane,
>   A thirsty evil; and when we drink we die.
> *Lucio:* If I could speak so wisely under an arrest, I would send for
>   certain of my creditors; and yet, to say the truth, I had as lief
>   have the foppery of freedom as the morality of imprisonment.
>   What's thy offence, Claudio?
> *Claudio:* What but to speak of would offend again.
> *Lucio:* What, is't murder?
> *Claudio:* No.
> *Lucio:* Lechery?
> *Claudio:* Call it so.

(1.2.118-132)

Yet five lines later he declares,

> Thus stands it with me: upon a true contract
> I got possession of Julietta's bed.
> You know the lady; she is fast my wife,
> Save that we do the denunciation lack
> Of outward order; this we came not to,
> Only for propagation of a dow'r
> Remaining in the coffer of her friends,
> From whom we thought it meet to hide our love
> Till time had made them for us. But it chances
> The stealth of our most mutual entertainment,
> With character too gross, is writ on Juliet.
> *Lucio.* With child, perhaps?
> *Claudio:*   Unhappily, even so.
> And the new deputy now for the Duke—
> Whether it be the fault and glimpse of newness,
> Or whether that the body public be
> A horse whereon the governor doth ride,
> Who, newly in the seat, that it may know
> He can command, lets it straight feel the spur;
> Whether the tyranny be in his place,
> Or in his eminence that fills it up,
> I stagger in. But this new governor

74

Awakes me all the enrolled penalties
Which have, like unscour'd armour, hung by th' wall
So long that nineteen zodiacs have gone round
And none of them been worn; and for a name,
Now puts the drowsy and neglected act
Freshly on me. 'Tis surely for a name.

What are we to make of this young man, who feels deeply sinful because he has cohabited with his wife, and at the same time sees himself as the only nominally guilty victim of a tyrannical ruler? Most commentators escape from the perplexity by ignoring Claudio's remarks about his marriage-contract. But once they are considered, how are we to account for the sense of guilt and shame, felt not only by Claudio but also by Juliet, who is made to declare of her transgression, 'I do repent me as it is an evil, / And take the shame with joy' (2.3.35-6)?[1] And, above all, if Claudio and Juliet are man and wife, what legal right has Angelo to arrest them and to sentence Claudio to death for fornication?

An answer to all these questions is, I believe, to be found in the complex and inherently contradictory nature of the contemporary laws and edicts relating to marriage, which had remained basically unchanged since the twelfth century. The contradictions sprang from two opposed and irreconcilable objectives on the part of the Church. On the one hand it wished to make the contraction of a legal marriage as easy as possible in order to encourage people to live in a state of matrimony rather than 'in sin'. It therefore decreed that any *de praesenti* contract (i.e. one in which a man and a woman declared that henceforth they were husband and wife) constituted a legal marriage. Such a contract did not need the presence of a priest, nor, indeed, of any third person to witness it, nor any deposition in writing. All that was required was the mutual consent of both parties. As Henry Swinburne puts it in his *Treatise on*

---

[1] It is worth noting that in Whetstone's play Andrugio and Polina, Claudio's and Juliet's counterparts, also express remorse for their transgressions. Each speaks of their sufferings, in an identical phrase, as 'penaunce of my mys' (Polina: Part II, 1.1.; Andrugio: Part II, 4.2.); and Polina, like Juliet, is depicted as devoutly religious and ready to endure her penance patiently. Shakespeare took over these attitudes and put them to his own uses.

75

Spousals: 'albeit there be no Witnesses of the Contract, yet the Parties having verily, (though secretly) Contracted Matrimony, they are very Man and Wife before God'.[1] But to counteract the obvious evils to which such laws were bound to give rise, the Church also insisted that, though valid and binding, such secret marriages were sinful and forbidden, and that, if they took place, the offenders were to be punished and forced to solemnize their marriage *in facie ecclesiae*. These inherent contradictions in the Church's attitude to clandestine marriages are well brought out by William Harrington in his *Commendacions of matrimony*: 'Yf that man & woman or theyr proctours do make matrymony secretly by them selfe without any recorde or but with one wytnesse that is called matrymony clandestinat the whiche for many causes is forboden by the lawe. And they whiche done make such matrymony are accused in that dede doynge; not withstondyng that matrymony is valeable and holdeth afore God in to so much that and the one of the same forsake the other and take other they lyue in a dampnable aduoutry.'[2]

If the Church denounced the contraction of clandestine marriages *per verba de praesenti*, it inveighed even more vehemently against their consummation before they had been publicly solemnized, an act which it regarded as fornication and a deadly sin. Again Harrington sums it up accurately: 'And whan matrymony is thus lawfully made yet the man maye not possesse the woman as his wyfe nor the woman the man as her husbonde nor inhabyte nor flesshely meddle togyther as man and wyfe: afore suche tyme as that matrymony be approued and solempnysed by oure mother holy chyrche and yf they do in dede they synne deadly.'[3]

---

[1] *A Treatise on Spousals*, p. 87. This treatise, published in 1686 but written *c.* 1600, is our chief source of knowledge of Elizabethan laws and legal opinions relating to the marriage-contract.

[2] *Commendacions of matrimony* (1528), A4-A4^v.

[3] *Ibid.*, A4^v. It is true that many people, and perhaps Shakespeare among them, paid little heed to the Church's commands on this topic. But it is quite erroneous to say with Halliwell-Phillipps (*Outlines of the Life of Shakespeare*, vol. 1, p. 62) that 'no question of morals would in those days have arisen, or could have been entertained', or to claim with J. Q. Adams that if Shakespeare 'took advantage of the privileges such a contract was supposed to give, it could not have offended the moral sensibilities of the

We see, then, that Claudio and Juliet are guilty in the eyes of the Church of two transgressions: of having contracted a secret marriage and of having consummated it. Being technically guilty of fornication, Claudio is therefore punishable under the law which Angelo has revived. When Arthur Underhill, in his chapter on Law in *Shakespeare's England*, declares that 'Angelo's condemnation of Claudio for alleged fornication was, and was intended by Shakespeare to be, absolutely tyrannical and illegal,'[1] it is only the first part of his statement which is correct. Angelo's condemnation of Claudio was—and no doubt was intended by Shakespeare to appear—absolutely tyrannical. But it was also unquestionably legal. Claudio knows this only too well, and never suggests that he could save himself by appealing to the legal circumstances of his case. It is by relying on Isabel's power to move the tyrannical ruler to mercy that he hopes to save his life.

We can now understand why it should be possible for Claudio to feel guilt and shame for having cohabited with his own wife, and at the same time to see himself as a judicial victim, condemned to die merely 'for a name'. Claudio is depicted as highly impressionable, easily swayed, and, like his counterpart in Whetstone's play, markedly religious. His very opening words, with their allusion to Paul's *Epistle to the Romans*, comment bitterly on the overweening ruler's usurpation of God's functions:

> Thus can the demigod Authority
> Make us pay down for our offence by weight.

Stratford folk' (*Life of Shakespeare*, p. 69). There is no justification for endowing Stratford folk with such monolithic moral sensibilities, and the same must be said of Shakespeare's audience when W. W. Lawrence writes of them: 'It seems clear that an Elizabethan or Jacobean audience would not have been repelled by sexual intercourse after formal betrothal but before the final ceremony, since this was a frequent and generally accepted occurrence' ('*Measure for Measure* and Lucio', *Shakespeare Quarterly*, vol. 9, 1958, p. 450). As E. I. Fripp points out, 'Puritan opinion was strong against the practice. . . . Stern laws were proposed on the lines of Old Testament legislation, and at Stratford, as elsewhere, clergy and churchwardens brought no light pressure to bear on erring couples' (*Shakespeare: Man and Artist*, vol. 2, p. 613).

[1] *Shakespeare's England* (1916), vol. 1, p. 408.

The words of heaven: on whom it will, it will;
On whom it will not, so; yet still 'tis just.

$$(1.2.114-17)^1$$

When he therefore finds himself condemned to death for fornication, and the instrument of Juliet's disgrace, it is not surprising that, in spite of his indignation at Angelo's legal tyranny, he should see himself as the Church saw him, a sinner who must suffer for his transgressions.

It seems to me, then, that the contradictions in Claudio's attitude towards the action for which he has been sentenced are not, as Professor Knights suggested, the result of 'feelings at war with themselves' in the poet, but rather spring from Shakespeare's exploitation, for his own purposes, of the contradictions inherent in the Church's edicts relating to the marriage-contract. What were these purposes? In order to show up in its blackest colours Angelo's legalism, his adherence to the letter rather than the spirit of the law, which is one of the main concerns of the play, Shakespeare needed a case in which the death-penalty could be lawfully imposed for an offence which would not lose for its perpetrator the sympathies of the audience, and one in which a proper regard for its circumstances should

---

[1] Dover Wilson calls these lines 'an insoluble crux' and thinks a whole passage may have been cut out, declaring, 'the resignation of ll. 118-19 ['The words of heaven . . . 'tis just'] is ill-suited with Claudio's fierce temper at this point' (*Measure for Measure*, *New Shakespeare* edition (1922), p. 121). But once we see that the mood of these lines is not one of resignation but of bitter indignation, they make perfectly good sense and follow quite naturally upon those that precede them. The only emendation that is needed is the insertion, first suggested by Warburton, of a full stop after 'weight'. Claudio is saying: 'Thus can authority, pretending to be like God, make us pay down for our offence in full measure (cf. Laertes' 'By heaven, thy madness shall be paid by weight', *Hamlet*, 4.5.153), arrogating to itself the words of Heaven: on whom this demi-god, authority, will have mercy, it will have mercy; on whom it will not, so—yet however wilful, it always claims to be just.' Claudio's words closely resemble, both in content and mood, Isabel's denunciation (2.2.110-23) of 'man, proud man, / Dress'd in a little brief authority', most ignorant of the frailty of his nature, though that is what Christian teaching most emphatically assures him of ('Most ignorant of what he's most assur'd, / His glassy essence'), acting like an angry ape, i.e. imitating God's wrath rather than his mercy (a return to the theme of the first half of her speech that men in authority like to imitate Jove's thunder but not his discrimination in punishment).

78

have earned him the judge's pardon. Claudio's counterpart in Cinthio's story had actually committed rape, though he was willing to make amends by marriage.[1] His counterpart in Whetstone's story and play had committed no rape, as Cassandra pleads, 'But with yeelding consent of his Mistresse, *Andrugio* hath onlye sinned through Loue, and neuer ment but with Marriage to make amendes'.[2] Shakespeare exculpates Claudio still further by making him actually the husband of Juliet, and supplying him with a strong reason why the marriage has not yet been solemnized. The fact that he should also have chosen to embody in Claudio something of the conflicting emotions which the Church's pronouncements must have aroused in many couples who had consummated an unsolemnized *de praesenti* contract, must, I think, be accounted for on dramatic grounds: apart from making him a more interesting and, to many, a more sympathetic character, it makes him a more perfect foil to Angelo. The self-incriminations of the comparatively innocent and lovable Claudio form a telling contrast to the self-righteousness of the guilty and repellent Angelo.

Another quality in Claudio which serves to make him a foil to Angelo is his sensuousness. This is manifested above all in the most famous lines he utters, his description of the terrors of the after-life. These are characteristically conceived wholly in sensory terms: the impact upon the body of the cold of the grave; the impact upon the soul of the tortures of fire, ice, and wind. These words, when joined to the Duke's preceding sermon on the miseries of life in *this* world, form an expanded version of Hamlet's 'To be or not to be' soliloquy. Critics, from Dr. Johnson onwards, have complained that in his great speech the Duke offers no hint of the Christian consolation, and that this is inconsistent with his assumed rôle of spiritual guide. But had he depicted the joys of Heaven he would have robbed Claudio's speech of much of its foundation. As it is, Claudio's fears of the torments awaiting him in the after-life, based on his feeling of guilt which he vents on his first appearance, can find unimpeded expression.[3]

[1] *Hecatommithi* (1574), Part II, R2ᵛ.
[2] *An Heptameron of Ciuill Discourses* (1582), N3ʳ.
[3] Whether he thinks of these torments as awaiting him in Hell or in Purgatory is of little dramatic importance. Miss Lascelles (*Shakespeare's*

The traditional sermon on death consisted conventionally of two parts: the *de contemptu mundi* part, depicting the worthlessness of the life in this world; and the *contemplatio mortis* part, which was made up of a contemplation of the physical act of dying and of the life to come. The Duke delivers the *de contemptu mundi* portion, and Isabel and Claudio between them the *contemplatio mortis* portion. Isabel points out that the pain of death is largely imaginary:

> The sense of death is most in apprehension;
> And the poor beetle that we tread upon
> In corporal sufferance finds a pang as great
> As when a giant dies.
>
> (3.1.79-82)

And Claudio delivers his impassioned speech on the terrors of the after-life.

Claudio is portrayed by Shakespeare with unfailing sympathy and affection. It is astonishing to find Coleridge describe him as 'detestable' and to hear other critics join in the chorus of abuse. The provost, himself upright and kindly, knows better than they when he calls him 'the most gentle Claudio' (4.2.67), an epithet which Shakespeare never bestows upon characters whom he wishes us to detest. We have seen that he first reduced the gravity of Claudio's transgression as far as was compatible with his need to make him subject to the death-penalty, and then further increased our sympathies for him by showing his remorse for what he had done. Similarly, while in Cinthio's story and Whetstone's play he experiences no inner conflict, but at once begs his sister to save his life by submitting to the deputy's demands, and in Whetstone's story he is reduced to silence by the conflict between his fear of death and the shame of receiving life under such conditions, in Shakespeare's play he at once exclaims, 'Thou shalt not do't', and only by degrees, when the full horror of death presents itself to his imagination, does he waver in his resolve. It is true that Shakespeare, by making the Duke the stage-manager of the *dénouement*, had to deny to

---

'*Measure for Measure*', 1953, p. 166) no doubt is right in saying that the reference to 'lawless and incertain thought' (3.1.128) indicates that at this point, at least, he is thinking of purgatorial pains.

Claudio the act which most endears Andrugio, his counterpart in Whetstone, to us: his return at the end of the play to save the life of the condemned Promos, although by revealing himself he expects his own death. (The assumption is that the death-sentence imposed by Promos upon Andrugio was not an act of judicial tyranny, and that the King would have it carried out should Andrugio reveal himself.) But he decides to jeopardize his life in order that his sister, who has meanwhile been married to Promos and come to love him, be spared the grief of widow-hood.[1] By means of this action Whetstone gives a balance to his play which is absent from *Measure for Measure*. Cassandra's sacrifice of her virginity to save the life of her brother is counter-poised by Andrugio's willingness to sacrifice his life to save his sister from a grief from which he thinks she would die. The relationship of brother and sister thus assumes a far greater importance in Whetstone's story and play than in either Cinthio's story (where the brother is really executed) and his play (where the brother does not appear on the stage at all) or in *Measure for Measure*. Indeed, one feels that it is this relation-ship which mattered most to Whetstone, and that instead of *Promos and Cassandra* the play ought to have been called *Andrugio and Cassandra* or *Love for Love*. In Shakespeare's play, though not as much as in Cinthio's, the relationship of Angelo and Isabella overshadows that of Claudio and Isabella,[2] and it might have been called after them, had Shakespeare been in the habit of calling his comedies, like his tragedies, after their protagonists.

Next a word about Lucio. He too has been much disliked by commentators. One of them, Dover Wilson, would indeed hand over most of his lines to an unknown reviser (though he is prompted in this less by literary than by textual considerations).[3] To me Lucio seems Shakespeare's throughout, and one of his most masterly and vivid creations. Dr. Johnson thought the

---

[1] *Promos and Cassandra*, p. 508. All page-references are to Geoffrey Bullough's reprint of the play in *Narrative and Dramatic Sources of Shakespeare*, vol. 2 (1958).

[2] Walter Pater takes a directly opposite view when he writes: 'But the main interest in *Measure for Measure* is not, as in *Promos and Cassandra*, in the relation of Isabella and Angelo, but rather in the relation of Claudio and Isabella' (*op. cit.*, p. 177).

[3] *Op. cit.*, pp. 98 ff.

comic scenes in the play 'very natural and pleasing',[1] but few of the later commentators share this view. Coleridge, as we saw, found them disgusting, and Edward Dowden declared that 'the humorous scenes would be altogether repulsive were it not that they are needed to present without disguise or extenuation the world of moral licence and corruption out of and above which rise the virginal strength and severity and beauty of Isabella'.[2] It is strange that critics who profess to delight in Falstaff should sternly refuse to be amused by Lucio. He has not only a touch of Falstaff about him (compare, for instance, the excellent scene in which he slanders the Duke to his face with the very similar scene in which Falstaff slanders the Prince), but also of Hal. His frivolities do not claim his entire being: they are partly a cloak for a nobler self which comes out in his conversations with Isabel, above all in his 'by my troth, Isabel, I lov'd thy brother' (4.3.153). He is a rather complex and, in some ways, contradictory character (which does not make him the less Shakespearian). Towards Claudio he shows himself to be a true and loyal friend, while towards Mrs. Overdone and Pompey he proves callous and perfidious, having them arrested, it would seem, in order to get out of the way these two incriminating witnesses to his own transgressions.[3]

There are two opposite attitudes towards sexual relations expressed through much of the play. There is the view of them as something natural, creative, and desirable. Of this view the chief spokesman is Lucio. And there is the view of them as something which leads to excess and thus to destruction. Of this the chief spokesman is Claudio, who sees this excess in the sexual appetite and the consequent self-destruction as something inherent in human nature:

> Our natures do pursue,
> Like rats that ravin down their proper bane,
> A thirsty evil; and when we drink we die.
>
> (1.2.122-4)

Just as rats are devoid of a natural instinct which warns them that the food they covet is poisoned, so man, according to

---

[1] *Johnson on Shakespeare*, ed. Walter Raleigh (1908), p. 81.
[2] *Shakespeare: His Mind and Art* (1875), p. 82.
[3] See 3.2.186 and, much less conclusively, 3.2.59-60.

Claudio, is devoid of the instinct which warns him that the free
indulgence of the sexual appetite leads to his destruction. And
in accord with this view is the conversation between Lucio and
the two gentlemen (1.2) about the diseases which they jestingly
accuse each other of having contracted as the result of their way
of life. The opposite attitude is most fully expressed in the great
lines spoken by Lucio to Isabel:

> Your brother and his lover have embrac'd.
> As those that feed grow full, as blossoming time
> That from the seedness the bare fallow brings
> To teeming foison, even so her plenteous womb
> Expresseth his full tilth and husbandry.
>
> (1.4.40-44)

The speech is a close counterpart, almost a reply, to Claudio's
description of the same event. Again the simile of feeding is
used, but here it is shown to lead not to death but to life, not to
self-destruction but to self-fulfilment. More prosaically, some
of Lucio's remarks to the Duke, such as his characterization of
Angelo, his 'it is impossible to extirp it quite, friar, till eating
and drinking be put down' (3.2.95-6) and Pompey's similar
words to Escalus (2.1.218 ff.) are expressions of the same
attitude.

Of the sex-nausea that occurs intermittently in the plays of
this period, from *Hamlet* to *Timon of Athens*, and which critics
have often regarded as a projection of Shakespeare's personal
mood, I can find little trace in this play. Apart from the just
quoted lines by Claudio it only receives expression in some of
the utterances of Angelo, the villain of the piece, which in itself
sufficiently 'places' it.

II

Lucio even more than Claudio serves as a foil to Angelo. In a
play which relies for many of its effects on contrast of characters
the two seem particularly marked out as opposites.

> This outward-sainted deputy,
> Whose settled visage and deliberate word
> Nips youth i' th' head, and follies doth enew
> As falcon doth the fowl,

as Isabel describes him (3.1.90-93); who takes pride in his
gravity and 'stands at a guard with envy' (i.e. is careful to give

no occasion to traducers); who 'scarce confesses / That his blood flows; or that his appetite / Is more to bread than stone', as the Duke puts it (1.3.51-3), is the exact opposite of the lapwing and jester, the reckless scandalmonger, the debauchee, and the loving friend. (His opposite, that is, in character. As a ruler and judge Angelo's opposite, as we shall see, is the Duke.)

Several of Angelo's most characteristic traits, such as his ingratitude, his cruelty, his lack of self-knowledge, his rigorous adherence to the letter of the law, are either data of the story or taken over by Shakespeare from one or several of his sources. Cinthio, in his narrative version of the tale, makes much of the ingratitude of Angelo's counterpart, Iuriste. The whole story is, in fact, told, to exemplify this crime, Iuriste's other offences being regarded as less monstrous. Fulvia, the young lady who tells the story, declares: 'Deurieno i Signori, che sono posti da Iddio a gouerno del mondo, non meno punire la ingratitudine, quall'hora viene loro a notitia, che puniscano gli Homicidi, gli Adulteri, i Ladronecci, i quali quantunque siano delitti graui, sono forse di minor pena degni che la ingratitudine.'[1] That Shakespeare was in general accord with these sentiments and that the theme of ingratitude had a peculiar fascination for him, several of his plays, culminating in *Lear* and *Timon*, bear witness. When Viola declares,

> I hate ingratitude more in a man
> Than lying, vainness, babbling drunkenness,
> Or any taint of vice whose strong corruption
> Inhabits our frail blood
>
> (*Twelfth Night*, 3.4.338-41)

there can be little doubt that she is also voicing the feelings of her creator. It seems likely, therefore, that the theme of ingratitude, of which Cinthio makes so much, was one of the facets of the story which first attracted Shakespeare to it.[2]

Angelo's cruelty, shown above all in his treatment of Mariana (3.1.219 ff.), but also in his parting wish in the suit of Elbow

---

[1] *Hecatommithi*, Part II, R2r.

[2] Of Shakespeare's knowledge of Cinthio's *novella* I think there can be little doubt. His whole opening scene, for instance, including the Duke's handing over of the commission ('lettere patenti' in Cinthio), seems broadly based on the *novella*. There is nothing corresponding to it in the other sources.

that all parties may be whipped (2.1.131) and in his threat to torture Claudio if Isabel does not yield to his desires (2.4.166-7), though less a datum of the story than his ingratitude, is also found in the sources. For instance, Whetstone in his *novella* calls him 'This Deuill, in humaine shape, more vicious than *Hyliogabalus* of *Rome*; and withall, as cruell as *Denis* of *Sicyll*'.[1]

Angelo's lack of self-knowledge, revealed above all in his first soliloquy (2.2.161 ff.), is basic to Shakespeare's conception of his character. Except for the short time at the end of the play in which he dissembles in order to save his skin, he is not a hypocrite, but is rather living up to the ideal of inhumanity which he has set himself. There is therefore nothing incongruous in the fact that even after his treatment of Mariana, which makes Isabel exclaim, 'What corruption in this life that it will let this man live!' (3.1.225), Angelo can refer to himself in soliloquy as a 'saint'. He is a self-deceiver rather than a deceiver of others. In this he is the opposite of the Duke, who takes pleasure in deceiving others (for good ends), but whose search for self-knowledge is, according to Escalus, his most notable characteristic ('One that, above all other strifes, contended especially to know himself'). The hint for Angelo's lack of self-knowledge seems to have come from Cinthio's *novella*, where Iuriste is described as being 'vie più lieto dell' vfficio, a che il chiamaua lo Imperadore, che buon conoscitore di se stesso'.[2]

For Angelo's rigorous adherence to the letter of the law at the expense of true justice Shakespeare also found suggestions in his sources. To Cassandra's plea that he should balance justice with pity Promos replies:

Cassandra, leave of thy bootlesse sute, by law he hath bene tride,
Lawe founde his faulte, Lawe judgde him death:

to which Cassandra answers:

Yet this maye be replide,
That law a mischiefe oft permits, to keepe due forme of lawe,
That lawe small faultes with greatest doomes, to keepe men styl
    in awe:
Yet Kings, or such as execute regall authoritie,
If mends be made may over rule the force of lawe with mercie.[3]

---

[1] *Heptameron*, O1ʳ.   [2] *Hecatommithi*, Part II, R2ᵛ.
[3] *Promos and Cassandra*, p. 452.

But in painting Angelo as a fanatical devotee of the Law Shakespeare seems to have been above all influenced by the figure of the Podestà in Cinthio's *Epitia*. A perusal of the scene between the Segretario and the Podestà (1.4), the one insisting on clemency and the need to consider the circumstances of each case, and pointing to the condemned youth's noble parentage ('Vico disceso è da progenie illustre'[1]; cf. Escalus's 'Alas! this gentleman, / Whom I would save, had a most noble father'), the other insisting on the necessity for the severest enforcement of the law, would, I think, by itself persuade many sceptics that Shakespeare was acquainted with Cinthio's play and influenced by it, especially in writing the dialogue between Angelo and Escalus (2.1.1-32).

To these character-traits of Angelo which he derived from his sources Shakespeare added others not found there. In the first place he turned Angelo into a Puritan; not the caricatured Puritan, all cant and hypocrisy, whom Jonson was to put on the stage a few years later, nor the comic figure with Puritan traits which Shakespeare had given us shortly before in Malvolio. Differences in social station and dramatic function prevent the two characters from having much in common beyond pride in their gravity, humourlessness, and a desire to interfere with the pleasures of their more indulgent fellow-creatures. Sir Toby's answer to Malvolio would serve for them both: 'Dost thou think, because thou art virtuous, there shall be no more cakes and ale?' Some commentators have denied Angelo's Puritanism, but his Pharisaical attitude towards the law, his particular harshness towards sexual offenders, and his revival of a statute imposing the death-penalty for fornication, seem to me to make it indisputable. The Duke calls him 'precise' (1.3.50), the normal Elizabethan word for 'puritanical', and Angelo refers to himself as a 'saint' (2.2.180), another unmistakable Puritan trait. As one scholar has pointed out, the death-sentence for adultery (though not for fornication), as laid down in the Old Testament, was a constant Puritan demand at the time, put forward by both Stubbes and Cartwright, and opposed by Anglican divines such as Whitgift. There seems much plausibility in his further conjecture that 'perhaps Shakespeare in his deputy is giving Elizabethan London a picture of

[1] *Epitia* (1583), A8v.

what they might expect if the Puritans were to wrench the sceptre from the hand of the civil magistrate'.[1]

Allied to Angelo's puritanism is another trait, which I have never seen mentioned by commentators, his cynicism. It is true that the chief evidence for this is found in one passage of somewhat doubtful meaning. It occurs towards the end of the great scene in which Angelo gradually unveils his desires to Isabel. At last he exclaims:

> I have begun,
> And now I give my sensual race the rein:
> Fit thy consent to my sharp appetite;
> Lay by all nicety and prolixious blushes
> That banish what they sue for; redeem thy brother
> By yielding up thy body to my will;
> Or else he must not only die the death,
> But thy unkindness shall his death draw out
> To ling'ring sufferance.
>
> (2.4.159-67)

What does Angelo mean by her blushes banishing what they sue for? Commentators fail to comment, yet the lines can clearly have two wholly different meanings. Angelo can either mean that Isabel's blushes at his infamous proposal, while suing for a change of heart in him, are banishing all chance of this (since they make her seem all the more desirable); or he can mean that Isabel's 'nicety and prolixious blushes' are a mere pose, that she is actually suing for what she pretends to banish,[2] his

[1] D. J. McGinn, 'The Precise Angelo', in *J. Q. Adams Memorial Studies* (1948), pp. 129 ff. Many years earlier a very young critic, Mary Suddard, in a remarkable essay, claimed that 'the play may be safely accepted as a forecast of the effect of Puritan rule on England'. And she went on to declare: 'How can the general scheme of *Measure for Measure* be interpreted save as an onslaught on Puritanism, if not as an individual yet as a social force? And does not the *dénouement* mean the downfall of Puritanic rule, the humbling of Puritanic pride, the restoration of the Renaissance?' ('*Measure for Measure* as a Clue to Shakespeare's Attitude towards Puritanism', in *Keats Shelley and Shakespeare Studies*, 1912, pp. 140, 151). A couple of years later Albrecht claimed that Shakespeare created the character of Angelo in order to personify in him the spirit of Puritanism, and that the whole play was born out of the inner need felt by the poet to come to grips with the whole issue of Puritanism (*op. cit.*, pp. 245 ff.). The first to suggest this seems to have been Ulrici (*op. cit.*, vol. 2, pp. 576 n. and 583).

[2] See *O.E.D.*, *banish* 4: 'To drive away, expel, dismiss (a thing)'; and cf. 'nor do not banish reason' (5.1.64).

embraces. I concede that the word 'banish' fits the first interpretation better. On the other hand the words 'lay by', suggesting that the nicety and blushes are merely 'put on', are more
in accord with the second interpretation. And so is the word
'prolixious', meaning 'long drawn out', for it suggests that her
blushes are merely postponing the moment of surrender with a
sort of mock-modesty.[1] This interpretation receives support
from another remark of Angelo's, the meaning of which is
unmistakable. Earlier in the scene, after Isabel has repeatedly
failed to see the hidden drift of his remarks, Angelo declares:

> Your sense pursues not mine; either you are ignorant
> Or seem so, craftily; and that's not good.
> *Isabel:* Let me be ignorant, and in nothing good
> But graciously to know I am no better.
> *Angelo:* Thus wisdom wishes to appear most bright
> When it doth tax itself; as these black masks
> Proclaim an enshell'd[2] beauty ten times louder
> Than beauty could, display'd.
>
> (2.4.74-81)

This passage seems to me all of a piece with that about the
'prolixious blushes' according to the second interpretation. In
the one Angelo cynically declares that Isabel's humility is
merely a pretence, and that she really longs for his praise; in
the other, with even greater cynicism, he claims that her
modesty is merely a pretence, and that she really longs for his
embraces. Such a reading of the lines does not conflict with the
fact that Angelo's lust for Isabel has been aroused by her purity
and that in his first soliloquy he speaks of her modesty and
goodness. For he does not, of course, really believe that her
chastity and humility are mere make-believe, but finds pleasure
in telling her that he thinks it. It is a state of mind akin to that
of Hamlet when he insults Ophelia in the nunnery- and 'mouse-
trap'-scenes. Both find a perverse pleasure in venting their

---

[1] This is how George Steevens understood the words: '*Prolixious blushes*
mean what Milton has elegantly called "sweet reluctant delay" ' (*apud* 1821
Variorum edition, vol. 9, p. 92). Hart in his Arden edition explains 'prolixious' as meaning 'superfluous', but this sense is not recorded in *O.E.D.*

[2] I have adopted the emendation of F's 'enshield' first proposed by
Tyrrwhit.

cynical view of womankind upon its one representative whom they know to be innocent and pure.

Another trait added by Shakespeare, Angelo's cold and calculated cunning, is chiefly revealed in fifty lines or so (2.4.30-80) of the scene just discussed. I do not think his manœuvring here, as carefully planned ahead as a game of chess, has ever been analysed by commentators. In the first section (ll. 42-57) his object is to trap her into declaring that fornication is not as great a sin as murder, so that he can then confront her with the fact that she must either commit the one or the other (for if she refused to yield to his demands she would, Angelo implies, be virtually guilty of murdering her brother) and that she had consequently better commit the lesser of the two sins. He therefore begins by denouncing fornication, declaring it to be just as bad as murder, in the hope that she will contradict him:

> Ha! Fie, these filthy vices! It were as good
> To pardon him that hath from nature stol'n
> A man already made, as to remit
> Their saucy sweetness that do coin heaven's image
> In stamps that are forbid; 'tis all as easy
> Falsely to take away a life true made
> As to put metal in restrained mints[1]
> To make a false one.

As he had hoped, Isabel declares that this is true according to divine law (lechery and murder are both deadly sins, and therefore equally damnable), but not according to human law:

> 'Tis set down so in heaven, but not in earth.

In other words, she tacitly reminds him that he is not God but a human judge, and that it is according to man-made law that her brother must be judged. Angelo at once takes her up and rapidly goes on to his next move:

> Say you so? Then I shall pose you quickly.
> Which had you rather—that the most just law
> Now took your brother's life; or, to redeem him,
> Give up your body to such sweet uncleanness
> As she that he hath stain'd?

[1] I have adopted Steevens's proposed emendation of F's 'meanes', which undoubtedly restores the true reading.

He thinks that he has now impaled her on the horns of a dilemma. For if she replies, as she is likely to do, that she would prefer her brother's death to her dishonour, he can quote back to her her own words, that in the eye of man murder is a greater sin than fornication. But Isabel defeats this move unwittingly in a way which Angelo had not anticipated. She simply does not answer his question at all, declaring:

> Sir, believe this:
> I had rather give my body than my soul.

Angelo is naturally annoyed at having his carefully built trap thus simply passed by, and he exclaims irritably: 'I talk not of your soul'. Then, seizing upon the new opening which she has suggested, he points out that she would not endanger her soul by yielding to his desires, since sins into which we are forced through necessity are not charged against us in the divine ledger:

> our compell'd sins
> Stand more for number than for accompt.

Again he is foiled by Isabel's inability to follow his drift. 'How say you?' she asks in bewilderment. He realizes at once that this argument will not prove effective, and, to return to the language of the chess-board, he takes his last move back.

> Nay, I'll not warrant that; for I can speak
> Against the thing I say.

A new move has to be thought of. Having first tried to make Isabel admit that fornication is a lesser sin than murder and therefore to be preferred, and having next maintained that sins into which we are forced are hardly sins at all, he now argues that a sin committed to save a brother's life partakes of virtue, a point of view more forcibly expressed later by Claudio:

> What sin you do to save a brother's life,
> Nature dispenses with the deed so far
> That it becomes a virtue.

> (3.1.135-7)

Angelo does not want to ruin his case through over-statement. He does not deny that it would be a sin, but merely argues that this sin would be counterbalanced by virtue. Again his move is defeated by Isabel's failure to see his true meaning:

> Answer to this:
> I, now the voice of the recorded law,
> Pronounce a sentence on your brother's life;
> Might there not be a charity in sin
> To save this brother's life?
> *Isabel:*   Please you to do't,
> I'll take it as a peril to my soul
> It is no sin at all, but charity.
> *Angelo:* Pleas'd you to do't at peril of your soul,
> Were equal poise of sin and charity.
> *ısabel:* That I do beg his life, if it be sin,
> Heaven let me bear it! You granting of my suit,
> If that be sin, I'll make it my morn prayer
> To have it added to the faults of mine,
> And nothing of your answer.

Angelo is now thoroughly exasperated. He feels like the chess-player who finds his most skilful and carefully calculated moves come to nothing, simply because his opponent fails to understand their purpose and therefore does not reply in the expected manner. Or is it possible that this girl is not really so slow-witted but is merely outmanœuvring him by pretending not to understand his meaning? And so Angelo exclaims:

> Nay, but hear me;
> Your sense pursues not mine; either you are ignorant
> Or seem so, craftily; and that's not good.

There follows the passage I have already discussed, and the rest of the game is played by Angelo in a much simpler style.

I have discussed these forty lines in such detail, partly because they shed light on an important side of Angelo's character, and partly because of Dr. Tillyard's remark that the scene 'is terribly obscure in places and simply cannot be read with unimpeded pleasure', and that this is the result of the 'imperfections of our only text, that of the First Folio'.[1] For though I admit the occasional obscurities in the scene, I do not think this due to any textual corruption, or, as Dover Wilson suggests, to any cuts by a reviser,[2] but to the fact that Angelo goes so darkly to work with the poor girl that he succeeds in mystifying not only her but also the audience.

---

[1] *Shakespeare's Problem Plays* (1951), p. 134.
[2] *Op. cit.*, pp. 132-4 *passim*.

Finally, Shakespeare added two other traits found, at best, very sketchily in his sources: Angelo's frigidity and his willed inhumanity. The latter is exhibited above all in the Duke's account of his desertion of Mariana upon the loss of her dowry: 'Left her in tears, and dried not one of them with his comfort; swallowed his vows whole, pretending in her discoveries of dishonour; in few, bestow'd her on her own lamentations, which she yet wears for his sake; and he, a marble to her tears, is washed with them, but relents not' (3.1.219-223). What we here learn of Angelo is wholly in accord with what we see of him in the course of the play. His perfidy and callousness towards Mariana is followed by his perfidy and callousness towards Isabel. The Duke's metaphor is telling: 'and he, a marble to her tears, is washed with them, but relents not'. Cold, hard, immovable, these are the very qualities on which Angelo prides himself. His ruling attribute is inhumanity in its most literal sense, a total absence of normal human feelings and desires. Lucio, who, throughout the play, acts as the spokesman of Nature, emphasizes this side of Angelo in his amusing gossip about his origins:

> They say this Angelo was not made by man and woman after this downright way of creation. Is it true, think you?
> *Duke:* How should he be made, then?
> *Lucio:* Some report a sea-maid spawn'd him; some, that he was begot between two stock-fishes. . . .
>
> (3.2.96-100)

And the Duke's description of him as one who

> scarce confesses
> that his blood flows, or that his appetite
> Is more to bread than stone
>
> (1.3.51-3)

in which, with his apparent allusion to the Temptation in the Wilderness, he seems to glance ironically at Angelo's pretensions to a Christ-like capacity to resist temptation, enforces the idea that his inhumanity is not merely a defect of Nature, but that Angelo is collaborating with Nature to achieve a willed and practised inhumanity.

That Angelo is thus a compendium of the human qualities which Shakespeare most disliked seems to me undeniable.

Cruelty, ingratitude, perfidy, judicial tyranny, calculated cunning, Pharisaism, humourlessness—the list could easily be prolonged. That in spite of all this we feel a measure of sympathy towards him even before his repentance at the end seems largely due to the way in which, in his three soliloquies, we are allowed to see him suffer and struggle, so that we feel towards him more as we do towards Macbeth and Claudius than towards Iago and Edmund. And if we can believe in his final conversion in the literal sense of a turning about of his whole character, that he is, in Isabel's words, 'like man new made' (2.2.79),[1] there is no reason why we should feel with Swinburne that in his pardon we have been 'defrauded and derided and sent empty away',[2] or grudge him Mariana as a wife. It is because this conversion is treated so perfunctorily, because Shakespeare, in the general bustle of the *dénouement*, has not allowed it sufficient space to bring it home to our imaginations, that the radical dissatisfaction, felt by many besides Swinburne, can take root. In his examination of Juliet's conscience the Duke had distinguished between two kinds of repentance:

> but lest you do repent
> As that the sin hath brought you to this shame,
> Which sorrow is always toward ourselves, not heaven,
> Showing we would not spare heaven as we love it,
> But as we stand in fear—
> *Juliet:* I do repent me as it is an evil,
> And take the shame with joy.

$$(2.3.30\text{-}36)$$

Had Shakespeare made us feel that Angelo could truthfully have echoed Juliet's words, that his repentance is not of the other sort, all would, I think, have been well.

Angelo is sometimes spoken of as a tragic character.[3] And it is true that, however sketchily, he is shown to undergo one of the two types of tragic experience which, in the previous chapter, we found to be recurrent in Shakespeare's plays: that of disillusion with the person or thing most dear to one in this

---

[1] Promos, in Whetstone's story and play, seems to undergo an equally radical conversion (see *Promos and Cassandra*, pp. 509 ff.; *Heptameron*, O3r).

[2] *A Study of Shakespeare* (1879), p. 203.

[3] Notably by W. M. T. Dodds, 'The Character of Angelo in *Measure for Measure*', *M.L.R.*, vol. 41 (1946), pp. 246 ff.

world. What makes his experience unique among Shakespeare's characters is that the object of this disillusion is his own person. The experience is expressed in his first and second soliloquies. In the first soliloquy (2.2.162 ff.) the disillusion is with the new self he has come to recognize within him. In the second soliloquy it is rather his old self, his former way of life, with which he has become disillusioned:

> The state whereon I studied
> Is, like a good thing being often read,
> Grown ser'd and tedious; yea, my gravity,
> Wherein—let no man hear me—I take pride,
> Could I with boot change for an idle plume
> Which the air beats for vain.

$$(2.4.7\text{-}12)^1$$

But in both cases the disillusion is with the person he most cherishes in this world, himself, and so conforms to the pattern of tragic experience in Shakespeare's plays. (It may here be added that Isabel's most tragic experience in this play also conforms to this pattern. The object of her disillusion is Claudio, the person she loves most in this world, an experience which vents itself in her terrible outburst (3.1.137 ff.).)

Shakespeare evidently intended the name of Angelo (perhaps suggested by Angela, Iuriste's sister, in Cinthio's play) to have a twofold connotation. He is both the 'angel on the outward side', as the Duke puts it (3.2.254), who is inwardly a devil, and also a false coin, not the angel (a ten-shilling gold coin in Shakespeare's day) that he appears to be. To the former there are repeated allusions. There is Isabel's 'This outward-sainted deputy . . . is yet a devil' (3.1.90-93); 'There is a devilish mercy in the judge' (3.1.66); 'You bid me seek redemption of the devil' (5.1.29); the Duke's 'let the devil / Be sometime honour'd for his burning throne!' (5.1.290-91); and above all Angelo's own much debated 'Let's write "good angel" on the devil's horn; / 'Tis yet the devil's crest' (2.4.16-17).[2] He is the fallen

---

[1] Cf. Macbeth's similar expression of disillusion with the state whereon he studied: 'My way of life / Is fall'n into the sere, the yellow leaf' (5.3.22-3), which supports the emendation of F's 'feard' to 'ser'd' or, less plausibly to my mind, 'sere'.

[2] That Shakespeare wrote 'yet' for F's 'not', as was first suggested by Johnson, seems to me a near-certainty. It alone fits the context and links

angel who, in the course of his fall, has turned into a devil. But
he is also the Angel of Death. To deal out death, to destroy is
his dominant function in the play, above all to destroy those
who create life, such as Claudio and Juliet. This lends added
meaning to his already quoted remark that

> It were as good
> To pardon him that hath from nature stol'n
> A man already made, as to remit
> Their saucy sweetness that do coin heaven's image
> In stamps that are forbid; 'tis all as easy
> Falsely to take away a life true made
> As to put metal in restrained mints
> To make a false one.

(2.4.42-49)

Apart from their immediate tactical purpose, these words also
seem to express Angelo's real convictions.

This passage serves as a bridge to the view of Angelo as a
false coin. It is not without piquancy to hear one false coin
denounce the making of others, though, whereas what is false
in Angelo is not the stamp which the Duke has put upon him
but the metal (he is not the gold that his glitter suggests), what
is false in the coins that he denounces is not the metal but the
stamp (they are illicitly minted). The references to Angelo as a
coin occur in the opening scene of the play. Before having him
called, the Duke asks Escalus: 'What figure of us think you he
will bear?' (1.1.17). And when acquainted with the office
entrusted to him Angelo exclaims:

> Now, good my lord,
> Let there be some more test made of my metal,
> Before so noble and so great a figure
> Be stamp'd upon it.

(1.1.48-51)

up with the preceding 'blood, thou art blood'. The blood, i.e. man's true
nature, remains the same, says Angelo, whatever the outward case, the
habit, in which it cloaks itself, and which deceives both foolish and wise.
The horn remains the crest of the devil, whatever deceiving motto we choose
to inscribe upon it. Dover Wilson's proposed emendation of 'not' to 'now'
and his explanation, 'By Angelo's fall "good Angel" has become "the devil's
crest"' (*op. cit.*, p. 132), involves, like the explanations of editors who retain
the reading of F, a confusion of crest with motto of which Shakespeare could
never have been guilty. For the horn as crest see *A.Y.L.*, 4.2.13-14. For 'n'
misprinted for 'y' see Leon Kellner, *Restoring Shakespeare* (1925), p. 86.

But the Duke, reversing the usual sequence, prefers to test his metal after the figure is stamped upon it, in order to see 'if power change purpose, what our seemers be' (1.3.54).

III

Let us look next at Isabel, the most controversial figure in the play. There is perhaps no other Shakespeare character about whom critics have disagreed so violently, and female critics no less so than male, as the following specimens will illustrate. Here are Una Ellis-Fermor's comments on Isabel:

> Hard as an icicle she visits Claudio in prison and lays before him the terms and her decision. . . . But because of her inhumanity she can watch unmoved while he faces the awful realization of immediate death, her pitilessness only growing with his pleading. Weak as he is, his self-indulgence cannot stand comparison with hers, with the pitiless, unimaginative self-absorbed virtue which sustains her. . . . We know from this moment that a nunnery contains no cure for Isabella's malady and we have a shrewd suspicion that she will not end there.[1]

And here are Mrs. Jameson's comments upon her:

> Isabel is like a stately and graceful cedar, towering on some Alpine cliff, unbowed and unscathed amid the storm. She gives us the impression of one who has passed under the ennobling discipline of suffering and self-denial: a melancholy charm tempers the natural vigour of her mind: her spirit seems to stand upon an eminence, and look down upon the world as if already enskyed and sainted. . . . Upon what ground can we read the play from beginning to end, and doubt the angel-purity of Isabella, or contemplate her possible lapse from virtue?[2]

Faced with such antithetical views of the same character, Quiller-Couch, who, on his own admission, swings back and forth between them in the course of reading the play, declares:

> We do not set ourselves up for umpires in this dispute. Our point is that the dispute itself—the mere fact that intelligent readers can hold such opposite views of a character which, on the face of it, should be simplicity itself—is proof that the play misses clearness in portraying its most important character.[3]

[1] *Op. cit.*, p. 226.
[2] *Shakespeare's Heroines* (1886), pp. 66, 75.
[3] *Measure for Measure, New Shakespeare* edition, pp. xxix-xxx.

But is not this very assumption that the character of Isabel should be simplicity itself the great mistake made by many critics, who proceed from the notion that the character *should* be simple to the conviction that it *is* simple, and consequently paint it all black or all white? When Quiller-Couch goes on to say that 'our own sense of the play has to admit the perplexity of Isabella', he ought to have written 'complexity' instead. Once we admit the latter, the former vanishes. Isabel, like the other main characters in the play, is complex, while her critics have, all too often, been simple. 'The ready judgments which are often passed on Shakespeare's most difficult characters and situations', writes Sir Walter Raleigh apropos of this play, 'are like the talk of children. Childhood is amazingly moral, with a confident, dictatorial, unflinching morality. The work of experience, in those who are capable of experience, is to undermine this early pedantry, and to teach tolerance, or at least suspense of judgement.[1]' Taking this wise piece of advice, and suspending our judgement a little, let us look at some of the issues raised by Shakespeare's depiction of Isabel.

Her detractors frequently use about her such words as 'icy' and 'glacial', when in reality she seems the most fiery of all Shakespeare's young women. At times this flame burns low, but most often it shoots up in a blaze of anger towards Angelo or Claudio or sinful man in general. The fierceness of Isabel's denunciation of her brother, however much it may pain us, therefore need not come as a surprise, in the face of similar outbursts by Isabel throughout the play. As R. W. Chambers, her ablest defender, remarks: 'For all her silence and modesty, Isabel has the ferocity of the martyr.'[2] That the outburst, unlike those directed at Angelo, *does* pain us, and was, I believe, intended by Shakespeare to do so, comes not so much from the vehemence or the nature of its invective as from the person at whom it is directed. Shakespeare has won our love and compassion for Claudio to such a degree that any except the gentlest of reproaches must jar upon us. Throughout the scene, as throughout the play, Shakespeare plays with our affection for Isabel, alternately arousing and chilling it. It is the technique discussed in the preceding chapter (p. 70) to which I have

[1] *Op. cit.*, p. 165.   [2] *Op. cit.*, p. 293.

there given the name of 'dramatic coquetry'. Quiller-Couch's description of his vacillating reactions to the character bears witness to Shakespeare's successful use of it with at least one reader. He declares that 'to us, in our day, it looks as if this virgin "enskied and sainted" had saved herself by a trick which denudes her own chastity of all but chastity's conventional (or conventual) religious trappings; that she is chaste, even fiercely chaste, for herself, without quite knowing what chastity means. We tell ourselves this; anon, as we read, we repent having said it; and, a page or so later, we say it again—or at least that "We do not love thee, Isabel. The reason why we cannot tell. . . ." '[1] Such a sequence of opposed feelings towards Isabel is, I think, exactly what Shakespeare was trying to evoke. Earlier in this scene the girl whom her detractors declare to be lacking in human feelings has drawn us to her by declaring,

> O, were it but my life!
> I'd throw it down for your deliverance
> As frankly as a pin.
>
> (3.1.105-7)[2]

R. W. Chambers's comparison of her to the Christian martyrs is most apt. She has their eagerness for self-sacrifice in the cause of her ideals, their utter contempt for life. At this moment and in the following lines, when we are watching her growing agony at Claudio's surrender to the lure of life, we are drawn closer to Isabel than anywhere else in the play, and we divide our love and compassion between these two tormented souls. Then comes the flow of savage invective and most of us are inevitably repelled.

Isabel has not only the ferocity and the contempt for life of the Christian martyrs, but also, as has been remarked by F. R. Leavis, she is capable of experiencing a 'kind of sensuality of martyrdom'[3]. When asked by Angelo what she would do if confronted with the choice between her brother's death and the sacrifice of her virginity, she replies:

[1] *Op. cit.*, p. xxx.

[2] Cassandra similarly declares in the corresponding scene:

> O would my life would satisfie his yre,
> *Cassandra* then, would cancell soone thy band. (p. 461)

[3] 'The Greatness of *Measure for Measure*', *Scrutiny*, vol. 10 (1942), p. 234.

> As much for my poor brother as myself;
> That is, were I under the terms of death,
> Th' impression of keen whips I'd wear as rubies,
> And strip myself to death as to a bed
> That longing have been sick for, ere I'd yield
> My body up to shame.
>
> (2.4.99-104)

Although she does not expressly call it a bridal bed, this seems implied by the context. The adornment of the bride ('Th' impression of keen whips I'd wear as rubies') is followed by her disrobing. The speech parallels Claudio's

> If I must die,
> I will encounter darkness as a bride
> And hug it in mine arms.

There is a significant contrast between the note of strenuousness, of a kind of moral athleticism, which appears in this as in so many of Isabel's utterances, and the softer and more lyrical quality of Claudio's words.

The thought of sacrifice also evokes in Isabel something of the gaiety of the Christian martyrs, as is suggested, to me at least, by the couplet which has repelled so many readers:

> Then, Isabel, live chaste, and, brother, die:
> More than our brother is our chastity.
>
> (2.4.184-5)[1]

Commentators have spoken of the callousness of these lines. But Isabel has just decided to sacrifice the person she loves most in this world rather than commit what she takes to be a deadly sin, and consequently can feel elated about her decision.

That Isabel could, apparently without a moment's hesitation, decide to sacrifice her brother rather than her virginity, has caused much offence among critics. Once we accept her postulate that the yielding to Angelo's demands would lead to

---

[1] One is reminded of that gay, dashing couplet in which Crashaw describes St. Teresa setting off in search of martyrdom:

> Farewell house, and farewell home!
> She's for the Moors and Martyrdom.

the eternal damnation of her soul, it is impossible to quarrel with her decision or to be surprised that she reaches it instantly and unhesitatingly.

> Better it were a brother died at once
> Than that a sister, by redeeming him,
> Should die for ever.
>
> (2.4.106-8)

But it is surely this very postulate that redemption of a brother under such circumstances would lead to eternal damnation which Shakespeare wishes us to question. Isabel takes as Pharisaical a view of the divine law as Angelo does of man-made law. In fact, she seems to imagine God as a kind of Angelo, a rigorous and legalistic judge, who will sentence her entirely according to the letter of the law rather than its spirit. It never occurs to her that it would be even more monstrous a perversion of justice for God to sentence her to eternal damnation for saving a brother's life by an act that has nothing whatever in common with the deadly sin of lechery except its outward form, than it is for Angelo to condemn Claudio to death for an act which can only in the most legalistic sense be said to fall within the law against fornication. Although Isabel eloquently stresses God's mercy when trying to move Angelo to imitate His example, when it comes to God's judgement of her own hypothetical sin she imagines Him as entirely rigorous and merciless. Her view of justice is indeed remarkably similar to that of Angelo: both seem to believe that the letter of the law and justice are synonymous. Her legalism is epitomized in her words to the Duke: 'I had rather my brother die by the law than my son should be unlawfully born' (3.1.187-8), a statement which tells us a lot about Isabel. She also shares Angelo's detestation of libertinism and his desire for a life of austerity and self-restraint. The Duke describes Angelo as 'A man of stricture and firm abstinence' (1.3.12), while Isabel in her opening words, always important with Shakespeare as an index to character, expresses her wish for 'a more strict restraint / Upon the sisterhood, the votarists of Saint Clare' (1.4.4-5), which she is about to join. And it is surely significant that, next to Angelo himself, she is the only person in the play who thinks the death-penalty a just punishment for fornication (2.2.41).

It is this fact and her detestation of libertinism which make her plea for her brother's life at first so half-hearted an affair:

> There is a vice that most I do abhor,
> And most desire should meet the blow of justice;
> For which I would not plead, but that I must;
> For which I must not plead, but that I am
> At war 'twixt will and will not.
>
> (2.2.29-33)

Isabel's inclination towards legalism is again shown in her exculpation of Angelo at the end of the play:

> My brother had but justice
> In that he did the thing for which he died;
> For Angelo,
> His act did not o'ertake his bad intent,
> And must be buried but as an intent
> That perish'd by the way. Thoughts are no subjects;
> Intents but merely thoughts.
>
> (5.1.446-52)

One's spirit recoils at hearing this girl, who had not a word to say in excuse of her brother but rather admitted the justice of his doom, now plead, with all the finesse of a seasoned attorney, on the most purely legalistic grounds for her would-be ravisher and the judicial murderer of her brother. It is particularly startling when put against her own words earlier in the scene:

> That Angelo's forsworn, is it not strange?
> That Angelo's a murderer, is't not strange?
> That Angelo is an adulterous thief,
> An hypocrite, a virgin-violator,
> Is it not strange and strange?
>
> (5.1.38-42)

Not as strange as that the person who has just called him these things should shortly afterwards plead that he is innocent in the eyes of the law and should therefore be pardoned. It is surely wrong to say with R. W. Chambers and others[1] that this is

---

[1] Elizabeth Pope, for example, declares: 'it is sheer, reckless forgiveness of the kind Christ advocates in the Sermon on the Mount' ('The Renaissance Background of *Measure for Measure*', *Shakespeare Survey*, vol. 2, 1949, p. 79).

simply Christian forgiveness. We are not here concerned with private forgiveness, the duty of every Christian, but with a judicial pardon. The Duke clearly brings out the distinction when he tells Isabel that she must pardon Angelo 'for Mariana's sake', but that the law demands his death (5.1.398 ff.). Isabel may or may not have pardoned Angelo. We are not told (in contrast to Cinthio's play, where the heroine declares explicitly, 'io gli perdono / Qualunque offesa'.[1]) Her prolonged silence in the face of Mariana's repeated appeals could certainly be taken to indicate that Isabel has not pardoned Angelo, and that she is torn by conflicting desires to see her enemy punished and to reciprocate Mariana's service to her by helping to save her husband—for this too is 'measure for measure' and thus a possible part of the complex meaning of the play's title. But all this is mere speculation. Indisputable is the fact that Isabel is here pleading for a judicial pardon, and not on the Christian grounds of the need to show mercy, as she does so eloquently in her first interview with Angelo, but on the legalistic grounds that Angelo is technically innocent of the crimes for which he is condemned to die. What repels us is not that Isabel should ask for Angelo to be pardoned. Had she done so on the same grounds on which she had pleaded for the pardon of her brother, we might have been surprised but we would not have been repelled. It is precisely the fact that her plea is *not* Christian but legalistic—'a string of palpable sophistry', as Quiller-Couch justly calls it[2]—which antagonizes so many spectators. (Isabel is decidedly more unselfish in her plea for Angelo's life than her counterparts in the sources. Epitia pleads because she fears her reputation would suffer if she consented to her husband's execution, Cassandra because she has come to love him. Isabel's plea alone is prompted by entirely unselfish motives. But unselfishness is not a Christian monopoly.)

It is significant that R. W. Chambers's defence of Isabel's plea for Angelo, in spite of his emphasis on its supposedly Christian nature, is as legalistic as Isabel's own. Much of the passage—on which I may be allowed to insert some comments —is a mixture of the half-truths and specious reasoning which

---

[1] *Epitia*, H2^v.　　　　[2] *Op. cit.*, p. xxxii.

seem to me to mar much of his in many ways so admirable essay on the play. He writes[1]:

> It is a postulate of our story that Claudio has committed a capital offence. Angelo has not committed a crime in letting the law take its course upon Claudio [that the Duke considers the promise-breach involved in 'letting the law take its course upon Claudio' as one of Angelo's two great crimes, his words make clear. Angelo, he tells Isabel, is
>
> > criminal in double violation
> > Of sacred chastity and of promise-breach,
> > Thereon dependent, for your brother's life
> > > (5.1.402-4)[2]];
>
> he has not committed a crime in his union with Mariana, to whom he has been publicly betrothed [in his union with Mariana Angelo has, in fact, committed fornication, and is thus as much subject to the death-penalty under the law which he has revived as Claudio had been. Whether his betrothal with Mariana was public or private is of no legal consequence]; those are assumptions on which the play is based. Angelo would be despicable if he put forward any such plea for himself, and he does not. But the fact remains that Angelo's sin has been, not in act, but in thought, and human law cannot take cognizance of thought: 'thoughts are no subjects' [among Angelo's crimes in act, not thought, is his gross abuse of his judicial powers in his relations with Isabel, the worst crime which *qua judge* he could have committed].

---

[1] *Op. cit.*, pp. 301-2.

[2] In this formulation of Angelo's principal crimes Shakespeare was, no doubt, influenced by his sources, chiefly, it would seem, Cinthio's *novella*, where the Emperor tells Iuriste:

'Due, sono stati i tuoi delitti, & ambidue molto graui: L'vno, l'hauer vituperata questa Giouane, con tale inganno, che si dee dire, che le habbi fatta forza; l'altro l'hauerle vcciso, contra la fede datale, il suo Fratello. . . . Però, poi che al primo peccato ho proueduto, con l' hauerti fatta sposare la violata donna, in emenda del secondo voglio, che cosi sia a te tagliata la testa, come al suo fratello la facesti tagliare.' (*Hecatommithi*, Part II, R5ᵛ).

Whetstone, in both his play and *novella*, follows Cinthio in making the King declare that Promos's forced marriage to Cassandra is 'to repayre her honour by thee violated' and that his subsequent execution is 'to make satisfaction for her Brother's death' (*Heptameron*, O2ᵛ; *Promos and Cassandra*, p. 499).

Besides, Isabel is conscious that, however innocently, she herself has been the cause of Angelo's fall:

> I partly think
> A due sincerity govern'd his deeds,
> Till he did look on me; since it is so,
> Let him not die.

[Chambers here confuses cause and occasion. A jeweller, by displaying his wares, is not the innocent cause of an attempted burglary.] And Angelo is penitent. There can be no doubt what the words of the Sermon on the Mount demand: 'Judge not, and ye shall not be judged.' That had been Isabel's plea for Claudio [like so many commentators on the play and like the early Anabaptists, Chambers here confuses public and private judgement. To prevent Anabaptist anarchy Protestant divines in the sixteenth century emphasized again and again that Christ's words merely applied to private judgement, and were by no means intended to abrogate the ruler's duty to pass judgement on all offenders.[1] Besides, Isabel had made no such plea for Claudio. She had not asked for an abstention from judgement but for the seasoning of Justice with Mercy.] It is a test of her sincerity, if she can put forward a plea for mercy for her dearest foe, as well as for him whom she dearly loves [by thus identifying the two pleas Chambers obscures the fact that, though they have the same object, they are utterly different in their nature: that for Claudio is predominantly Christian, while that for Angelo is purely legalistic].

This strain of legalism in Isabel has been remarked by Professor Charlton: 'Too frequently she seems to regard the letter as the fundamental thing in the law', he comments.[2] And Isabel's Puritanism—which also manifests itself at times in her diction, e.g. 'I have spirit to do anything that appears not foul in the truth of my spirit' (3.1.201-2)—has also not gone unnoticed. Lascelles Abercrombie, in his excellent British Academy Lecture for 1930, says of it: 'When we come to Shakespeare's use of the feeling against puritanism in *Measure for Measure*, we find that the antagonist who brings into odium the popular idea of

---

[1] For a valuable discussion of this point see Miss Pope's article cited above, p. 69.

[2] *Shakespearian Comedy* (1938), p. 254.

puritanism in Angelo is actually puritanism itself—the splendid and terrible puritanism of Isabella'.[1]

I am not suggesting that we should do what Quiller-Couch confesses he was once almost driven to do: to examine Isabel and Angelo 'as two pendent portraits or studies in the ugliness of Puritan hypocrisy'.[2] For Isabel is no hypocrite, nor is there anything ugly about her Puritanism. It is, as Abercrombie says, 'splendid and terrible'. I am merely maintaining that throughout the play Shakespeare is showing up certain likenesses between the two characters, that he is manipulating our feelings towards Isabel by alternately engaging and alienating our affection for her, and that he is doing all this mainly to make us question her decision to sacrifice her brother rather than her virginity. He makes us question it without forcing an answer upon us. The majority of critics have, in fact, felt that Isabel could have acted in no other way than she did. R. W. Chambers, who must speak for all these, declares that 'whether she remains in the Convent or no, one who is contemplating such a life can no more be expected to sell herself into mortal sin, than a good soldier can be expected to sell a stronghold entrusted to him'.[3] (By taking it for granted that it would be a mortal sin, Chambers begs the question. Hence the analogy with the soldier is a false one.) There have been others—a minority among critics, but much more numerous, I suspect, among those mute, inglorious Bradleys that constitute the bulk of Shakespeare's readers—who have thought that Cinthio's Epitia and Whetstone's Cassandra made the more admirable choice. The manner in which Shakespeare manipulates his material, as well as the evidence of his other plays, suggest to me very strongly that he, too, preferred Cassandra's choice. How he felt towards a legalistic conception of Divine Justice is suggested by his treatment of the churlish priest in *Hamlet*, who refuses Ophelia's

---

[1] 'A Plea for the Liberty of Interpreting', in *Aspects of Shakespeare* (1933), p. 236. Many years earlier Mary Suddard had written: 'In Isabella and Angelo Shakespeare not only embodies two main types of Puritan, but sets forth all the advantages and defects of Puritanic training. . . . Different as its results may seem on Angelo and Isabella, the two studies point to the same conclusion: Puritanism, in its present state, unmodified, is unfit to come into contact with society. To borrow the words of Lamb, "it is an owl that will not bear daylight" ' (*op. cit.*, p. 149).

[2] *Op. cit.*, p. xxx. [3] *Op. cit.*, p. 292.

body full burial rites because technically her death may come
under the heading of suicide:

> Her death was doubtful;
> And, but that great command o'ersways the order,
> She should in ground unsanctified have lodg'd
> Till the last trumpet; for charitable prayers,
> Shards, flints, and pebbles, should be thrown on her . . .

with Laertes' splendid reply:

> I tell thee, churlish priest,
> A minist'ring angel shall my sister be
> When thou liest howling.

(5.1.221 ff.)

It is the kind of reply which one would like Isabel to have made
when Angelo denounces the 'filthy vices' of her brother. Instead
we get her 'My brother had but justice, / In that he did the
thing for which he died'. By depicting first the inhumanity of
Angelo's legalism, followed by numerous parallels between
Isabel's and Angelo's characters, and then showing Isabel's
legalistic view of Divine Justice, Shakespeare is, it would seem
to me, strongly suggesting his own attitude towards her choice.
But he leaves it sufficiently unobtrusive to allow the audience
to respond to it in an uncertain, divided, or varied manner.

Measure for Measure is thus seen to conform to the definition
of the Problem Play given in the Introduction (p. 6). We have
found in it 'a concern with a moral problem which is central to
it, presented in such a manner that we are unsure of our moral
bearings, so that uncertain and divided responses to it in the
minds of the audience are possible or even probable'. This view
of the play is supported by Raleigh when he writes of it: 'Of all
Shakespeare's plays, this one comes nearest to the direct treatment of a moral problem.'[1] It finds its sharpest opponent in
E. E. Stoll, who declares that *Measure for Measure* is 'a tragi-
comedy, still less than *All's Well* a problem play. No question
is raised, no casuistry is engaged in, no "dilemma", whether
intolerable or tolerable, is put. . . . By his deviation from his
source . . . Shakespeare has made the play even less of the
problem kind than it had been. . . . In fact, the moral rigour in
the heroine—the want of a problem—is . . . what some un-

[1] *Op. cit.*, p. 169.

sympathetic contemporary critics complain of.'[1] Professor Stoll fails to see that the moral rigour of the heroine, as Shakespeare presents it, is itself at the root of the problem. That Isabel's choice does not appear to her in any way problematic—that she is shown free from all inner conflict and doubt—in no way implies that Shakespeare presents it as unproblematic and that the same freedom from conflict and doubt is experienced by the audience. This truism—that the response of the audience and of the protagonist to a moral choice confronting him may be opposed and must be distinguished—can be most neatly illustrated by a comparison of Whetstone's presentation in his play of Cassandra's choice with Shakespeare's presentation of the choice of Isabel.

Like Epitia in Cinthio's *novella*, Cassandra, when faced with the judge's infamous proposal, is concerned solely about her 'honour', i.e. her reputation in the eyes of the world, where Isabel is concerned solely about the salvation of her soul. Like Epitia, Cassandra declares that she would rather die than lose her honour: 'Honor farre dearer is then life, which passeth price of golde', she tells Promos (p. 460). And in the scene with her brother she justifies this conviction:

> Yet honor lyves when death hath done his worst,
> Thus fame then lyfe is of farre more emprise:

(p. 462)

Andrugio replies that her honour will not suffer:

> Nay *Cassandra*, if thou thy selfe submyt,
> To save my life, to *Promos* fleashly wyll,
> *Justice* wyll say thou dost no cryme commit:
> For in forst faultes is no intent of yll.

(In Whetstone's *novella* he even argues: 'if this offence be known, thy fame will bee enlarged, because it will lykewise bee knowne, that thou receauedst dishonor to giue thy Brother lyfe'.[2]) Cassandra replies that

> *Dispite* wyll blase my crime, but not the cause:
> And thus although I fayne would set thee free,
> Poore wench, I feare the grype of slaunders pawes.

---

[1] '*All's Well* and *Measure for Measure*', in *From Shakespeare to Joyce* (1944), pp. 259-60.

[2] *Heptameron*, N4ᵛ.

But out of love for her brother she consents to 'kill her credit' and to 'slay her honour'.

Cassandra never considers the action as sinful until after she has committed it. Then she speaks of 'my guilt' and 'my crime', and declares that 'my selfe, my conscience doth accuse'. But she is still primarily concerned about her reputation:

> And shall *Cassandra* now be termed, in common speeche, a stewes?
> Shall she, whose vertues bare the bell, be calld a vicious dame?
> O cruell death, nay hell to her, that was constraynd to shame!
>
> (p. 469)

But immediately afterwards, upon deciding to complain to the King and make public her wrong, she declares:

> So doing yet, the world will say I broke *Dianas* lawes,
> But what of that? no shame is myne when truth hath showne
> my cause.
>
> (p. 470)

Cassandra's attitude towards her action is thus seen to be complex and divided. Fear that her fame will suffer, a feeling of guilt and shame, are mingled with the conviction that her action was honourable and her conduct irreproachable. Yet I do not think that there is anything in the least problematic in Whetstone's presentation of her choice. We are never made to question its rightness or to doubt that her act of self-sacrifice deserves our deepest admiration. We accept without questioning the King's description of it,

> Thy forced fault was free from evil intent,
> So long, no shame can blot thee any way
>
> (p. 499),

which closely echoes Andrugio's words I have quoted:

> *Justice* wyll say thou dost no cryme commit;
> For in forst faultes is no intent of yll.

We find, then, a complete antithesis between Shakespeare's and Whetstone's presentation of their heroine's choice. To put it crudely and, perhaps, oversimply, but not, I think, unjustly: whereas Whetstone keeps his heroine divided and wavering but his audience single-minded and free from doubts, Shakespeare keeps his heroine single-minded and free from doubts but his audience divided and wavering. In other words, *Measure for Measure* is a problem-play, whereas *Promos and Cassandra* is not.

Shakespeare made two main alterations in the story he took over from his sources. The first was to introduce the motif of the substituted bride, common in folk-tale and ballad, and used by himself probably only a few months earlier in *All's Well*. What made Shakespeare devise this 'bed-trick', as it is commonly referred to? Critics are apt to tell us that it was his desire to preserve his heroine's virginity, 'to make more gentle', as R. W. Chambers puts it, 'one of the quite horrible situations of the pre-Shakespearean drama'.[1] I do not believe that, had it suited his dramatic conception, Shakespeare would have hesitated to let Isabel follow Cassandra's course. But the whole conception for which I have argued, his desire to make us question Isabel's choice and to turn *Measure for Measure* into a problem play, demanded that she should persist in her refusal, and therefore a substitute had to be found if Angelo was fully to act out his villainy and yet a happy ending was to be contrived. And by means of the 'bed-trick' Shakespeare was able at the same time to avoid the one element which is most repugnant in what critics condescendingly like to call 'the barbarous old story' (though I find nothing barbarous in either Cinthio's or Whetstone's treatment of it): the heroine's forced marriage to the villain she hates in order to 'repair her crased honour', whether she continues to hate him after her marriage, as in Cinthio's two versions, or whether, as Whetstone, with much less psychological plausibility, has it, she is 'tyed in the greatest bondes of affection to her husband'[2] the moment she becomes his wife. Only through the 'bed-trick' is Shakespeare able to avoid this and to bring about a much more satisfying ending than was possible in any of the earlier versions.

One of the purposes of the 'bed-trick' seems explicable by a point of law which commentators have overlooked. Where, as we have seen, Claudio and Juliet were made husband and wife by a *de praesenti* contract, the marriage-contract between Angelo and Mariana seems to have been a case of sworn spousals *per verba de futuro* (in which the couple promise under oath to

[1] *Op. cit.*, p. 279.
[2] *Promos and Cassandra*, 'The Argument', p. 445.

become husband and wife at a future date).[1] Now any *de futuro* contract was turned into matrimony and became as indissoluble as a *de praesenti* contract as soon as cohabitation between the betrothed couple took place. This point of law seems to be basic to the Duke's substitution-plot, and appears to be alluded to when he declares, 'If the encounter acknowledge itself hereafter, it may compel him to her recompense' (3.1.242-3). And its recognition may make the expedient more acceptable to those who have been distressed by it and by Isabel's immediate consent to it.

The apparent contradiction between Isabel's condemnation of her brother's offence and her ready connivance in what would appear to be an identical transgression on the part of Mariana has often worried commentators, and has even been called by one scholar 'the central problem of *Measure for Measure*'.[2] His suggested solution is that her inconsistency in condemning the one and abetting the other 'exactly mirrors a national inconsistency. The Elizabethans recognized and acknowledged the ideal, but *Usus efficacissimus rerum omnium magister*, and they, a practical people, readily accepted the reality.' I should prefer to account for it in other ways. Isabel appears to be ignorant throughout of her brother's marriage-contract. Lucio fails to mention it in his report of Claudio's arrest, while the words he uses, 'He hath got his friend with child', 'Your brother and his lover have embraced' (1.4.29, 40), would, on the contrary, suggest that there was no matrimonial bond between them. But why did Shakespeare choose to keep Isabel ignorant of the marriage-contract? Because had she known of it her entire plea before Angelo would have had to be different, an appeal to equity rather than to mercy. And it would have much lessened her inner conflict, 'At war 'twixt will and will not'. For not even the 'enskied and sainted' Isabel could have called the consummation of a *de praesenti* contract 'a vice that most I do abhor' and have thought of it as justly deserving the death-penalty. It is apparently the situation of the saintly novice exculpating the seeming libertine which

---

[1] For arguments in support of this view see my article on 'The Marriage-Contracts in *Measure for Measure*', *Shakespeare Survey*, vol. 13 (1960), pp. 84-86.

[2] D. P. Harding, 'Elizabethan Betrothals and *Measure for Measure*', *J.E.G.P.*, vol. 49 (1950), p. 156.

above all kindles Angelo's lust and gives him his opening in the seduction-scene. And all this Shakespeare would have had to forgo, had he made Isabel aware of the circumstances of Claudio's transgression.

To Isabel, therefore, her brother's 'vice' and Mariana's nocturnal encounter with Angelo, with its multiple benefits ('by this', the Duke tells her, 'is your brother saved, your honour untainted, the poor Mariana advantaged, and the corrupt deputy scaled') would not have seemed by any means identical, or indeed to have much in common. And the fact that the scheme is put forward by the Friar-Duke as spokesman of the Church would have helped to counteract any possible scruples raised in her mind by the Church's commands in this matter.

And yet there remains a basic contradiction: not between Isabel's attitude to her brother's 'vice' and to the 'bed-trick', but rather between her ready acceptance of the scheme and her equally ready refusal to fulfil herself Angelo's demand. For Mariana is as much guilty of the deadly sin of fornication by her action as Isabel would have been. And the same legalistic view of Divine Justice which made Isabel assume that she would be eternally damned for it ought to have made her postulate the same about Mariana. It is difficult to see how Shakespeare could have avoided this inconsistency once he had decided on the 'bed-trick', for which Isabel's consent is needed. Shakespeare at this point required an Isabel with a liberal view of morality; elsewhere one with a narrowly legalistic view.

I do not believe that this inconsistency can be explained by postulating a change of outlook in Isabel. Several critics, notably Wilson Knight[1] and Donald A. Stauffer,[2] have seen her undergoing such a change in the course of the play. Wilson Knight, the only 'Christian' interpreter of the play who is among her detractors, maintains that 'Isabella, like Angelo, has progressed far during the play's action: from sanctity to humanity'. He speaks of her 'self-centred saintliness', her 'ice-cold sanctity', and her lack of human feelings in the first part of the play. Then, towards the end, 'confronted by that warm, potent, forgiving human love, Isabella herself suddenly shows

[1] *Op. cit.*, p. 93.
[2] *Shakespeare's World of Images* (1949), pp. 152-6.

a softening, a sweet humanity'.[1] Since I can see no lack of human feelings, nothing self-centred or ice-cold about the Isabel of the first part of the play, nor 'a sudden softening, a sweet humanity' in her plea for Angelo's life, it is not surprising that I cannot follow Professor Knight in this view. To me Isabel, like the other main *dramatis personae*, with the important exception of Angelo, seems essentially a static character. She possesses that remarkable integrity in the literal sense which would make any great change in her come as a surprise.

IV

Next to the introduction of the 'bed-trick', Shakespeare's other main departure from his sources has been the turning of the Duke from a mere *deus ex machina*, who arrives at the end to judge and finally to pardon his corrupt subordinate, into the most omnipresent figure in the play, who is given more lines to speak than Isabel and Angelo combined.

Most criticism of the Duke has been, like that of Isabel, of a mutually contradictory nature. 'Christian' interpreters regard him usually as the embodiment of Providence, Divine Justice, or Grace, while many of those who see him as a purely human figure are repelled by his un-British love for disguises, secret stratagems, and the telling of lies. (Sir Edmund Chambers uniquely combines these two attitudes by finding the Duke both repellent *and* an embodiment of Divine Providence. He is thus driven to conclude that the play expresses 'a satirical intention of Shakespeare towards theories about the moral government of the universe which, for the time being, at least, he does not share'.[2])

The real answer to the contention that the Duke is a quasi-allegorical figure representing Providence is surely that given by Elizabeth Pope in her valuable article on 'The Renaissance Background of *Measure for Measure*': 'Any Renaissance audience would have taken it for granted that the Duke did indeed "stand" for God, but only as any good ruler "stood for" Him; and if he behaved "like power divine", it was because that was the way a good ruler was expected to conduct himself.'[3] Like

---

[1] *Loc. cit.*   [2] *Shakespeare: A Survey* (1925), p. 215.
[3] *Op. cit.*, p. 71.

the other main characters of the play, the Duke is too complex a figure to allow us to see him as the embodiment of an abstraction, whether we call it Providence, or Justice, or Good Rule, or Divine Grace. Only if we abandon these abstractions can we, for instance, reconcile such apparent inconsistencies as the Duke's report of his earlier misrule with his evident rôle throughout the play of representing the model prince.

As for the attack on the Duke's questionable moral conduct, the true defence is not, I believe, to be found in the claims made by W. W. Lawrence,[1] E. M. W. Tillyard,[2] and others, that he must not be judged by the standards of actual life, but is to be regarded as 'a convenient stage machine' or folk-tale motif. For it was Shakespeare's business as dramatist to turn his stage-devices and folk-tale motifs into psychologically plausible and coherent human beings (as he does, for instance, consummately in the case of Lear and the initial folk-tale situation of the love-test), and any character that repels a large portion of the audience when it is supposed to attract them must be accounted an artistic failure. The true defence seems to me rather again that made by Miss Pope, who points out that one of the privileges enjoyed by the Renaissance ruler was that of using extraordinary means to achieve his ends, and that there would have been no need to apologize for the Duke's practices to an Elizabethan audience. It is, then, not the claim that we must not judge the Duke according to the ideals of conduct of actual life, but rather the fact that these ideals differed in the Renaissance from those of later centuries which constitutes to my mind the real defence of his actions.

Apart from relying on these privileges of the monarch, Shakespeare has made the Duke's conduct still more plausible by showing it to be also rooted in his character.[3] As so often, Shakespeare makes a virtue of a necessity, and shows him to have a native relish for the scheming, the cat-and-mouse play,

---

[1] *Shakespeare's Problem Comedies* (1931), p. 120.

[2] *Op. cit.*, p. 118.

[3] The opposite view is taken by W. W. Lawrence, who writes: 'Shakespeare has not succeeded in making the Duke both serviceable to the purposes of drama, and psychologically consistent. . . . He is essentially a puppet, cleverly painted and adroitly manipulated, but revealing, in the thinness of his colouring and in the artificiality of his movements, the wood and pasteboard of his composition' (*op. cit.*, p. 112).

and all the mystery-mongering that are required in the interests
of dramatic suspense. Lucio's name for him, 'the old fantastical
duke of dark corners' (4.3.154), is no part of his slander of the
Duke's character, but an accurate and vivid description of it.
The evident relish with which he conducts the proceedings
comes out most fully in the final scene, when as Duke he calls
for himself as Friar, leaves the stage, returns as Friar and calls
for himself as Duke, accuses his *alter ego* of injustice, and caps
it all by declaring,

> the Duke
> Dare no more stretch this finger of mine than he
> Dare rack his own.
>
> (5.1.311-13)

Chiefly, it would seem, for reasons of dramatic economy,
Shakespeare has made the Duke both the ideal ruler, wise,
omniscient, and beneficent, and also the exemplar of one kind
of misrule, which consists in a neglect to enforce the law with
sufficient vigour. (The plot did not require the Duke to have
been over-merciful. His handing over to Angelo could have
been sufficiently motivated, as it partly is, by his desire to test
and watch him. Hence his lax law-enforcement seems mainly
designed to fill out the pattern of types of misrule.) It was a
commonplace in Renaissance literature on the subject that the
good ruler follows the golden mean between excessive severity
and excessive clemency in the punishment of offenders. As
William Perkins puts it in his *Treatise on Christian Equity and
Moderation*, published in 1604, the very year in which *Measure
for Measure* was written, bad judges are of two kinds: the first
are 'such men as by a certain foolish kind of pity are so carried
away, that would have nothing but *mercy, mercy*, and would . . .
have the extremity of the law executed on no man'. The second
kind are 'such men as have nothing in their mouths, but the
law, the *law*: and *Justice, Justice*: in the meantime forgetting
that Justice always shakes hands with her sister mercy, and that
all laws allow a mitigation'.[1] '*Nam in medio stat virtus*', writes
King James in the *Basilikon Doron*. 'What difference is betwixt
extreame tyrannie, delighting to destroy all mankinde; and
extreame slacknesse of punishment, permitting euery man to

---

[1] Quoted by Miss Pope, *op. cit.*, p. 74.

tyrannize ouer his companion?'[1] 'A magistrate', declares Calvin, 'must take hede to both, that he do neither with rigorousness of minde wound rather than heale, or by superstitious affectation of clemency fall into a most cruell gentlenes, if with soft and loose tendernes he be dissolute to the destruction of many men.'[2] As Miss Pope has pointed out, Shakespeare dramatizes this in the opposition of the Duke and Angelo as rulers. Whether it was the result of lethargy or of 'a certain foolish kind of pity' (and the metaphors of the 'o'ergrown lion' and the 'fond fathers', which he uses in his speech to Friar Thomas, 1.3.19 ff., suggest that it was a mixture of both), the Duke's neglect of law-enforcement was, in the words of Perkins, 'the high way to abolish laws, and consequently to pull down authority, and so in the end to open a door to all confusion, disorder, and to all licentiousness of life', a state vividly described by the Duke as one where

> liberty plucks justice by the nose;
> The baby beats the nurse, and quite athwart
> Goes all decorum.

(1.3.29-31)

The other and much more common vice among judges, that of judicial tyranny, is exemplified by Angelo. Of this Bacon speaks in his essay *Of Judicature* (1612) in words which are peculiarly applicable to this play:

Judges must beware of hard constructions and strained inferences; For there is no worse torture than the torture of laws. Specially in case of laws penal, they ought to have care, that that which was meant for terror be not turned into rigour: and that they bring not upon the people that shower whereof the scripture speaketh, *Pluet super eos laqueos*. For penal laws pressed, are a shower of snares upon the people. Therefore let penal laws, if they have been sleepers of long, or if they be grown unfit for the present time, be by wise judges confined in the execution: *Iudicis officium est, ut res, ita tempora rerum*, etc. In causes of life and death, judges ought (as far as the law permitteth) in justice to remember mercy, and to cast a severe eye upon the example, but a merciful eye upon the person.[3]

[1] *The Political Works of James I*, ed. C. H. McIlwain (1918), p. 38.
[2] *The Institution of Christian Religion*, transl. Thomas Norton (1578), p. 625. Quoted by E. T. Sehrt, *op. cit.*, p. 43.
[3] *Essays*, World's Classics edition, pp. 223-4.

Angelo is guilty of all the judicial misdemeanours against which Bacon particularly warns. First, he revives a law which has been a sleeper of long.[1] Next, in condemning Claudio under it, he is guilty of a signal neglect of the Ovidian maxim quoted by Bacon, which insists on the judge's duty to enquire not only into the fact but also the circumstances of the case. And finally he disregards Bacon's special admonition to remember mercy in causes of life and death, and 'to cast a severe eye upon the example, but a merciful eye upon the person', or, as Isabel puts it,

> I have a brother is condemn'd to die.
> I do beseech you, let it be his fault,
> And not my brother.
>
> (2.2.34-6)

It is Escalus who in this play illustrates the *via media* between the two excesses in the administration of justice. He possesses the proper mixture of severity and mercy which marks the ideal judge. He is 'accounted a merciful man', as Mrs. Overdone tells him, but in this very scene he shows that he can also be severe: 'Away with her to prison. Go to; no more words' (3.2.193). The Elbow-Pompey-Froth scene, excellent comedy though it is, seems to have been introduced mainly to show the ideal judge at work. Escalus is full of patience, humanity, and tolerance, in sharp contrast to Angelo, who leaves half way through the hearing, declaring,

> This will last out a night in Russia,
> When nights are longest there; I'll take my leave,
> And leave you to the hearing of the cause,
> Hoping you'll find good cause to whip them all.
>
> (2.1.128-31)

Escalus, kindly, humorous, yet firm and severe when necessary, deals with the defendants quietly and efficiently. In his plea for Claudio's life he uses much the same metaphor as that in which Calvin warns the magistrate against rigorousness which wounds rather than heals:

[1] Shakespeare twice (1.2.162-4; 2.2.90) uses this metaphor about the law Angelo has revived, three times if we adopt Theobald's tempting if unnecessary emendation of F's 'slip' to 'sleep' in 1.3.21.

> Let us be keen, and rather cut a little
> Than fall and bruise to death.

(2.1.5-6)

The metaphors suggest that the duty of the magistrate is to wield the surgeon's knife rather than the cudgel, in other words to heal, not to wound. Escalus's true mercy is contrasted both with the 'devilish mercy' of Angelo and the dangerous mercy formerly exercised by the Duke. (Angelo is thus placed in significant contrast to four main persons in the play: to Claudio and Lucio chiefly in terms of character, to the Duke and Escalus chiefly in his rôle as judge.)

The main intellectual concern of *Measure for Measure* is clearly with the nature of Justice and Good Rule, a concern which is expressed at once in the opening lines ('Of government the properties to unfold . . .'), which are, as often in Shakespeare, an important index to the play's dominant preoccupations. The law, in Shakespeare's plays, is frequently shown to be a stalking-horse for every form of cruelty and persecution, whether by the state, as in our play and *Timon* (3.5), or by a private citizen, as in *The Merchant of Venice* (4.1.) and *A Midsummer Night's Dream* (1.1.39 ff.). And repeatedly, but above all in *Measure for Measure*, the poet's plea seems to be for a more humane and less literal interpretation of the law, both manmade and divine, in accordance with the circumstances of each case, and for the seasoning of Justice with Mercy. Much of this is summed up by the single word 'equity' and Aristotle's description of it in the *Nicomachean Ethics* (Bk. 5, ch. 14):

> While that which is equitable is just, it is not just in the eye of the law, but is a rectification of legal justice. And the reason is that all law is couched in general terms, but there are some cases upon which it is impossible to pronounce correctly in general terms.

This contrast between equity and the 'surly Law', which was a commonplace in Renaissance literature on the subject, is stated in noble verse by Samuel Daniel in his 'Epistle to Sir Thomas Egerton':

> Which Equitie being the soule of Law
> The life of Iustice, and the Spirite of right,

Dwells not in written Lines, or liues in awe
Of Bookes; deafe powres that haue nor eares, nor sight:
But out of well-weigh'd circumstance doth draw
The essence of a iudgement requisite:
And is that Lesbian square, that building fit,
Plies to the worke, not forc'th the worke to it.

Maintaining still an equall parallel
Iust with th'occasion of humanitie,
Making her iudgements euer liable
To the respect of peace and amitie:
When surly *Law*, sterne, and vnaffable,
Cares onely but itselfe to satisfie:
And often, innocencie skarse defends,
As that which on no circumstance depends.[1]

That the enforcement of this contrast is one of the main
concerns of our play was recognized by three critics already in
the last century: by the German, Gervinus, who wrote in 1849:
'And this indeed is not only the spirit of the Duke, but that of
our whole play, in which the Duke is, as it were, the chorus:—
namely, that true justice is not jealous justice, but that circum-
spect equity alone, which suffers neither mercy nor the severe
letter of the law to rule without exception, which awards
punishment not *measure for measure*, but *with* measure. Neither
the lax mildness which the Duke had allowed to prevail and
which he himself condemns, nor the over-severe curb which
Angelo applied, is to be esteemed as the right procedure; the
sluggishness which gives licence to sin, and the system of in-
timidation which destroys the sinner with the sin, meet with
the same condemnation'[2]; by F. S. Boas, when he wrote: 'In
the years passed since *The Merchant of Venice* was written
Shakspere had reached a loftier conception of justice. The
earlier play had furnished an ideal illustration of "measure for
measure". Shylock took his stand upon the letter of the law,
and by the letter he was overthrown. But here the fanatical
worship of the letter is shown to conflict with the genuine
principle of equity, and we realize that codes and charters may
become a curse instead of a blessing to society, unless they are

---

[1] *Poems*, ed. A. C. Sprague (1930), pp. 104-5.
[2] *Shakespeare Commentaries*, transl. F. E. Bunnett (1903), p. 502.

applied in a remedial and not a nakedly retributive spirit'[1]; and above all by Walter Pater, whose essay on *Measure for Measure*, written in 1874, contains still some of the best comments on the play that we possess. He writes:

> The action of the play, like the action of life itself for the keener observer, develops in us the conception of this poetical justice, and the yearning to realize it, the true justice of which Angelo knows nothing, because it lies for the most part beyond the limits of any acknowledged law. . . . It is for this finer justice, a justice based on a more delicate appreciation of the true conditions of men and things . . . that the people in *Measure for Measure* cry out as they pass before us; and as the poetry of this play is full of the peculiarities of Shakespeare's poetry, so in its ethics it is an epitome of Shakespeare's moral judgements.[2]

In his views on Justice Shakespeare is by no means an isolated figure in his own day, but has most humanist writers, from Sir Thomas Elyot to Bacon and King James, behind him. A thesis directly opposite to this is advanced by E. T. Sehrt in the work previously cited. He argues that Shakespeare's view of the relation of Justice and Mercy is essentially at odds with the prevailing view of his own day, whether Puritan or humanist. For while the Puritans turned to the Old Testament conception of Justice, with its insistence on severe and rigorous punishment, and the humanists pleaded for equity and clemency, Shakespeare returned to the medieval conception of

---

[1] *Shakspere and his Predecessors* (1896), p. 368. With Boas's contention that Shakespeare's conception of Justice in *Measure for Measure* is different and 'loftier' than in *The Merchant of Venice* and that the latter 'had furnished an ideal illustration of "measure for measure" ' I cannot agree. Shakespeare's conception of Justice seems to me to remain essentially the same throughout his plays. Portia's mercy-speech (*M.V.*, 4.1.179 ff.), much like Isabel's (2.2.58 ff.), is a plea not for the abrogation of the law but for the mitigation of its rigour, for the seasoning of Justice with Mercy ('And earthly power doth then show likest God's / When mercy seasons justice. . . . . I have spoke thus much / To mitigate the justice of thy plea . . .'). The punishment meted out to Shylock is not a violation of this ideal, as some critics have argued (notably E. T. Sehrt, *op. cit.*, pp. 96 ff.), but an exact fulfilment of it. Under the *ius strictum* both Shylock's life and all his possessions were forfeit. The mercy that seasons justice and mitigates the rigour of the law first, in the person of the Duke, spares Shylock's life and then, in the person of Antonio, allows him to retain half his possessions.

[2] *Op. cit.*, p. 183.

Mercy as abrogating rather than mitigating punishment. This conception, almost unique in Shakespeare's day, he finds expressed in Portia's and Isabel's mercy-speeches. It stems from Shakespeare's increasing sense of man's weakness and his dependence on God's grace. I have no space to dispute at length the validity of this thesis, which is argued cogently, learnedly, and throughout an entire book. I would merely make two points, as far as it affects *Measure for Measure*: First, had Shakespeare's concern in this play really been to stress man's need for a mercy which does not 'shake hands with her sister Justice', but which abrogates rather than mitigates it, it seems more than unlikely that he would have introduced into the same play the Duke's insistence on the evils to which his past failure to punish offenders has given rise, or have made the wise and kindly Escalus declare, 'Mercy is not itself that oft looks so; / Pardon is still the nurse of second woe' (2.1.269-70). Secondly, the fact that Isabel, in her plea for her brother's life, talks of mercy and *not*, like her counterparts in Cinthio and Whetstone, of equity, seems to me not, as Professor Sehrt claims, to be an expression of the mature Shakespeare's Christian outlook, his sense of man's frailty and his need for absolute pardon, but rather to stem from his wish, for reasons discussed above, to make Isabel consider the sentence just, and therefore not to be disputed on the grounds of equity. But though she talks of mercy and not of equity, I do not think that she speaks of a mercy that takes the place of justice, but rather, like Portia, of a mercy that seasons and mitigates it. (In the final pardon extended by the Duke to Angelo and to Barnardine such an abrogation of Justice by Mercy no doubt is found. But we are surely to see this neither, with some commentators, as an expression of the play's teachings on the relation of Mercy and Justice, nor, with others, as a sign that the Duke has learnt nothing and has lapsed again into his old habit of excessive clemency, but rather as an amnesty, which allows the play to end as happily as Shakespeare could contrive.[1])

I come now to my final point about the Duke in *Measure for Measure*. In 1799 the Scottish antiquarian George Chalmers

[1] Though I have taken issue with its main thesis, Professor Sehrt's book contains much that is valuable and from which I have profited, including an exemplary discussion of the sources of *Measure for Measure*.

wrote: 'The commentators seem not to have remarked, that the character of *the Duke*, is a very accurate delineation of that of King James, which Shakespeare appears to have caught, with great felicity, and to have sketched, with much truth.' And he added, 'Knowing that King James's writings; his *Basilikon Doron*; his *True Law of Free Monarchies*; and other treatises; had been, emulously, republished in 1603, by the London book-sellers, in many editions, Shakspeare could not fitly give a closer parody.'[1] This claim, though echoed by Charles Knight,[2] received little attention until it was taken up and developed at great length by the German scholar Louis Albrecht in his study of the play published in 1914. Albrecht maintained that *Measure for Measure* was written as an act of homage to the King upon his accession to the throne of England, that James's tract on 'the properties of government', the *Basilikon Doron* (written *c.* 1598), constitutes one of the chief sources of the play, that the Duke was intended to be recognized as an idealized portrait of James, and that the whole play was written, from first to last, with an eye upon the King's special interests and predilections.[3] This thesis, too, was largely ignored by commentators, or referred to only to be curtly dismissed. Quite recently an American scholar, David L. Stevenson, unaware, apparently, of the existence of both Chalmers' and Albrecht's discussions, has put forward a very similar thesis, declaring that *Measure for Measure* 'is a play in which the political element bears the conscious and unmistakable imprint of the predilections of James I himself as Shakespeare and his London audience were aware of them in the first flush of the post-Elizabethan era'; that the poet 'deliberately sketched in Duke Vincentio a character whose behaviour as a ruler would be attractive to James (and therefore to a Jacobean audience) because it followed patterns which the King had publicly advocated'; and that 'Shakespeare, we may infer, was as anxiously (if more subtly)

---

[1] *A Supplemental Apology for the Believers in the Shakespeare-Papers* (1799), pp. 404-5.

[2] *Studies of Shakespeare* (1849), p. 319.

[3] Albrecht's thesis, like so many of the doctoral kind, suffers from being pushed too far (e.g. when he argues that Isabel represents an idealized image of James's wife, Queen Anne, even the most sympathetic must cry a halt), and from his failure to discriminate between important and trivial or between persuasive and wholly unpersuasive points of resemblance.

courting James I with *Measure for Measure* as was a Bilson, for example, in his flattering repetition of James's opinions in his "Coronation Sermon", or as was a Barlow in his flattering portrait of James's role in the Hampton Court Conference'. Quoting many of the same parallels between *Measure for Measure* and the *Basilikon Doron* as Albrecht, Stevenson comes to much the same conclusion: 'One is forced to think that Shakespeare carefully mined the *Basilikon Doron* in order to be able to dramatize the intellectual interests of his new patron in his comedy.'[1]

In discussing the validity of these theses it will be useful to distinguish between two quite separate though related claims: (1) that *Measure for Measure* was deliberately made to turn upon themes which were of special interest to James, whether this was done in order to pay homage to the King, as Albrecht claims, or to court his favour by flattery, as Stevenson maintains, or to exploit the current public interest in the theory of government which was inspired by the accession of James, as Miss Pope suggests[2]; and (2) that the Duke is drawn as an image of James, whether this is to be regarded as an idealized image, as Albrecht and Stevenson contend, or as 'a very accurate delineation', as Chalmers asserts.

The first of these claims seems to me to have a great deal of plausibility (among the three I would favour Albrecht's hypothesis of the play's principal *raison d'être*, which, of course, does not exclude Miss Pope's). And it is much strengthened by the analogous case of *Macbeth*, where again Shakespeare seems deliberately to have written a play on themes that were of special interest to the King and on which the latter had published erudite works (indeed, it could be said that the *Basilikon Doron* is to *Measure for Measure* what it and the *Daemonology* together are to *Macbeth*). That Shakespeare had read the *Basilikon Doron* before writing *Measure for Measure* is inherently probable. It was unquestionably the Book-of-the-Year in 1603, when it went through one Scottish and two English editions. 'This book,' wrote Francis Bacon, 'falling into every man's hand, filled the whole realm as with a good perfume or incense

[1] 'The Role of James I in Shakespeare's *Measure for Measure*', *ELH*, vol. 26 (1959), pp. 188, 189, 207, 196.
[2] *Op. cit.*, p. 70.

before the King's coming in. . . .'[1] But though many of the
views on Justice and Good Rule in the *Basilikon Doron* find
fairly exact parallels in Shakespeare's play, these are of too
commonplace a nature to prove indebtedness in the absence of
close verbal echoes. (As a typical instance of this tantalizing
relationship compare the Duke's

> Thyself and thy belongings
> Are not thine own so proper as to waste
> Thyself upon thy virtues, they on thee.
> Heaven doth with us as we with torches do,
> Not light them for themselves; for if our virtues
> Did not go forth of us, 'twere all alike
> As if we had them not.

> (1.1.29-36)

with the following passage from the *Basilikon Doron*: 'For it is
not ynough that ye haue and retaine (as prisoners) within your
selfe neuer so many good qualities and vertues, except ye
employ them, and set them on worke, for the weale of them that
are committed to your charge: *Virtutis enim laus omnis in actione
consistit.*'[2])

As for the second claim—that the Duke is drawn as an image
of James—I think both Albrecht *and* Chalmers are right: that
it is an idealized image, made up of the qualities in a ruler
which James in his writings had particularly praised; and that
it is yet sufficiently particularized, and endowed with traits
peculiar to the King, to enable Shakespeare's audience and
James himself to recognize the likeness. Several of these
idiosyncrasies, such as the Duke's dislike of the people's 'loud
applause and Aves vehement' (1.1.71), his fondness for mystifying his subjects and playing cat-and-mouse with them, his
description of himself, 'let him be but testimonied in his own
bringings-forth, and he shall appear to the envious a scholar, a
statesman, and a soldier' (3.2.133-5), in that significant order[3]

---

[1] *Works*, ed. Spedding (1878), vol. 6, pp. 278-9.

[2] *Op. cit.*, p. 30. Both Albrecht and Stevenson compare the two passages.

[3] This has also been pointed out by Albrecht (*op. cit.*, pp. 188-9). An
additional point, which I have not seen made by anyone, is the use of the
word 'bringings-forth'. For what can the Duke's 'bringings-forth' that bear
testimony to his scholarship refer to except publications, or, less plausibly,
public disputations, on learned matters? In either case, few people in the
audience could have failed to be reminded of James.

(compare also the order of his words to Lucio at the end of the play, 'You, sirrah, that knew me for a fool, a coward, / One all of luxury, an ass, a madman!' What smarts most is Lucio's denial of his sagacity)—all these when taken together seem to me too uniquely characteristic of James to be dismissed as mere accidental likenesses. Even the one trait in the Duke which does not accord with the presentation of him as a model ruler, his failure to enforce the laws with sufficient severity, fits James, who in the *Basilikon Doron* confesses to have been over-lax in punishing offenders at the beginning of his reign, and to have reaped only disorder.[1]

What further supports the hypothesis that the Duke is de-liberately drawn as an image of James is the fact that it may help to explain the presence in the play of at least two some-what puzzling passages. One is the Duke's denunciation of 'newfangledness', which seems curiously isolated, not linking up with any of the satiric preoccupations of the rest of the play. To Escalus's question, 'What news abroad i' th' world?', the Duke replies, 'none, but that there is so great a fever on good-ness that the dissolution of it must cure it. Novelty is only in request; and it is as dangerous to be aged in any kind of course as it is virtuous to be inconstant in any undertaking.'[2] (3.2.208-11). But James was much given to denouncing newfangledness. In the *Basilikon Doron*, for instance, Shakespeare would have read: 'But vnto one fault is all the common people of this kingdome subiect, as well burgh as land; which is, to iudge and speake rashly of their Prince, setting the Common-weale vpon foure props, as wee call it; euer wearying of the present estate, and desirous of nouelties.'[3] The other puzzling passage is the Duke's words upon first hearing of Barnardine: 'How came it that the absent Duke had not either deliver'd him to his liberty or executed him? I have heard it was ever his manner to do so' (4.2.124-6). This *penchant* for the two extremes of free pardon

---

[1] *Op. cit.*, p. 20.

[2] I have adopted the emendation, first proposed by Staunton, of F's 'constant' to 'inconstant', which seems to me imperative. For the Duke to be saying that the danger of constancy is equal to its virtue is much too tame for the satiric context.

[3] *Op. cit.*, p. 27. The parallel has been pointed out by Albrecht (*op. cit.*, p. 160).

and immediate execution, surprising in a model ruler, may, perhaps, be explained as an allusion to an action by James upon first coming into England (April 25, 1603) which caused much comment: at Newark he had a cutpurse, taken in the act, hanged at once without trial, while at the same time he commanded all the prisoners in the Castle to be set free.[1]

Lastly, the hypothesis helps to explain the sentence initially imposed upon Lucio by the Duke (5.1.505 ff.). Its extreme harshness (whipping and hanging) comes as a shock, especially through its juxtaposition with the free pardon which Angelo has just received. It becomes much more comprehensible in the light of James's notorious sensitiveness to slander, which led to the passing of a Scottish Act of Parliament in 1585 that made slander of the King a treasonable offence, punishable with death. Several people were, in fact, executed under this act, one in 1596 for calling James 'ane bastarde'.[2]

It seems to me, then, that the view that in the Duke Shakespeare drew an image of James, partly as he was, partly as he would like to have been or was then thought to be, is supported by too much evidence to be dismissed. And it may help to account for another fact often remarked upon by critics: the shadowiness of the Duke, compared to the other main *dramatis personae*. For, paradoxically, dramatic characters become less 'real' the more they are modelled on living persons and the less they are conceived wholly in the poet's imagination.[3]

An acceptance of the belief (which I share with Albrecht and Stevenson) that *Measure for Measure* deliberately turns upon themes which were of special interest to James, and that the views on Justice and Good Rule which it expresses are closely similar to those found in the political writings of the King, in no way compels one to see the play less as an expression of Shakespeare's most personal and sincerely held convictions.

[1] See *A Jacobean Journal*, ed. G. B. Harrison (1941), p. 15. Stevenson oddly refers to this incident—without relating it to the passage in the play—as an example of how 'James had actually put theory into action' (*op. cit.*, p. 202). To me it seems rather an example of the notorious lack of accord between James's precepts and his practice.

[2] See Craigie's note in his edition of the *Basilikon Doron* (1950), vol. 2, p. 208.

[3] It is, of course, true that the Duke's shadowiness is partly—but not, I think, entirely—due to his functions in the play.

For, as I have said, Shakespeare's own views on these matters seem to have been in close accord with those of the King and other humanist writers of his day. I do not find anything peculiarly Christian in these views. James's own references in support of them are to ancient, pre-Christian writers, such as Aristotle, Cicero, and Seneca. They are views held by humane and enlightened men in all ages.

Indeed, the claim, which has been reiterated so much in recent years, that *Measure for Measure* expresses a specifically Christian ethos seems to me without foundation. Those who argue in its favour tend to point to four main elements in the play:

1. Isabel's plea for her brother's life, which, unlike that of Cinthio's and Whetstone's heroine, is explicitly Christian.
2. Isabel's plea for Angelo, which is said to be motivated by Christian forgiveness and the need to love one's enemies.
3. The Duke's rôle throughout the play of controlling and leading events towards a happy conclusion, which makes him seem an image of Divine Providence.
4. The Duke's action of testing Angelo and then Isabel, as God tests His servants by submitting them to severe trials.

About the first point I shall say something below. The second and third points have, however briefly and inadequately, already been dealt with in the course of this chapter. As for the fourth point, there is nothing inherently unlikely about the notion that Isabel is tested by the Duke as Angelo had been tested by him. It would certainly be in character for him to do so. But I fail to find any evidence for it in the play. That which is usually cited as evidence, the Duke's deliberate omission to tell Isabel of the preservation of her brother, rather seems to me to make against the notion. For when in Act IV the Duke is left alone upon the stage solely in order to explain to the audience why he inflicts this unnecessary sorrow upon the poor girl, all that he says is:

> But I will keep her ignorant of her good,
> To make her heavenly comforts of despair
> When it is least expected.

(4.3.105-7)

Had the important notion that 'the Duke, an earthly Providence, tortures Isabel till he wrings her agonized forgiveness out of her', as R. W. Chambers puts it,[1] been part of Shakespeare's conception, he would surely have made the Duke say so in this soliloquy, just as in his testing of Angelo he leaves us in no doubt about it (1.3.50-54), rather than make him give a quite different, and to the audience much less satisfying, explanation. It may be that it would have been a better play if Shakespeare had adopted this notion of the testing of Isabel by the Duke. And it may be that Shakespeare would have welcomed the suggestion. As it is, one is forced to conclude that if he made the Duke keep Isabel ignorant of her good it was not in order to wring out of her every drop of Christian forgiveness, but rather in order to wring out of the play's final scene every drop of dramatic excitement.[2]

It scarcely needs pointing out that the mere introduction of more 'religious' characters than are found in the sources, such as friars, a nun, and a novice, who fitfully—though none too frequently—voice Christian sentiments, does not make *Measure for Measure* a more Christian play. It could, indeed, had Shakespeare so desired, have made it a more anti-Christian play. We can only guess at his reasons for the introduction of these characters. In the case of the Friar-Duke two alternative explanations seem possible: Having once decided on the 'bed-trick', Shakespeare needed someone who would not only have access to the prison to overhear the scene between brother and sister, but who would also have sufficient moral authority to persuade Isabel and Mariana to accept the scheme. The obvious person for such a part, if the Duke was to remain *incognito*, is a friar. And since Shakespeare intended to make the question of how the just and virtuous ruler conducts himself one of the chief concerns of the play, he hit upon the idea of investing the Duke himself with the friar's hood, thus making him at the same time carry out all the counter-intrigue that the plot demanded and provide an *exemplum* of the conduct of the

---

[1] *Op. cit.*, p. 302.

[2] This is also Raleigh's view, who declares, tersely but not unjustly: 'So Isabella, who deserved to hear the truth, is sacrificed to the plot' (*op. cit.*, p. 158).

good ruler. Alternatively, it may be that the motif of the dis-
guised ruler spying upon his subordinates, and supplying both
a pattern of Good Rule and an image of King James, had
primacy in Shakespeare's mind; that the suggestion for making
the disguise that of a friar came to him from Whetstone's *novella*,
where we read that Andrugio, upon hearing of Promos's impending execution, came 'covertly in the habyt of an hermyt'
and was one of the ghostly fathers who strengthened Promos
with 'comfortable perswasions' before his imminent death[1]
(this may well have suggested the Duke's similar service to
Claudio); and that the device of the 'bed-trick' only occurred
to him at a later point.

The question why Shakespeare turned Cinthio's philoso-
phical and humanistic maiden into a novice of the Order of
St. Clare is less readily answered. His intention, for which I
have argued, of paralleling Angelo's legalism in matters secular
with Isabel's legalism in matters divine, and to paint two
portraits of contrasting types of Puritan, would make it necessary that she was at least a devout Christian. By making her a
novice Shakespeare renders her quick choice more natural (but
not therefore the less problematic), as well as giving added
plausibility to Angelo's perverted lust for her, and making his
project seem even more criminal. Having turned Isabel into a
devout Christian and a novice of St. Clare, it is natural that
Shakespeare should make her plead for her brother's pardon
on specifically Christian grounds, all the more as he was pre-
vented, for the reasons I have given earlier, from making her
follow Epitia and Cassandra in exculpating her brother and
pleading that equity demanded his pardon.

But I do not think that this introduction of more 'religious'
characters makes *Measure for Measure* a more Christian play.
We do not call *Julius Caesar* a stoical or *Timon of Athens* a cynical
play because its protagonists voice stoic and cynic sentiments.
Only if the orientation of the material suggested that the play
itself endorses and presses home these sentiments could we
speak of it in such terms. And I can find no evidence of this in
Measure for Measure. Shakespeare's attitude in this play seems
to me most justly described by Raleigh: it is 'critical and iron-

[1] This influence has been claimed by Albrecht (*op. cit.*, pp. 90-92).

ical, expressed in reminders, and questions, and comparisons.'[1]
It is the attitude befitting a problem play.

As for Shakespeare christianizing his source-material, it
seems to me at least arguable that *Promos and Cassandra* is the
more Christian play. For, unlike *Measure for Measure*, it provides
explicitly Christian comment on its main action, first through
the mouth of its kindly gaoler, who declares,

> Such a just, good and righteous God is he:
> Although awhyle he let the wicked raygne,
> Yet he releeves the wretch in misery,
> And in his pryde he throwes the tyraunt downe
>
> (p. 471)

and then through the words of Andrugio:

> For God we see styll throwes the Tyrant downe
> Even in the heyght and pride of his renowne.
>
> (p. 504)

And we are nowhere made to question the justness of this
summing up, or to doubt that it conveys the point of view of
the entire play. In *Measure for Measure* the Duke has taken the
place of God as a controller and orderer of events, and to that
extent Shakespeare has de-christianized his source-material.

And Cassandra's choice, if not more Christian, is certainly
more Christ-like than Isabel's (if such a distinction is, in fact,
permissible), especially as it is described in Whetsone's *novella*:
Cassandra, 'who werie of her owne life, and tender ouer her
brothers, with the teares of her louely eyes, bathed his Cheekes,
with this comfortable sentence.

Lyue Andrugio, and make much of this kisse, which breatheth
my honour into thy bowels, and draweth the infamie of thy
first trespasse into my bosome.'[2] (What would Christian
allegorizers not have made of these words, had they been found
in Shakespeare's play? One can already see them working out
their equations: 'thy first trespass' = the Fall of Man; Cassandra
= Christ; Andrugio = fallen mankind, etc. Lacking such hopeful
material, Professor Battenhouse is reduced to finding an allegory
of the Atonement in Mariana's nocturnal encounter with
Angelo in the garden-house.[3])

---

[1] *Op. cit.*, p. 172.   [2] *Heptameron*, N4ᵛ.   [3] *Op. cit., passim.*

To sum up: I have tried to plead in the course of this chapter for a fuller recognition of the complexity of the main characters of *Measure for Measure*. Such a recognition prevents us from seeing them as simple embodiments of virtues and vices, and hence from turning the play into a quasi-morality. Though *Measure for Measure* is throughout concerned with moral issues, these are of such a complex nature that it is at a far remove from the Moralities and Interludes. As Walter Pater has so well said, 'the old "moralities" exemplified most often some rough-and-ready lesson. Here the very intricacy and subtlety of the moral world itself, the difficulty of seizing the true relations of so complex a material, the difficulty of just judgment, of judgment that shall not be unjust, are the lessons conveyed'.[1]

I have tried to show that *Measure for Measure* has two main concerns: in the field of public ethics it is with the nature of Justice and Good Rule; in the field of private ethics it is with the choice of Isabel. The two concerns are united by a common reprobation of legalism in favour of a more humane, more truly just interpretation of the Law, whether man-made or divine. And whereas the private moral issue is treated problematically, the public moral issue is not. We are never in doubt of our moral bearings in the controversy over the proper relation of Justice and Mercy.[2]

Considered as a problem play, *Measure for Measure* reveals a marked though unobtrusive likeness to *Julius Caesar*. In Isabel's choice between the death of her brother and the loss of her virginity, as in Brutus's choice between the death of Caesar and what he believes to be the loss of his country's liberty, personal ties, human loyalties and affections, are made to clash with high ideals and moral principles which, if adhered to, involve the death of the loved person. In both plays the protagonists choose to sacrifice these human loyalties and ties to what they consider

---

[1] *Op. cit.*, p. 184. For an opposite view see M. C. Bradbrook, 'Authority, Truth, and Justice in *Measure for Measure*', *R.E.S.*, vol. 17 (1941), pp. 385 ff.

[2] Just the opposite is found in Cinthio's *Epitia*, where the heroine's choice, presented as a *fait accompli* when the play opens, is treated quite unproblematically, whereas in the controversy between the Podestà and the Segretario—though it seems to me weighted heavily in favour of the latter, who defends clemency—it is at least possible to experience some doubt, so that Professor Bullough can speak of *Epitia* as 'a problem-play about Justice and Mercy' (*op. cit.*, p. 402).

their higher loyalties. And in both plays, by the orientation of his material and the manipulation of our responses, Shakespeare seems to me to suggest, strongly but not compulsively, his siding against the choice which is made.

But in other ways, especially in the absence of any marked inner conflict within the protagonist when faced with a difficult and crucial moral choice, *Measure for Measure* bears a greater kinship to the next and last of Shakespeare's Problem Plays, *Antony and Cleopatra*, which we must now consider.

III

ANTONY AND CLEOPATRA

I

IN THE case of *Julius Caesar* and *Measure for Measure* I have proceeded to a consideration of their main concerns by way of a discussion of their principal characters. In the case of *Antony and Cleopatra* I shall approach them by way of a discussion of its structural pattern. For it is the road which in this play takes us most quickly and surely to the heart of these concerns.

'The events of which the principal are described according to history, are produced without any art of connection or care of disposition', wrote Dr. Johnson of this play.[1] Nearly a century and a half later A. C. Bradley expressed a very similar view when he called it 'the most faultily constructed of all the tragedies', and pointed to it as exemplifying Shakespeare's 'defective method' of stringing together a 'number of scenes, some very short, in which the *dramatis personae* are frequently changed; as though a novelist were to tell his story in a succession of short chapters, in which he flitted from one group of his characters to another'.[2] What can explain such extraordinary blindness in these two great critics, and in the others who have echoed them? It seems partly to stem from a false expectation, the expectation of a 'linear' structure, like that preached by Aristotle and found in much Greek and classical French tragedy. But, as H. T. Price insists in his excellent essay on *Construction in Shakespeare* (1951), the structure of Shakespeare's plays, comedies and tragedies alike, is not linear but multilinear, not based on a unity of action but on a unity of design. When Elizabethan playwrights began to take their subject-

[1] *Johnson on Shakespeare*, ed. Raleigh (1908), p. 180.

[2] *Shakespearean Tragedy* (1904), pp. 71, 260. In his discussion of the play in his *Oxford Lectures on Poetry* (1905) he singles out the third and fourth acts as being 'very defective in construction' (p. 283).

matter from narrative romance or chronicle history, with their multitude of characters and incidents, they were inevitably confronted with the vexed problem of imposing shape and coherence upon so heterogeneous a material. Shakespeare solved this problem more brilliantly than any of his fellow-playwrights. He does it mainly by establishing a series of parallels and contrasts. Character is compared and contrasted with character, incident with incident. Dramatic irony is called into play, so that action comments implicitly upon action, situation upon situation, speech upon speech. Sometimes, as in *Lear* and *Timon*, a whole subplot is invented to comment, both by its likenesses and its contrasts, upon the main plot. At other times, as in the Laertes and Fortinbras scenes in *Hamlet*, such parallels and contrasts are more closely integrated into the main action, but serve the same function of implicit commentary. The structural pattern thus helps not only to give the play shape and coherence but also, more importantly, it becomes a silent commentator, a means of expressing the playwright's attitudes and concerns.[1]

Nowhere is this principle of construction better illustrated than in *Antony and Cleopatra*. Of all Shakespeare's plays this is probably the one in which the structural pattern is most perfectly adjusted to the theme and has, in fact, become one of the chief vehicles for its expression. This pattern consists (*a*) of a series of contrasts between Rome and Egypt; and (*b*) of a series of parallels between Antony and Cleopatra. Let us deal with the second class first.

This may be divided into three groups: (i) echoes of each other by the lovers, both in words and actions; (ii) similarities in descriptions of them; (iii) parallels in relations with them. But the function of all three is much the same: to bring out the extraordinary likeness, the near-identity of Antony and Cleopatra, in feeling, in imagination, in tastes, in their responses to people and events, and in their modes of expressing these responses. The total effect of all this is to make us see their relationship as something more than a sensual infatuation, more even than an exalted passion. Professor Peter Alexander has defined its precise quality better than any other critic known to

[1] Much the same could, of course, be said of the structural pattern of *The Faerie Queene* or of *Paradise Lost*.

me when he writes of Antony: 'Having enjoyed all the world can give to unlimited power and the richest physical endowment, he finds in Cleopatra's company a joy beyond anything he has known. And the world, whatever it may say of those who sacrifice reputation and wealth for such a satisfaction, does not readily forget their story, guessing dimly no doubt at the truth with which Aristophanes entertained Socrates and his friends, when he told the fable of the creatures cut in half by Zeus and condemned to go as mere tallies till they find and unite with their counterpart . . . "for surely", he concludes, "it is not satisfaction of sensual appetite that all this great endeavour is after: nay, plainly, it is something other that the soul of each wisheth—something which she cannot tell, but, darkly divining, maketh her end".'[1]

The lovers' echoes of each other's words and sentiments, though found scattered throughout the play, increase greatly in the last two acts, at the very time that the other main element in the structural pattern, the contrast between Rome and Egypt, diminishes. For towards its end the play becomes much less concerned with the presentation of the choice between two opposed modes of life and increasingly with the glorification of the choice which Antony has made. The following is a brief list of some of the most notable of these echoes:

> *Antony:* Let Rome in Tiber melt, and the wide arch
> Of the rang'd empire fall!
>
> (1.1.33-4)
>
> *Cleopatra:* Melt Egypt into Nile! and kindly creatures
> Turn all to serpents!
>
> (2.5.78-9)
>
> *Antony:* Kingdoms are clay; our dungy earth alike
> Feeds beast as man. The nobleness of life
> Is to do thus when such a mutual pair
> And such a twain can do't . . .
>
> (1.1.35-8)
>
> *Cleopatra:*   'Tis paltry to be Caesar:
> Not being Fortune, he's but Fortune's knave,
> A minister of her will; and it is great

[1] *Shakespeare's Life and Art* (1939), p. 176. In applying Aristophanes' fable to the lovers Alexander follows M. W. MacCallum, *Shakespeare's Roman Plays* (1910), pp. 445-7.

> To do that thing that ends all other deeds,
> Which shackles accidents and bolts up change,
> Which sleeps, and never palates more the dung,
> The beggar's nurse and Caesar's.
>
> (5.2.2-8)

(The echo here is accompanied by a contrast. Suicide has taken the place of love-making as 'the nobleness of life'. The quite unjustified change of 'dung' to 'dug', initiated, on Warburton's suggestion, by Theobald and followed by the majority of subsequent editors, eliminates the echo and with it the contrast.[1])

Cleopatra's

>   Broad-fronted Caesar,
> When thou wast here above the ground, I was
> A morsel for a monarch; and great Pompey
> Would stand and make his eyes grow in my brow . . .
>
> (1.5.29-32)

is echoed in Antony's

> I found you as a morsel cold upon
> Dead Caesar's trencher. Nay, you were a fragment
> Of Cneius Pompey's . . .
>
> (3.13.116-18)

Both lovers, characteristically, look on death as an erotic experience.

> *Antony:*   But I will be
> A bridegroom in my death, and run into't
> As to a lover's bed.
>
> (4.15.99-101)
>
> *Cleopatra:* If thou and nature can so gently part,
> The stroke of death is as a lover's pinch,
> Which hurts and is desir'd.
>
> (5.2.292-4)

Each sees the death of the other as the extinction of the source of all light:

> *Antony:*   Since the torch is out,
> Lie down, and stray no farther.
>
> (4.14.45-6)

[1] On this point see Dover Wilson's Introduction to his edition of the play, pp. xxi-xxii.

> Cleopatra: Ah, women, women, look,
> Our lamp is spent, it's out!
>
>   (4.15.84-5)

Antony's

> Unarm, Eros; the long day's task is done,
> And we must sleep
>
>   (4.14.35-6)

finds a close echo—though this time by the maid, not the mistress—in Iras's

> Finish, good lady; the bright day is done,
> And we are for the dark.
>
>   (5.2.192-3)

Of echoes in the actions of the two lovers the most notable instance is Cleopatra's treatment of the messenger who brings her the news of Antony's marriage to Octavia (2.5) and Antony's treatment of Caesar's messenger, Thyreus (3.13). Both actions are prompted by jealousy and a sense of betrayal and desertion by the other, and both are marked by uncontrolled fury, coupled with a relished cruelty towards the innocent messenger, as shown in Cleopatra's

> Thou shalt be whipp'd with wire and stew'd in brine,
> Smarting in ling'ring pickle
>
>   (2.5.65-6)

and in Antony's

>   Whip him, fellows,
> Till like a boy you see him cringe his face,
> And whine aloud for mercy.
>
>   (3.13.99-101)

Now for the chief parallels in the descriptions of the two lovers: Cleopatra's words about Antony,

>   Be'st thou sad or merry,
> The violence of either thee becomes,
> So does it no man else
>
>   (1.5.59-61)

echo (and hence also belong to the previous group) Antony's words about her:

> Fie, wrangling queen!
> Whom everything becomes—to chide, to laugh,
> To weep; whose every passion fully strives
> To make itself in thee fair and admir'd.
>
> (1.2.48-51)

The great set-piece describing Cleopatra's transcendent perfections, Enobarbus's barge-speech, finds its counterpart in Cleopatra's equally hyperbolical description of Antony to Dolabella. In both speeches the same conceit is used: the person described is declared superior to anything the artist's imagination could create, Nature in this instance surpassing fancy. Cleopatra was

> O'erpicturing that Venus where we see
> The fancy out-work nature.
>
> (2.2.204-5)

Of Antony we are told,

> Nature wants stuff
> To vie strange forms with fancy; yet t'imagine
> An Antony were nature's piece 'gainst fancy,
> Condemning shadows quite.
>
> (5.2.97-100)

Both lovers at their death are identified with the star most appropriate to them. At the death of Antony the guards exclaim:

> 2 *Guard:* The star is fall'n.
> 1 *Guard:* And time is at his period.
>
> (4.14.106-7)

The reference here is presumably to the day-star, the sun, which measures time, and to which Antony has been repeatedly compared in the course of the play. When Cleopatra dies, Charmian exclaims:

> O Eastern star! (5.2.306)

The appositeness of this identification of the Egyptian queen, mistress of the East, with Venus, the 'Eastern star', needs no emphasis.

Among the third group, the parallels in the relations of others with Antony and Cleopatra, the most notable instances are found in the deaths of their companions and servants. Eros and Charmian do not even consider the possibility of surviving them. This is the supreme tribute paid to the pair in the play. And, to complete the pattern, Iras, like Enobarbus, appears to die merely from grief, of a broken heart. Suicide, though contemplated, is not found necessary.

> This blows my heart.
> If swift thought break it not, a swifter mean
> Shall outstrike thought: but thought will do't, I feel.
> (4.6.34-6)

And thought does it, we are led to believe. Enobarbus dies with Antony's name on his lips (4.9.23). The lack of a stage-direction in the Folio leaves the cause of Iras's death more obscure. But the absence of any aside like that given to Charmian ('O, come apace, dispatch. I partly feel thee') suggests that we are not meant to regard it as suicide. And the structural pattern, which plays such an important rôle in the play, corroborates this view.

Let us now turn to the other main element in the play's structural pattern, the series of contrasts between Rome and Egypt. These contrasts between Roman and Egyptian attitudes and values, Roman and Egyptian ways of feeling and thinking, find their simplest expression in the constant alternation of scenes located in Rome and Alexandria.[1] But the Roman world sometimes invades Egypt, as at the play's opening, where the hostile comments of the Roman soldier, Philo, are delivered in the very stronghold of the enemy, the court at Alexandria; and occasionally Egypt invades Rome, as in the person of the sooth-sayer (2.3), or in Enobarbus's barge-speech, where the most glowing tribute to Cleopatra is delivered in Rome and by a Roman soldier, though one partly under the spell of the East. And the pattern of simple opposition between Rome and Egypt is further complicated by the fact that in her last hours of life Cleopatra, without surrendering any of her Eastern guile and sensuousness, acquires some Roman qualities, becoming

---

[1] As H. T. Price remarks, this is a device frequently used by Shakespeare. 'It was a normal part of Shakespeare's construction to establish two points of contrast, as, for instance, Belmont and Venice, Egypt and Rome, court and country, and, by regularly switching from one to the other, to enforce his idea' (*op. cit.*, p. 28). It occurs, he points out, as early as the First Part of *Henry VI*.

'marble-constant' (5.2.239) and doing 'what's brave, what's noble' 'after the high Roman fashion' (4.15.87), though with some concession to an Eastern concern for 'easy ways to die', preferring the indigenous and kindred serpent (' "Where's my serpent of Old Nile?" / For so he calls me', 1.5.25-6) to the Roman sword. And standing between the two opposed worlds, and combining them in his person, there is Antony. What in him they have in common is their extravagant, hyperbolic nature. 'The greatest soldier of the world' (1.3.38) is also its greatest lover. The same Antony who amazes his fellow-soldiers when, during a famine in his wars, he drinks 'the gilded puddle / Which beasts would cough at', and eats 'strange flesh, / Which some did die to look on' (1.4.62-9) amazes them equally by his feats of drinking and eating in his Alexandrian revels (2.2.183-6). Hyperbole is the mark of his own words and deeds, as well as of what is said by others about him, finding its climax in Cleopatra's great speech to Dolabella.

What above all unites the two worlds in Antony is the intense vitality which he brings to his rôle of voluptuary as well as to that of statesman and soldier. Professor L. C. Knights puts it admirably when he writes of it: 'What Shakespeare infused into the love story as he found it in Plutarch was an immense energy, a sense of life so heightened that it can claim to represent an absolute value. . . . This energy communicates itself to all that comes within the field of force that radiates from the lovers, and within which their relationship is defined.'[1] The opposition is never one between sensual sloth and the life of action. That is why the stock-image presented by Spenser of the knight in the arms of Acrasia (*F.Q.*, II, 12, lxxvi-lxxx) fits Antony's case so little, in spite of its surface similarities. Pompey thinks of the relationship in this conventional way when he calls upon Cleopatra to

> Tie up the libertine in a field of feasts,
> Keep his brain fuming. Epicurean cooks
> Sharpen with cloyless sauce his appetite,
> That sleep and feeding may prorogue his honour
> Even till a Lethe'd dullness.
>
> (2.1.23-7)

[1] *Some Shakespearean Themes* (1959), p. 145. Also in the Penguin *The Age of Shakespeare* (1955), p. 245.

Caesar in his account, for all his patrician contempt for the
'democratic' Antony, and in spite of much that he leaves out,
conveys the energy and vitality of this life much more truly:

> Let's grant it is not
> Amiss to tumble on the bed of Ptolemy,
> To give a kingdom for a mirth, to sit
> And keep the turn of tippling with a slave,
> To reel the streets at noon, and stand the buffet
> With knaves that smell of sweat.

(1.4.16-21)

A further complication of the simple pattern of contrasts
results when Shakespeare, after showing Antony's Love and
Honour (meaning chiefly military glory) in continuous conflict, with Honour disastrously routed by Love at the battle of
Actium, proceeds to give us a series of scenes in which Love and
Honour have for a time joined forces. In 4.4. Cleopatra, the
armourer of his heart, has also become the armourer of his
body, and his love for her the spur to his valour. The scene was,
I believe, influenced by Plutarch's implied contrast of Antony's
behaviour with that of Demetrius, in his 'Comparison of
Demetrius with Antonius': 'They were both in their prosperitie
very riotously and licentiously given: but yet no man can euer
say, that *Demetrius* did at any time let sleep any opportunitie or
occasion to follow great matters, but only gaue himselfe indeed
to pleasure, when he had nothing else to do . . . but indeed
when he was to make any preparation for war, he had not then
Iuie at his darts end, nor had his helmet perfumed, nor came
out of the Ladies closets pricked and princt to go to battell:
but he let all dancing and sporting alone, and became as the
Poet Euripides saith: *The souldier of Mars, cruell and bloudie.*'[1]
Plutarch's unfavourable contrast is here turned by Shakespeare
in Antony's favour. For he is shown capable of sporting and
feasting all night *and* fighting a victorious battle the next day,
of being in quick succession a devotee of Venus and Bacchus
and a soldier of Mars.

The temporary fusion of Love and Honour in these scenes is
epitomized by the astonishing image in Antony's speech of
welcome to Cleopatra after his victorious return from battle:

[1] Plutarch's *Lives*, transl. North, 1612 ed., p. 950. The first part of the
quotation may have suggested Caesar's words about Antony at 1.4.25-33.

> Leap thou, attire and all,
> Through proof of harness to my heart, and there
> Ride on the pants triumphing.
>
> (4.8.14-16)

The image also forms an ironic contrast to Antony's imprecations uttered the following morning (only about a hundred lines separate the two passages):

> Vanish, or I shall give thee thy deserving
> And blemish Caesar's triumph. Let him take thee
> And hoist thee up to the shouting plebeians . . .
>
> (4.12.32-4)

Another element that complicates the pattern of contrasts between the two worlds is the fact that certain qualities, such as cruelty and deceit, are shown to belong to both. For instance, Caesar's cruel treatment of Alexas (4.6.12-16) has its counterpart in Antony's treatment of Thyreus and his offer concerning Hipparchus (3.13.147-51). The whole last act is given over to the contest between Caesar's guile and Cleopatra's, each determined to outwit the other. 'Policy' and duplicity is used just as much by Cleopatra in the service of Love as by Caesar in the service of the State. The truth is that Cleopatra is less Caesar's complete opposite than is Antony. It is Caesar's sister, Octavia, who is her opposite in every way.[1]

This juxtaposition of opposed characters, Antony and Caesar, Cleopatra and Octavia, forms another essential part of the play's dualistic structure, another means by which Shakespeare brings out the all-pervasive contrast between East and West. He achieves the contrast between Antony and Caesar by burying the Antony of *Julius Caesar* and creating an entirely new and different dramatic character. In spite of the attempts of many critics to find links and similarities between them, I do not see how a belief in the unity of conception of the two

[1] J. F. Danby also remarks that 'Octavia is the opposite of Cleopatra as Antony is the opposite of Caesar', and neatly formulates one of the contrasts between the two women: Octavia 'is woman made the submissive tool of Roman policy where Cleopatra always strives to make the political subservient to her' (*Poets on Fortune's Hill* (1952), ch. 5, p. 142). This is probably the most illuminating essay on the play known to me, and my debt to it is considerable, in spite of my radical disagreement with some of its conclusions.

Antonies can be maintained. As we have seen in Chapter I
(pp. 43-44), the Antony of *Julius Caesar* has scarcely a trait in
common with the Antony depicted by Plutarch, except a fondness for revelry, and this is also his only link with the Antony
of our play, who is largely based on Plutarch's depiction of him.
He is basically what Plutarch calls him, and what the Antony
of *Julius Caesar* only pretends to be (3.2.218), 'a plaine man
without subtilty'.[1] The Machiavellism of the Antony of *Julius
Caesar* has in the later play been transferred to Caesar, who had
shown no traces of it in the earlier drama. The ruthless treatment of Lepidus there advocated by Antony (*J.C.*, 4.1.19-27)
is in fact carried out by Caesar in *Antony and Cleopatra* (3.5.6-12).
We need only to think of this cynical advice on the treatment
of Lepidus in the mouth of the Antony of the later play, or to
imagine that 'mine of bounty' planning to defraud Caesar's
heirs of part of their legacies (*J.C.*, 4.1.8-9), to realize how
impossible it is to entertain the notion that the Antony of our
play is a development and continuation of the Antony of *Julius
Caesar*. Nor is it very difficult to see why Shakespeare should
have made the change. Had Antony instead of Caesar been
made the calculating politician, the deceitful Machiavel, it
would have destroyed the presiding conception of the play.
This demanded that the value of all that Antony loses through
his love for Cleopatra, such as political power, wordly glory,
should be called into question by a display of the ruthlessness,
the deceit, the calculating inhumanity that goes with the
acquisition and maintenance of such power and glory. Caesar,
therefore, had to be the Machiavel,[2] and Antony, by contrast,
the simple, generous, impulsive, chivalrous soldier; one who is
willing to stake his worldly fortunes upon a sea-fight where he
is at a grave disadvantage, merely because Caesar 'dares us
to't' (3.7.29) and his chivalric code obliges him to accept this

[1] *Shakespeare's Plutarch*, ed. Tucker Brooke (1909), vol. 2, p. 35.
[2] For Caesar as the Machiavel Shakespeare could also have derived
suggestions from Garnier's play. This is how Antonius there describes him:

> His vertue, fraude, deceit, malicious guile,
> His armes, the arts that false *Ulisses* us'de.

(ll. 1102-3)

No doubt the germ of this conception is found in Plutarch's account of
Caesar's double-dealing towards Cleopatra after Antony's death.

challenge; one who seems genuinely surprised when 'the full Caesar' refuses to 'answer his emptiness' and meet him in personal combat (4.2.1-4).

Yet, as one would expect with Shakespeare, who, even at his most schematic, refuses to paint in black and white, Caesar is depicted not merely as the cold-blooded, calculating politician. He is also shown to be a tender and loving brother (for, unlike some commentators, I do not think Shakespeare means us to question the sincerity of this love) and at least the *post mortem* admirer of Antony and Cleopatra, capable of true and deep feeling.

Professor Danby has shown how what he calls 'the Shake-spearean dialectic' is the informing structural principle of the entire play. 'It comes out in single images, it can permeate whole speeches, it governs the build-up inside each scene, it explains the way one scene is related to another.'[1] It also extends to the emotional pattern exhibited by the two lovers (this is another way in which they resemble and echo each other). In no other play by Shakespeare do we meet characters given to such persistent oscillation of feelings, such violent veering between emotional extremes.[2] In the case of Cleopatra it is at times deliberately practised, part of her technique of exhibiting her infinite variety in order to keep monotony at bay, her method of tantalizing Antony by providing moods that are emotional foils to his own.

> If you find him sad
> Say I am dancing; if in mirth, report
> That I am sudden sick.
>
> (1.3.3-5)

But it also expresses her essential nature, dominated by her planet, the fleeting moon. With Antony the oscillation of feel-ings is even more pronounced and is linked to, and partly expressive of, his veering between East and West, which exert their rival pull upon him. The remarkable absence of any inner conflict in Antony when faced, at several points in the play, with the necessity to choose between Rome and Egypt is an

---

[1] *Op. cit.*, p. 139.

[2] Wilson Knight likewise stresses 'a strange see-saw motion of the spirit, an oscillating tendency, back and forth' (*The Imperial Theme* (1931), p. 265).

expression of this emotional polarity, this pendulum swing of the feelings. As A. C. Bradley remarks, Shakespeare 'might have made the story of Antony's attempt to break his bondage, and the story of his relapse, extremely exciting, by portraying with all his force the severity of the struggle and the magnitude of the fatal step'.[1] But he chose not to do so. Instead he shows us Antony's complete devotion to Cleopatra in the opening scene, followed by his sudden resolution to break free from her: 'These strong Egyptian fetters I must break, / Or lose myself in dotage' (1.2.113-14). In the leave-taking that follows his fetters are shown to be as stoutly knit as ever:

> By the fire
> That quickens Nilus' slime, I go from hence
> Thy soldier, servant, making peace or war
> As thou affect'st.
>
> (1.3.68-71)

In the message he sends her by Alexas he promises to 'piece her opulent throne with kingdoms' (1.5.46). Then comes Agrippa's marriage-plan, Antony's immediate acceptance of it, and his protestation to Caesar:

> Further this act of grace; and from this hour
> The heart of brothers govern in our loves
> And sway our great designs!
>
> (2.2.151-3)

When we meet him next he confesses to Octavia,

> I have not kept my square; but that to come
> Shall all be done by th' rule.
>
> (2.3.6-7)

Directly upon this follows the encounter with the soothsayer, and Antony's instant resolution:

> I will to Egypt;
> And though I make this marriage for my peace,
> I' th' East my pleasure lies.
>
> (2.3.39-41)

---

[1] *Oxford Lectures on Poetry*, p. 285.

When we find him next in the company of Octavia, at their leave-taking from Caesar, the following exchange takes place between the two men:

> *Caesar:* Most noble Antony,
> Let not the piece of virtue which is set
> Betwixt us as the cement of our love
> To keep it builded be the ram to batter
> The fortress of it; for better might we
> Have lov'd without this mean, if on both parts
> This be not cherish'd.
> *Antony:* Make me not offended
> In your distrust.
> *Caesar:* I have said.
> *Antony:* You shall not find,
> Though you be therein curious, the least cause
> For what you seem to fear.
>
> (3.2.27-36)

A few scenes later Octavia hears from her brother that Antony is back in Egypt, that 'Cleopatra / Hath nodded him to her' (3.6.65-6). I feel sure it would be a gross falsification of Shakespeare's conception to see Antony in these changes as a conscious deceiver, hiding his true feelings and intentions from Caesar, Octavia, or Cleopatra. Rather should we see him as sincere in all his protestations, believing each to be true at the moment it is uttered, until he is suddenly drawn into a contrary allegiance. Instead of being 'with himself at war', like Brutus, or Macbeth, or Othello, he is like a chronic deserter, forever changing sides in the struggle, and this emotional pattern mirrors and underlines the structural pattern of the entire play.

II

The dualistic structure of *Antony and Cleopatra* also helps to make it Shakespeare's problem play *par excellence*. Let us remind ourselves of L. C. Knights's dictum quoted in the *Introduction*: 'In *Macbeth* we are never in any doubt of our moral bearings. *Antony and Cleopatra*, on the other hand, embodies different and apparently irreconcilable evaluations of the central experience.' Throughout the play, and to an extent far exceeding anything found in *Julius Caesar* and *Measure for Measure*, we are confronted with these opposed evaluations, and in such a way as to exclude—at least in those open to the play's full imaginative impact—a simple or consistent response. Indeed, Antony's great speech to Eros ('Sometime we see a cloud that's dragonish') not only expresses his sense of an utter loss of identity as a result of Cleopatra's supposed betrayal of him, but, as Professor Danby suggests,[1] also describes our experience in watching the play. As applied to the ever-changing outlines of Cleopatra's character it is only another way of describing her infinite variety. But it extends to the play's whole moral landscape, our shifting attitudes towards its events, our ever-changing feelings towards its main characters, Antony, Cleopatra, and Caesar. Here the technique of 'dramatic coquetry', consisting in an alternate enlisting and repelling of the audience's affections for a character, which we have studied in the two preceding chapters and which, when strongly in evidence, is one of the hallmarks of the Shakespearian Problem Play, reaches its climax. As regards the two lovers, it is employed from the very beginning until the fourth act. As for Caesar, it extends through the entire play up to its closing lines.

To Professor Knights's contrast between *Macbeth* and our play may be added a secondary contrast between them: In *Macbeth* Shakespeare depicts in his hero's mind a complex response to a simple, unproblematic, moral issue. In *Antony and Cleopatra*, as in *Measure for Measure*, the reverse is found: A complex, problematic, moral issue confronting Antony and Isabella evokes a simple response, one apparently arrived at without any inner conflict. But the simplicity of the response, the absence of inner conflict in the hero and heroine of these plays, in no way prevents a complex and divided response in the minds of the audience or the taking of opposite sides among its members. As with *Julius Caesar* and *Measure for Measure*, the opposition of attitudes in the play, the conflicting presentation of its moral issues, is reflected in the polarity of views among its commentators. A substantial body of critics, especially of the last century (with even Arthur Symons, oddly, among them[2]), adhere, with varying degrees of emphasis, to the Roman view

[1] *Op. cit.*, p. 131.
[2] See his introduction to the play in the *Henry Irving Shakespeare* (1894), vol. 6, pp. 119-20.

of Caesar, Pompey, and Philo, seeing Antony's love for Cleopatra very much as Plutarch saw it. This attitude may be prompted by a personal response to the play, or, in more recent times, by an attempt to see it 'historically', to respond to it as it is supposed an Elizabethan audience (always by such critics thought of as a monolith, incapable of divided feelings or varying reactions) would have responded.[1] On the opposite side there is the at present more influential body of critics who see the love-affair as the glorious culmination of Antony's life. This group, whose doyen is Swinburne, includes such names as Wilson Knight, Dover Wilson, S. L. Bethell, and, across the Atlantic, Donald Stauffer and Harold S. Wilson.[2]

But, once again, there is also a *tertium quid*, a group of critics who feel that the play conveys no clear-cut, unequivocal attitude to the love-story. A. C. Bradley may be allowed to speak for all these when he declares that 'Neither the phrase "a strumpet's fool", nor the assertion "the nobleness of life is to do thus", answers to the total effect of the play. But the truths they exaggerate are equally essential; and the commoner mistake in criticism is to understate the second.'[3] Since these words were written (1905), the critical pendulum has swung the other way and today the commoner mistake is to understate the first. But Bradley's essay, despite a few lapses, remains one of the sanest and justest comments on the play.

Another set of oppositions in the play's effect upon its audience is brought out by Professor Knights when he writes: 'This, then, is what the play asks of us: to be true to both these impressions of the presented relationship. On the one hand, a closed circle of passion, of which the boasted "variety" is, in the end, entirely dependent on the application of fresh stimulants; on the other hand, natural force and fertility and spontaneous human feeling, all apparently inextricably tied

[1] An example of this attitude is provided by F. M. Dickey's *Not Wisely but too Well* (1957), pp. 144 ff.

[2] A. C. Swinburne, *A Study of Shakespeare* (1880), p. 188; Wilson Knight, *op. cit.*, chapters 7 and 8; Dover Wilson, *op. cit.*, pp. xviii ff.; S. L. Bethell, *Shakespeare and the Popular Dramatic Tradition* (1944), pp. 128-30; Donald A. Stauffer, *Shakespeare's World of Images* (1949), pp. 232 ff.; H. S. Wilson, *On the Design of Shakespearian Tragedy* (1957), p. 177.

[3] *Op. cit.*, p. 293.

("this knot intrinsicate") with passions directed to death. . . .
If we do not feel both the vitality and the sham vitality, both
the variety and the monotony, both the impulse towards life
and the impulse towards death, we are missing the full experience of the play.'[1]

Professor Danby provides a *tertium quid* of a different sort.
After pointing to 'the ambiguity which invests everything in
Egypt equally with all things in Rome' and declaring that 'If it
is wrong to see the "mutual pair" as a strumpet and her fool,
it is also wrong to see them as a Phoenix and a Turtle', he goes
on to argue that both the Roman and Egyptian attitudes are
shown to be inadequate and mistaken. 'Egypt is the Egypt of
the biblical glosses: exile from the spirit, thraldom to the
flesh-pots, diminution of human kindness. . . . The fourth and
fifth acts of *Antony and Cleopatra* are not epiphanies. They are
the ends moved to by that process whereby things rot themselves
with motion—unhappy and bedizened and sordid, streaked
with the mean, the ignoble, the contemptible. Shakespeare
may have his plays in which "redemption" is a theme (and I
think he has), but *Antony and Cleopatra* is not one of them.'[2] I
do not find it possible to follow him in this view. If the desola-
tion that begins to make a better life for Cleopatra (5.2.1-2)
does not take her away from the flesh-pots, if she does not
undergo an ennoblement (if we prefer to confine the word
'redemption' to religious contexts) which carries with it an
increase in human kindness and a diminution of selfishness and
pride, and so is kindred to the change in Lear (a comparison
which Professor Danby dismisses as blasphemous), it is difficult
to see what Shakespeare was doing in the last act.

Bernard Shaw achieves a unique combination of the opposed
critical views when he claims that 'after giving a faithful
picture of the soldier broken down by debauchery, and the
typical wanton in whose arms such men perish, Shakespeare
finally strains all his huge command of rhetoric and stage
pathos to give a theatrical sublimity to the wretched end of the
business, and to persuade foolish spectators that the world was

---

[1] 'On *The Tragedy of Antony and Cleopatra*,' *Scrutiny*, vol. 16 (1949),
pp. 321-2.
[2] *Op. cit.*, pp. 130, 148.

well lost by the twain'.[1] Shaw's account is based on a fundamental distortion of Shakespeare's procedure in this play. For
from the opening scene until Antony's death the two views are
presented side by side. The theatrical sublimity is as manifest
in the lovers' first words (1.1.14-17) or in Enobarbus's 'barge-
speech' as in what Shaw calls 'the wretched end of the business'.
(His account applies far better to the Countess of Pembroke's
Antonius, where for the play's first three quarters chiefly the
hostile, Roman view of Antony's infatuation is presented, while
in the last quarter we are given the 'romantic', sympathetic
view.)

I do not share Professor Knights's feelings that in the last
resort Shakespeare 'places' and condemns the love-affair. 'It is,
of course', he comments, 'one of the signs of a great writer that
he can afford to evoke sympathy for what, in his final judgment,
is discarded or condemned. In *Antony and Cleopatra* the sense of
potentiality in life's untutored energies is pushed to its limit,
and Shakespeare gives the maximum weight to an experience
that is finally "placed".'[2] So definite, so unequivocal a response
does not seem to me to emerge. Shakespeare does not prevent
those who wish to do so from applying to his play the subtitle
of Dryden's adaptation, 'The World Well Lost'.

The nature of Shakespeare's treatment can be perceived more
clearly when it is contrasted with the handling of a very similar
moral issue by two other great poets. In *Paradise Lost* the protagonist has also to choose between a woman whom he loves
and who threatens his very existence and a contrasted set of
values allegiance to which assures his self-preservation and
prosperity. And there, too, he chooses immediately, unhesitatingly, to follow the woman. *Paradise Lost* could well have been
called *All for Love*. But it could never have been called *The
World Well Lost*. For though Milton enlists our utmost sympathy
for Adam's decision to sacrifice all for his love of Eve, this
decision is presented in a context of values which leaves no
room for a problematic response by the reader. The whole
ethical framework of the poem is too explicit in its condemnation of the action. And it is just because it is so explicit

---

[1] Preface to *Three Plays for Puritans* (1925), p. xxviii.
[2] *Some Shakespearean Themes*, p. 149.

and we are never in doubt of our moral bearings that Milton can afford to evoke such a degree of sympathy for Adam's choice. And much the same may be said of Virgil's treatment of Dido and Aeneas. His deeply compassionate presentation of the plight of the abandoned Queen is not, so it seems to me, an indication that the poet was 'swept away irresistibly' beyond his intentions, that the moralist's overt purposes have been foiled by the artist's hidden sympathies, as some critics have asked us to believe; but on the contrary, and much as with Milton, it is an expression of Virgil's confidence in the clarity and force of the poem's ethical postulates and in the reader's ability to share them imaginatively, at least to suspend his disbelief in them. In the case of some readers this has proved an over-confidence. Just as a number of Romantic critics have applauded Adam's decision to die with Eve, there are some who have deplored Aeneas's decision to abandon Dido.[1] But their response is not the result of any ambiguity or uncertainty in the moral framework of the two poems, but rather of the critics' lack of sympathy with it, which makes them anxious to enlist the poet as an ally in their revulsion against it, makes them eager to discover in him conflicts between the conscious moralist and the intuitive artist, between the planner and the maker.

Adam's and Aeneas's decisions are 'placed' by the moral framework of the poem in a way that Antony's never is. *Antony and Cleopatra* remains securely within the area of the problem play. It is interesting to compare it in this respect with two of its English predecessors, with both of which Shakespeare was acquainted, the Countess of Pembroke's *Antonius* (1590),[2] and its companion-piece, Daniel's *Cleopatra* (1594).

In its general presentation of the love-story the Countess of Pembroke's *Antonius*, a translation of Garnier's *Marc Antoine*

---

[1] J. W. Mackail may be allowed to speak for all these when he declares: 'Apology may be invented,—palliations may be urged; defence of Aeneas is impossible' (p. lxvii of his edition of the *Aeneis*, 1930). The most eloquent statement and most extensive defence of the Romantic critics' attitude to Adam's choice is made by A. J. A. Waldock in his *'Paradise Lost' and its Critics* (1947), pp. 45-57.

[2] For evidence of Shakespeare's knowledge of this play see my note on '*Antony and Cleopatra* and the Countess of Pembroke's *Antonius*', *Notes and Queries*, vol. 201 (1956), pp. 152-4.

(1578), is, surprisingly, not at such a far remove from Shakespeare's as one would expect. It is certainly closer to it than it is to that of Plutarch, its principal source. It differs chiefly from Shakespeare's presentation in its omission of anything that derogates from its eulogistic portrayal of Cleopatra. Though, of course, more simple and less vital, she is basically Shakespeare's Cleopatra of Act V, with no hint of Shakespeare's Cleopatra of Acts I-IV. Her love for Antonius has been deep and true from the first, his suspicions of her betrayal are unfounded, and her motives for suicide simple and unalloyed: To have her body closed 'in one selfe tombe, and one selfe chest' (l. 1968)[1] with that of Antonius, while her spirit is reunited with his in 'the hellish plaine' (l. 1951). In essence this Cleopatra, who invokes Antonius by 'our holy mariage' (l. 1948), is indistinguishable from Chaucer's, the martyr and one of the saints of Love.[2] To this picture of her as a devoted and faithful wife Garnier has added that of the loving mother in a pathetic scene of leave-taking from her children (ll. 1834 ff.).

Apart from the deluded Antonius when he thinks himself betrayed by her, nobody in the play except she herself utters a word of blame or criticism of Cleopatra; not even the chief victims of her actions, the chorus of Egyptians, who, in laments full of Sophoclean pessimism, repeatedly bewail their fate; not even Caesar and Agrippa, who have a great many harsh things to say about Antonius. And her self-blame is not for her past relations with Antonius but for her flight at Actium, which led to his overthrow. The equivalent to Enobarbus's tribute to Cleopatra in his 'barge-speech' is found in Diomede's extended praise of her perfections:

> Nought liues so faire. Nature by such a worke
> Her selfe, should seme, in workmanship hath past.
> She is all heau'nlie: neuer any man
> But seeing hir was rauished with her sight, *etc.*

> (ll. 709-12)

While the picture of this paragon among women thus remains untarnished, Antonius's part in the love-affair is severely con-

---

[1] Line-references are to Alice Luce's edition of the play (1897). I quote throughout from her text, an edited reprint of the first edition of 1592.

[2] *The Legend of Good Women*, I. 'The Legend of Cleopatra'.

demned by various speakers: by his friend, Lucilius; by Caesar and Agrippa; but chiefly and most vehemently by himself while in revulsion against his love for the woman whom he believes to have betrayed him. Nothing that Caesar or Philo say in Shakespeare's play is stronger in its condemnation than Antonius's

> Nay, as the fatted swine in filthy mire
> With glutted heart I wallow'd in delights,
> All thoughts of honor troden under foote.
> So I me lost.

(ll. 1155-8)

The tributes to Antonius come chiefly from Cleopatra, but are also to be found in Dircetus's account of the 'plaints and out-cries horrible to heare' with which 'Men, women, children, hoary-headed age' received the news of his death (ll. 1661-2).

In *Antonius*, then, as in Shakespeare's play, we find side by side both condemnation and glorification of the love of Antony and Cleopatra. What we do not find in Garnier's play, and what is all-important in Shakespeare's, is a weighing of what Antony loses against what he gains, an alternate calling into question of the values of wordly glory and of the glory of their love. There is scarcely anything in *Antonius* of the 'World Well Lost' attitude, which is epitomized by Antony's words to Cleopatra after Actium,

> Fall not a tear, I say; one of them rates
> All that is won and lost

(3.11.69-70)

and which is caught well enough by Dryden in his Antony's exclamation,

> Give, you Gods,
> Give to your Boy, your *Caesar*,
> This Rattle of a Globe to play withal,
> This Gu-gau World, and put him cheaply off:
> I'll not be pleas'd with less than *Cleopatra*.
> (*All for Love*, II, 443 ff.)

Much the same contrast is also found between Shakespeare's play and Daniel's *Cleopatra*, which equally lacks a problematic attitude towards the love-story. Its chief difference from

Antonius lies in its treatment of Cleopatra. She is seen as a much more complex creature, driven on to suicide by a mixture of motives, as she herself confesses.

> So shall I shun disgrace, leaue to be sorry,
> Flye to my loue, scape my foe, free my soule,
> So shall I act the last of life with glory,
> Die like a Queen, & rest without controule.
>
> (ll. 1382-5)[1]

Dying like a Queen seems to mean more to her than flying to her love. Unlike the Cleopatra of *Antonius* (and of Shakespeare's play), she has only come to love Antony after his death. She repents of her former way of life, speaks of its infamy (l. 461), and sees herself as an *exemplum* of princes 'As please themselues, and care not what become' (l. 465). Nor do others spare her in their comments. The Chorus of Egyptians, in marked contrast to that in *Antonius*, fiercely condemns her for her vices, which have led to the destruction of them all.

> *And Cleopatra now,*
> *Well sees the dangerous way*
> *She tooke, and car'd not how,*
> *Which led her to decay:*
>   *And likewise makes us pay*
> *For her disordered lust,*
> *The int'rest of our blood:*
> *Or liue a seruile pray,*
> *Vnder a hand vniust,*
> *And others shall thinke good.*
> *This hath her riot wonne,*
> *And thus she hath her state, herselfe, and vs vndone.*
>
> (ll. 336-47)

'For now is nothing hid', they declare,

> *The scene is broken downe,*
> *And all vncouered lies,*
> *The purple Actors knowne*
> *Scarce men, whom men despise.*
>
> (ll. 360-3)

Nothing said by their detractors in Shakespeare's play is as savage in its denunciation of the lovers as these lines by the Chorus of Egyptians.

---

[1] All quotations follow the 1611 version in M. Lederer's edition (1911).

The chief tribute to her perfections comes from Cleopatra's last conquest, Dolabella. She is, he declares,

> The wonder of her kind, of powerfull spirit,
> A glorious Lady, and a mighty queene.
>
> (ll. 1620-1)

The divided response towards his Cleopatra which Daniel thus evokes in his reader is one of repugnance for what she has been and of admiration for what she has become, something quite different therefore from our divided response to Shakespeare's Cleopatra.

One's moral bearings are never in doubt. Her liaison with Antony is seen as infamous, though perhaps only the means used by the divine powers to punish the Egyptians for their sins by causing their country's enslavement (ll. 450-57). For the repentant, regenerate Cleopatra our utmost sympathy and admiration is evoked. At the same time Daniel turns us against Caesar by giving us the soliloquy of his innocent victim, Caesario, who predicts that the heavens will revenge the crime of his execution.

> And then *Augustus* what is it thou gainest
> By poore *Antillus* blood, and this of mine?
> Nothing but this, thy victory thou stainest,
> And pulst the wrath of heauen on thee and thine.
>
> (ll. 1444-7)

But the effect of this is merely to draw us closer to Cleopatra, not to make us question the comparative value of Love and Empire. It does not bring Daniel's *Cleopatra* any nearer to being a problem play.

In describing *Antony and Cleopatra* as such it must be insisted that the problem it raises is not general but unique. I cannot agree with S. L. Bethell's statement that in '*Antony and Cleopatra* Shakespeare returns to the old problem: What are the positive bases of the good life?'[1] The problem, as presented by Shakespeare, seems to me a much more specific one, confined to the choice by a uniquely endowed individual, placed in a unique

---

[1] *Op. cit.*, p. 130.

historical situation. The play is not a Morality, presenting the choice of Everyman, or Rex, between Love and Empire. By means examined at the beginning of the chapter, it conveys, on the contrary, a sense of an unexampled, near-miraculous fitness of the lovers for one another, and hence of the singularity of their case. 'The nobleness of life', exclaims Antony,

> Is to do thus when such a mutual pair
> And such a twain can do't . . .
>
> (1.1.37-8)

The force of the restrictive clause, obscured if not entirely obliterated by the habit of editors, misled by the punctuation of the Folio-text, of placing a heavy stop after 'thus',[1] is all-important and too often ignored by commentators on the play.

III

An insistence on Shakespeare's presentation of Antony's choice as not a representative case but as unique and singular does not imply, however, that analogues did not play their part in influencing this presentation. It seems, in fact, probable to me that two such analogues especially were a good deal in Shakespeare's mind when he wrote *Antony and Cleopatra*: that of the choice of Hercules between Pleasure and Virtue, and that of the kindred choice of Aeneas between Dido and the fulfilment of his divine mission.

The story of *Hercules in bivio*, of the youthful Hercules arrived at the fork in the road and forced to choose between the path of virtue and that of pleasure, enjoyed, after a period of neglect in the Middle Ages, considerable popularity in the Renaissance upon its rediscovery by fifteenth-century humanists. There is a good deal of evidence that it was well known to the Elizabethans (though not, it would seem, as widely as the nature of the story would lead one to expect), chiefly owing to Cicero's reference to it in the first book of the *De Officiis* (I. 32) and its inclusion in a number of emblem-books, including Whitney's

---

[1] For a brief discussion of this point see my note in *Notes and Queries*, vol. 205 (1960), p. 20.

Choice of Emblemes (1586).[1] Shakespeare nowhere refers to the story, but it seems likely that he was not unfamiliar with it. Consciously or not, it may have played its part in shaping his presentation of the Antony and Cleopatra story in terms of the hero's choice between two opposed ways of life, seen at least from the Roman point of view as the opposition between the path of *virtus* and of *voluptas*, as well as the hero's position between two women embodying these values (the play's abundance of allusions linking Antony with his ancestor Hercules, culminating in 4.12.43-7, strengthens this conjecture). It is in the *locus classicus* of the *Hercules in bivio* story, Xenophon's version of it in his *Memorabilia* (which had not, however, been translated into English but was available in several Latin translations) that the greatest kinship to Shakespeare's presentation is to be found. Here is part of Xenophon's story in a modern English translation:

> When Heracles was passing from boyhood to youth's estate, wherein the young, now becoming their own masters, show whether they will approach life by the path of virtue or the path of vice, he went out into a quiet place, and sat pondering which road to take. And there appeared two women of great stature making towards him. The one was fair to see and of high bearing; and her limbs were adorned with purity, her eyes with modesty; sober was her figure, and her robe was white. The other was plump and soft, with high feeding. Her face was made up to heighten its natural white and pink, her figure to exaggerate her height. Open-eyed was she; and dressed so as to disclose all her

[1] An admirable discussion of the variants and fortunes of the legend, especially as reflected in pictorial representations, is found in Erwin Panofsky's *Herkules am Scheidewege* (1930). A reference to the story (with woodcut illustration) is found in English literature as early as 1509 in Alexander Barclay's *The Shyp of Folys of the Worlde* (1874 reprint, vol. 2, p. 287). Of major English writers during the Renaissance only Ben Jonson refers to it explicitly (in *Pleasure Reconciled to Virtue*, *Works*, ed. Herford and Simpson, vol. 7, especially ll. 115-18, 257-60). For references to the story by other Elizabethans see Hallett Smith's *Elizabethan Poetry* (1952), pp. 296 ff. Professor Smith seems to me, however, greatly to exaggerate the centrality of the story in Renaissance conceptions of Hercules when he declares that 'the Renaissance stressed, not the twelve labors or the other feats familiar to us, but a legend in which the hero is shown deliberately choosing the kind of life he will lead' (*ibid.*, p. 293).

charms. Now she eyed herself; anon looked whether any noticed her; and often stole a glance at her own shadow.

When they drew nigh to Heracles, the first pursued the even tenor of her way: but the other, all eager to outdo her, ran to meet him, crying: 'Heracles, I see that you are in doubt which path to take towards life. Make me your friend; follow me, and I will lead you along the pleasantest and easiest road. You shall taste all the sweets of life; and hardship you shall never know. First, of wars and worries you shall not think, but shall ever be considering what choice food or drink you can find, what sight or sound will delight you, what touch or perfume; what tender love can give you most joy, what bed the softest slumber; and how to come by all these pleasures with least trouble . . .'

Virtue on her part offers only toil and sweat on the road that leads to her.

And Vice, as Prodicus tells, answered and said: 'Heracles, mark you how hard and long is that road to joy, of which this woman tells? but I will lead you by a short and easy road to happiness.'

And Virtue said: 'What good thing is thine, poor wretch, or what pleasant thing dost thou know, if thou wilt do nought to win them? Thou dost not even tarry for the desire of pleasant things, but fillest thyself with all things before thou desirest them, eating before thou art hungry, drinking before thou art thirsty, getting thee cooks, to give zest to eating, buying thee costly wines and running to and fro in search of snow in summer, to give zest to drinking; to soothe thy slumbers it is not enough for thee to buy soft coverlets, but thou must have frames for thy beds. For not toil, but the tedium of having nothing to do, makes thee long for sleep. Thou dost rouse lust by many a trick, when there is no need, using men as women: thus thou trainest thy friends, waxing wanton by night, consuming in sleep the best hours of day. Immortal art thou, yet the outcast of the gods, the scorn of good men. . . .'[1]

And this is followed by a contrasting description of the simple joys of the virtuous life. If Shakespeare knew the story in Xenophon's narrative, a possibility that cannot be ruled out, it may have influenced not only the thematic orientation of his

[1] *Memorabilia*, transl. E. C. Marchant, Loeb Classical Library (1923), pp. 95-7, 99-101.

material but also his presentation of the contrast between Octavia and Cleopatra.

But Hercules was to the Renaissance not only the great representative of 'that virtue and strength of mind which casts out all vices and conquers all voluptuous desires'[1] through the story of his choice, but, through the legend of his servitude to Omphale, was also one of the chief examples of the heroic warrior who becomes unmanned, losing all thoughts of worldly honour and renown, fallen into effeminate subjection to the woman he loves. The parallel between the Hercules-Omphale story and that of Antony and Cleopatra is drawn explicitly by Plutarch in his *Comparison of Demetrius with Antonius* when he writes of Demetrius: 'But to conclude, he neuer had ouerthrow or misfortune through negligence, nor by delaying time to follow his owne pleasure; as we see in painted tables, where *Omphale* secretly stealeth away *Hercules* clubbe, and took his Lyons skinne from him: euen so *Cleopatra* oftentimes vnarmed *Antonius*, and enticed him to her, making him lose matters of great importance, and very needfull iournies, to come and be dandled with her.'[2] The parallel is developed at length by Lucilius in Garnier's play, causing the repentant Antonius to exclaim,

> In onelie this like *Hercules* am I,
> Of this I proue me of his lignage right:
> In this himselfe, his deedes I shew in this,
> In this, nought else, my ancestor he is.

ll. 1232-5

The twin pictures of Hercules and Antony as love's victims in Tasso's description of the panels on the gate of Armida's palace (*Gerusalemme*, XVI, 3-7)[3] and the coupling of them by Spenser in the *Faerie Queene*,

---

[1] Hallett Smith, *op. cit.*, p. 295.
[2] Plutarch's *Lives*, transl. North, 1612 ed., p. 951.
[3] That Shakespeare was not unfamiliar with this passage, at least in Fairfax's translation, seems indicated by a probable echo, in the image of Cleopatra's barge burning on the water, of Tasso's description of how, at the battle of Actium, 'D'oro fiammeggia l'onda', which Fairfax renders, 'The Water burn'd about the Vessels good, / Such Flames the gold, therein inchased, threw'. (The similarity was first pointed out by R. H. Case in his Arden edition of the play, p. 53.)

So also did that great Oetean Knight
For his loues sake his Lions skin vndight:
And so did warlike *Antony* neglect
The worlds whole rule for *Cleopatras* sight.

(Bk V, 8. ii. 3-4)

would further strengthen the link between the two pairs of
lovers in Shakespeare's mind, a link which seems to have found
expression in Cleopatra's 'Then put my tires and mantles on
him, whilst / I wore his sword Philippan' (2.5.22-3).[1] The
exchange of clothes, with Omphale carrying Hercules' club and
quivers and wearing his lion's skin, belongs to their story as
narrated by Ovid in his *Fasti* (II, 317), which Shakespeare
appears to have remembered, for none of the passages just
mentioned speak of an exchange of clothes between the lovers
or of Hercules wearing Omphale's attire.

Next to the *Hercules in bivio* story, the chief *exemplum* for the
Renaissance of the hero forced to choose between *virtus* and
voluptas was probably the tale of Dido and Aeneas, at least as
seen through Virgilian, not medieval, eyes. And here the evidence that Shakespeare had this analogue much in mind while
writing *Antony and Cleopatra* is much more conclusive than with
the Choice of Hercules. There is, first of all, the overt comparison of the two pairs of lovers, put into the mouth of
Antony:

Where souls do couch on flowers, we'll hand in hand,
And with our sprightly port make the ghosts gaze.
Dido and her Aeneas shall want troops,
And all the haunt be ours.

(4.14.51-4)

Next, there is a series of apparent echoes of Marlowe's *Dido,
Queen of Carthage*, a play that seems to have been echoed also in
A Midsummer Night's Dream[2] and in the Pyrrhus speech in
Hamlet (2.2.467-8; *Dido*, 2.1.253-6). The force of these echoes,

---

[1] Conversely, when Thomas Heywood dramatized the Hercules-Omphale
story in *The Brazen Age*, he seems to have drawn on memories of a stage-
performance of *Antony and Cleopatra*, as a number of echoes indicates. See
my discussion of this in 'Heywood's *Ages* and Shakespeare', *R.E.S.*, N.S.,
vol. 11 (1960), pp. 23-4.

[2] See E. I. Fripp, *T.L.S.*, August 1928, p. 593.

which have been listed by Professor T. P. Harrison,[1] is cumulative, and, though no single instance by itself convinces, in aggregate they seem to me to leave little room for doubt that Marlowe's play was much in Shakespeare's mind during the writing of *Antony and Cleopatra*. Thirdly, there is an apparent echo of a line in Dido's letter to Aeneas in Ovid's *Heroides*,[2] 'Sed iubet ire deus, vellem vetuisset adire', in Cleopatra's

> What says the married woman? You may go.
> Would she had never given you leave to come!
>
> (1.3.20-21)[3]

That Shakespeare should have had the Dido and Aeneas story so much in mind in writing *Antony and Cleopatra* is not surprising. Apart from their similarity as *exempla* of the hero's choice between Love and Empire, the two stories have so many other points in common that a number of commentators on Book IV of the *Aeneid* have suspected Virgil to be glancing at Cleopatra's relations with Antony and Julius Caesar.[4] Shakespeare had already coupled the two African Queens in *Romeo and Juliet* ('Dido, a dowdy: Cleopatra, a gipsy', 2.4.41-2). The

[1] *Texas Studies in English* (1956), pp. 58 ff.

[2] *Heroides*, VII, l. 139. This was first pointed out by T. Zielinski, *Philologus* (1905), vol. 64, p. 17.

[3] The similarity is increased if we punctuate with Dover Wilson (following Thistelton), 'What, says the married woman you may go?' instead of, with Rowe and most subsequent editors, 'What says the married woman? You may go'. (The Folio has 'What sayes the married woman you may goe?') But the notion that Fulvia should give Antony permission to leave Cleopatra makes little sense. And that the permission comes from Cleopatra is borne out by the immediately following lines: 'Let her not say 'tis I that keep you here— / I have no power upon you; hers you are'. Hence the conventional punctuation is almost certainly correct.

[4] Mackail (*op. cit.*, p. lxvii), for instance, writes: 'In the venomous description given by Rumour of Aeneas and Dido,

> nunc hiemem inter se luxu, quam longa, fovere
> regnorum immemores turpique cupidine captos,

one can hardly fail to see an oblique reference to Antony and Cleopatra at Alexandria; and it is worth notice that in the Sousse mosaic of Aeneas and Dido, she is represented, like Cleopatra, with the *uraeus* or sacred asp in her head-dress.' See also A. S. Pease's list of parallels between Virgil's Dido and the historical Cleopatra in his edition of Book IV of the *Aeneid* (1935), pp. 24-6.

link between them was, no doubt, strengthened in his mind by their joint appearance (in first and third place) as Love's martyrs in Chaucer's *Legend of Good Women*, on which Shakespeare had almost certainly drawn in *A Midsummer Night's Dream* (5.1.126 ff.), in *The Merchant of Venice* (5.1.1-14), and again in our play. For there can be very little doubt that Shakespeare derived his knowledge of Cleopatra's marriage to Ptolemy and her subsequent widowhood from Chaucer's 'Legend of Cleopatra'.[1]

A third analogue to Antony's situation which seems to have been a good deal in Shakespeare's mind while writing this play is the story of the love of Mars and Venus[2] (though here the choice between *virtus* and *voluptas* is, at best, only implicit. Its true parallel is the Hercules-Omphale story rather than that of Hercules' Choice.) Once again there is an overt reference to the story, Mardian's 'Yet have I fierce affections, and think / What Venus did with Mars' (1.5.17-18). Next, Antony is repeatedly compared to Mars (1.1.4; 2.2.6; 2.5.117) and Cleopatra to Venus (2.2.204; and to Venus as the morning-star, 5.2.306). And lastly the play contains echoes of *Venus and Adonis*. I have not seen it pointed out that in Enobarbus's words (which come close upon his comparison of Cleopatra to Venus),

> Age cannot wither her, nor custom stale
> Her infinite variety. Other women cloy
> The appetites they feed, but she makes hungry
> Where most she satisfies,
>
> (2.2.239-42)

Shakespeare is manifestly recalling Venus's words to Adonis:

> And yet not cloy thy lips with loath'd satiety,
> But rather famish them amid their plenty,
> Making them red and pale with fresh variety.
>
> (ll. 19-21)

And it is difficult to read the opening thirteen lines of the play without feeling that it owes something, in thought and structure

---

[1] For evidence of this see my note on '*Antony and Cleopatra* and *The Legend of Good Women*', in *Notes and Queries*, vol. 205 (1960), pp. 335-6.

[2] J. F. Danby goes so far as to declare that 'the play is Shakespeare's study of Mars and Venus—the presiding deities of Baroque society, painted for us again and again on the canvasses of his time' (*op. cit.*, pp. 150-1).

if not in wording (but notice the image of tempered steel in both passages), to Venus's description of her relations with Mars in the earlier poem (ll. 97-114).

But far more important than any of these analogues in its effect on the play's structure and on the whole organization of its material was, I believe, Shakespeare's own two-part play of *Henry IV*.

There are, it seems to me, two main ways of looking at the structural pattern of *Henry IV*. With Quiller-Couch,[1] Dover Wilson,[2] and Tillyard,[3] one can see the two-part play as possessing the basic structure of a Morality, turning on Hal's choice between Vanity and Government. 'In the first part the Prince . . . is tested in the military or chivalric virtues. He has to choose, Morality-fashion, between Sloth or Vanity, to which he is drawn by his bad companions, and Chivalry, to which he is drawn by his father and his brothers. And he chooses Chivalry. . . . Near the end of the play the Prince ironically surrenders to Falstaff the credit of having killed Hotspur, thus leaving the world of arms and preparing for the motive of the second part. Here again he is tested, but in the civil virtues. He has to choose, Morality-fashion, between disorder or misrule, to which he is drawn by his bad companions, and Order or Justice (the supreme kingly virtue) to which he is drawn by his

---

[1] *Shakespeare's Workmanship* (1918), p. 148: 'The whole of the business is built on the old Morality structure, imported through the Interlude. Why, it might almost be labelled, after the style of a Morality title, *Contentio inter Virtutem et Vitium de anima Principis.*'

[2] *The Fortunes of Falstaff* (1943), pp. 17-20, 74-5.

[3] *Shakespeare's History Plays* (1944), p. 265. Dr. Tillyard's views on this matter are broadly the same as Dover Wilson's, except that in Part I he takes Hal to represent the Aristotelian middle way between the excess of the military spirit, represented by Hotspur, and its defect, represented by Falstaff. To me it seems that, rather than representing such an Aristotelian mean, Hal embodies Shakespeare's ideal of true chivalry in contrast to Hotspur's false ideal, which is little more than a thirst for personal glory and fame. This contrast is epitomized in Hal's willingness to let Falstaff claim the glory of Hotspur's overthrow, in the 'fair rites of tenderness' with which he honours his dead opponent, and in his act of setting free the captured Douglas without ransom, none of which is found in the play's sources (in Holinshed it is the King who releases the Douglas without ransom). Here, Shakespeare is saying by implication, you have true chivalry, not in Hotspur's narrow, selfish ideal.

father and by his father's deputy the Lord Chief Justice. And he chooses Justice.'[1] With this way of looking at the play we have not only a Morality structure (two groups of characters embodying opposed moral values are seen struggling for the Prince's allegiance, with the action oscillating between the two groups), but also a Morality *ethos* (the contrast between the moral values of the two groups is seen as a clear-cut opposition of good and evil). I do not wish to deny that this structural pattern is to be found in the play (though it must be insisted that there is only a mock-drama of salvation, for the audience knows that the protagonist is secretly 'converted' and 'saved' from the very outset. The element of suspense, central to any true Morality play, is thus entirely lacking, its place being taken, as is customary with Shakespeare, by dramatic irony). But it is overshadowed by a structural pattern which is considerably more important to the play's total effect: this consists of the juxtaposition of the same two worlds as in the other pattern, that of Eastcheap, epitomized by Falstaff, and that of Westminster, epitomized by the King; but now not seen through the eyes of a writer of Moralities but through the eyes of a Shakespeare. Here the moral issues are no longer simple and clear-cut. Both worlds and their representatives are made to appear attractive and repulsive in turn and serve as foils to each other. Looked at in this way, the play still has a Morality structure but no longer a Morality *ethos*. It is this structural pattern which, among all Shakespeare's plays, bears the closest similarity to that of *Antony and Cleopatra* (where again we find a Morality structure without a Morality *ethos*). It is this very remarkable similarity—which, oddly enough, seems never to have been noted by commentators—that I wish to bring out in what follows.

Like Antony, Hal is seen standing between two opposed worlds: Eastcheap (the East where his pleasure lies) represents above all a life of varied enjoyments, of freedom from social and moral restraints. Like Antony, Hal mixes freely, democratically, with the common people. His father's reproaches of him for being 'So common-hackney'd in the eyes of men, / So stale and cheap to vulgar company' (1 *Henry IV*, 3.2.40-41) are much

---

[1] Tillyard, *loc. cit.*

like Caesar's denunciation of Antony for reeling the streets at
noon and standing 'the buffet / With knaves that smell of
sweat' (*A. & C.*, 1.4.20-1). In these censures there is the same
mixture of the fastidious patrician's disdain for 'the rabble' and
the calculating politician's concern for keeping up appearances
in public. The pleasures of Eastcheap and of Alexandria are
not of the senses only but include practical jokes, such as Hal's
of the robbery of the robbers at Gadshill and Cleopatra's trick
of the salt-fish in the angling-wager (*A. & C.*, 2.5.15-18); and
masquerades, such as Hal and Poins's dressing-up as drawers
to spy on Falstaff and Antony and Cleopatra's wandering in
disguise through the streets of Alexandria to 'note / The qualities of people' (*A. & C.*, 1.1.53-4). Falstaff and Cleopatra have
been at times compared by critics.[1] What they chiefly have in
common is their infinite variety, which is not only theirs by
nature but is also deliberately practised and calculated to
banish boredom in the companion on whom they wish to
maintain their hold.

This life of pleasure is contrasted throughout both plays with
the life of power-politics, represented by Caesar in the one
play, by the King and Prince John of Lancaster in the other.
This does not stop short of the use of treachery for 'reasons of
state', as is seen, for instance, in Caesar's betrayal of Pompey
and Lepidus (*A. & C.*, 3.5.4-12) and Prince John's betrayal
of the rebels at Gaultree Forest (2 *Henry IV*, 4.2.106-23). It is
marked by sobriety and mirthlessness (cf. Falstaff's description
of Prince John as a 'young sober-blooded boy' whom no man
can make laugh [2 *Henry IV*, 4.3.86-7] and Shakespeare's
portrayal of 'the boy Caesar', especially during the feast on
Pompey's galley). On the more positive side this life involves
self-control, a sense of duty and service, an ideal of 'Honour'
which is not wholly selfish.

In both plays the same structural pattern of constant oscillation between the two worlds is found, the same device of
making them comment on each other. And the same technique
of 'dramatic coquetry' is used towards the representatives of the
two opposed ways of life, Falstaff and the King in the one play,

[1] See, for example, F. S. Boas, *Shakspere and his Predecessors* (1896), p. 475;
A. C. Bradley, *Oxford Lectures on Poetry*, pp. 299-300; and H. S. Wilson,
op. cit., pp. 172-3.

Cleopatra and Caesar in the other. (For example, after having engaged our sympathies for Falstaff by his speech on the virtues of sherris-sack, Shakespeare promptly repels them again on his next appearance by showing him plotting to defraud Shallow.[1])

Set over against the politicians (Bolingbroke, Caesar) and the voluptuaries (Falstaff, Cleopatra) stands in each play a third person, dissociated from both: Hotspur and Pompey. Each is presented as attempting to gain political power by means of war, but as caring less for Power than for Honour, as is shown in Pompey's refusal to gain power at the expense of his honour by murdering his guests, and in Hotspur's refusal to increase his chances of victory at the expense of personal glory by postponing the battle until the arrival of reinforcements. Hal, like Antony, shares this concern for Honour, though, again like Antony, he asserts it only fitfully. The Percy rebellion plays a part equivalent to that of Pompey's. It makes Hal temporarily abandon the pleasures of Eastcheap to return to Court and take up arms. Just as with Antony, the world of 'Honour' and power-politics regains him for a time.

As in *Antony and Cleopatra* so in *Henry IV*, the character of its hero, on which everything, including the fate of the common people, turns, is constantly discussed, by Falstaff, the King, Vernon (1 *Henry IV*, 5.2.52 ff.), Warwick (2 *Henry IV*, 4.4.67 ff.) and others. The King's description of him,

> He hath a tear for pity and a hand
> Open as day for melting charity;
> Yet notwithstanding, being incens'd, he is flint;
> As humorous as winter, and as sudden
> As flaws congealed in the spring of day
>
> (2 *Henry IV*, 4.4.31-4)

with its seasonal images and its contrast of moods, is reminiscent of Cleopatra's description of Antony in her great speech to Dolabella:

> His voice was propertied
> As all the tuned spheres, and that to friends;
> But when he meant to quail and shake the orb,

[1] A neat epitome of the opposed attitudes to Falstaff, presented throughout the two parts of the play, is provided by Hal's indictment and Falstaff's self-defence in 1 *Henry IV*, 2.4.431-64.

He was as rattling thunder. For his bounty,
There was no winter in't; an autumn 'twas
That grew the more by reaping.

$$(A \ \& \ C, \ 5.2.83\text{-}8)$$

As in *Antony and Cleopatra*, the contrasted worlds are shown
to be not in every way opposed. 'Policy', the manipulation of
human beings for personal advantage, plays just as prominent
a part in the actions of Falstaff as in those of Bolingbroke.
Duplicity is exhibited not only by Prince John in his dealings
with the rebels and by 'the indirect crook'd ways' by which his
father gained the crown, but also by Falstaff in his dealings with
Shallow and Mistress Quickly. Similarly, Cleopatra as well as
Caesar is shown to be a consummate politician, while the whole
final act, in one of its aspects, presents a contest between the
rival duplicities of East and West. A main difference between
the two plays is that in *Henry IV* the central character, Hal,
himself shares in this 'policy' (in his calculated debauchery)
and duplicity (in leading Falstaff and his companions by the
nose), whilst Antony is quite free from either.

Another main difference is that Hal's attitude towards the
two opposed worlds is quite different from Antony's, who is not
a sheep in wolf's clothing, merely playing at debauchery in
order to make a dramatic rejection of it in time. Nor does
Shakespeare anywhere suggest that 'the nobleness of life' is to
do as Hal is doing in Falstaff's company. And that is one of the
reasons why *Henry IV*, unlike *Antony and Cleopatra*, is not a
problem play. The life of Eastcheap, though an important
corrective to that of Westminster and a welcome release from
it, is never presented as a valid possible alternative once Hal is
king. Falstaff, whatever his similarities in rôle and character
to the Queen of Egypt, is not Hal's Cleopatra (except in the
estimation of some romantic critics) but only his licensed jester.

Another reason why *Henry IV* is not a problem play lies in the
fact that it does not impose upon the hero (or the audience) a
choice between the two moral orders which it presents, but
envisages the possibility of a third order, exemplified in the
Chivalry which Hal displays at the end of Part I and the
Justice which he embraces at the end of Part II.[1] It is here that

---

[1] In fact, in *Henry V* we find him uniting these virtues with the Machiavellism of Bolingbroke (over the French war) and his old Eastcheap *penchant*

the Dover Wilson-Tillyard pattern asserts itself, the pattern in which Morality *ethos* is joined to Morality structure. For whereas the juxtaposition of Eastcheap and Westminster, as we have seen, is one of parallels as well as contrasts, and leaves us in continuous doubt of our moral bearings, the contrasted be- haviour of Falstaff and Hal at Shrewsbury in Part I and the juxtaposition of Falstaff and the Lord Chief Justice in Part II is devoid of all moral ambiguity and leaves us in no such doubt.

No third moral order of this kind is envisaged in *Antony and Cleopatra*. For Pompey's moral code is too much like Antony's and plays too subordinate a part to fulfil this function; whereas Octavia, though she represents all that is best in Rome without any of its deficiencies, is too slightly—even if magnificently— sketched to be considered a fit vehicle for suggesting such a third order. The choice before Antony is presented in the play as solely one between Rome and Egypt and the values which they stand for.

But in spite of these important differences between the two plays, I hope that the preceding pages have brought out enough of their essential kinship in themes and in the characters and the structural pattern through which these are expressed, to substantiate my claim that of all Shakespeare's plays *Henry IV* provides the closest analogue to *Antony and Cleopatra* and that it served as the rough model on which, consciously or not, he patterned his later play.

IV

Finally, I want to consider *Antony and Cleopatra* as a tragedy, looking in turn at each of its three main aspects as tragedy, the 'formal', the 'experiential', and the 'affective',[1] and comparing it in each case with the corresponding elements in Garnier's *Antonius* and Daniel's *Cleopatra*.

Looked at 'formally', *Antony and Cleopatra* contains both a

for practical jokes (over the business of the glove). His chivalry is now less like the ideal embodied by himself at Shrewsbury and more like Hotspur's, consisting above all of covetousness of Honour and a love of fighting. It is as a kind of Hotspur, a plain, blunt, fighting man, who has not 'well the gift of tongue', that he portrays himself in the wooing-scene (5.2.132-66).

[1] See Chapter I, pp. 57 ff.

De Casibus tragedy in the medieval manner and a tragedy of *hubris* and *ate* in the manner of the Greeks. Let us look first at the *De Casibus* tragedy. To Professor W. E. Farnham this provides the basic pattern of the play. He argues that 'Shakespeare organizes his tragedy as Antony's struggle for world rulership and gives it a pyramidal form showing a rise and fall in the hero's fortunes'.[1] This pattern is undoubtedly present (and it is amplified by the corresponding rise and fall in the fortunes of Cleopatra) though it is more of a zig-zag movement than the figure of a pyramid suggests. For instance, Shakespeare magnifies what is in Plutarch a minor skirmish outside Alexandria into a major victory for Antony (4.6-4.8), largely, it would seem, to heighten the anguish of his experience on the following morning, when he finds all his new-born hopes irrevocably dashed through what he takes to be Cleopatra's treachery. But Antony's struggle for world rulership, while it provides the main action of the play, is not the sole focus of our attention, but shares this with the playwright's exploration of Antony's relationship with Cleopatra. If we are searching for a single image to convey the basic pattern of the play, I would prefer to that of a pyramid, representing the rise and fall of Antony's fortunes, that of a pair of scales, representing the balancing of the values of Love and Empire.

Garnier's *Antonius* concerns itself almost as much with the *De Casibus* tragedy of Cleopatra as with that of Antonius, while in Daniel's play Cleopatra's fall is at the centre of our attention. As for the cause of the tragedy, blind Fortune, Fate, and man's transgressions are all adduced and their respective share in the catastrophe debated at great length in both these plays.

In *Antonius* it is the lovers who insist on their own responsibility for their misfortunes, in opposition to their comforters, who argue that they are the victims of Fate or blind Fortune. There is an extended altercation between Charmian, who declares that 'Things here belowe are in the heau'ns begot' and that the Gods are responsible for Cleopatra's misfortunes, and her mistress, who asserts that

> They neuer bow so lowe, as worldly cares.
> But leaue to mortall men to be dispos'd

[1] *Shakespeare's Tragic Frontier* (1950), p. 177.

Freelie on earth what euer mortall is.
If we therin sometimes some faultes commit,
We may them not to their high maiesties,
But to our selues impute.

(ll. 472-7)

This is balanced by a similar altercation between Lucilius, who declares that Fortune, who has 'all things fast enchaind / Unto the circle of hir turning wheele' (ll. 1124-5), is especially powerful in War, and Antonius, who exclaims:

> *It was not fortunes euer chaunging face,*
> *It was not Dest'nies chaungles violence*
> *Forg'd my mishap. Alas! who doth not know*
> *They make, nor marre, nor any thing can doe.*
> *Fortune, which men so feare, adore, detest,*
> *Is but a chaunce whose cause unknown doth rest.*
> *Although oft times the cause is well perceiu'd,*
> *But not th'effect the same that was conceiu'd.*
> *Pleasure*, nought else, the plague of this our life,
> Our life which still a thousand plagues pursue,
> Alone hath me this strange disastre spunne,
> Falne from a souldior to a Chamberer,
> Careles of vertue, careles of all praise.

(ll. 1142-54)

But elsewhere in the play the two lovers express the opposite view. It opens with Antonius's lament:

> Since cruell Heav'ns against me obstinate,
> Since all mishappes of the round engine doo
> Conspire my harme: since men, since powers divine,
> Aire, earth, and Sea are all iniurious . . .

And Cleopatra, towards its end, declares that 'the wrath / Of all the Gods at once on vs is falne' (ll. 1800-1) and speaks of 'fortune's hate' for her. Caesar is depicted as a consistent fatalist, from his opening words, 'You euer-liuing Gods which all things holde / Within the power of your celestiall hands . . .' (ll. 1346-7) to his last speech (ll. 1706-13). He believes that he bears his sway at the behest of heavenly powers (l. 1377), and is encouraged in this view by Agrippa, who asserts that the Gods have given Caesar his victory and 'grace / To raigne alone, and rule this earthlie masse' (ll. 1530-1). The first Chorus of

Egyptians voices the belief that the miseries of human existence are caused by 'heauens hate', springing from anger at Prometheus' theft of sacred fire (ll. 213-21), while their third Chorus declares that 'mightie Destinie' will eventually overthrow the Roman power, for Time's 'great scithe mowes all away' (ll. 821-6) and 'All things fixed ends do staie' (l. 860). Philostratus is alone in introducing the notion of divine punishment, thus reconciling his fatalist view that destiny decreed their miseries (ll. 299-300) with the belief that they spring from human sinfulness and that love, as harmful as Paris's love for Helen, is the cause of their misfortunes (ll. 285-96).

This view, subordinate in *Antonius*, where all blame is carefully deflected from Cleopatra, becomes the presiding conception of Daniel's play. His Antony (ll. 275-7), Cleopatra (ll. 95-8, 450-7), and Caesario (ll. 136-9) are all fatalists, viewing themselves as the playthings of destiny. But the second Chorus of Egyptians (ll. 714 ff.) makes clear to the reader that this 'destiny' is but Divine Justice, punishing the evil-doer through its daughter Nemesis. Caesario in his soliloquy (especially ll. 1432-5, 1444-9) also voices his belief in Divine Justice, which punishes all human transgressions. This belief is married to the basically opposed concept of the cyclical revolution of man's fortunes, his inevitable fall from prosperity into wretchedness, in the speech by the philosopher Arius to his friend Philostratus. He achieves this by arguing that sinfulness is the inevitable accompaniment of man's prosperity:

> For senslesse sensualitie doth euer
> Accompanie our loose felicity,
> A fatall whitch, whose charmes doth leaue vs neuer
> Till we leaue all confus'd with miserie.

(ll. 860-3)

Man's transgressions that lead to his downfall, the inevitable turn of Fortune's wheel, the decree of Fate, and the intervention of Divine Justice are thus all reconciled and we have the seeming paradox that

> Although the same be first decreed on hie,
> Our error still must beare the blame of all,
> Thus must it be, earth aske not heauen why.

(ll. 865-7)

In the final lines of the Chorus that ends the play Daniel brings together the various concepts which, clearly and consistently, he has been reiterating throughout: belief in an all-seeing, all-controlling Providence, in Divine Justice ('Right') that punishes human pride, in the self-destructive nature of greatness, in the inevitable overthrow of Disorder by Order, which is the Divine Government of the Universe.

> *O thou al-seeing light,*
> *High president of Heauen,*
> *You Magistrates the starres*
> *Of that eternall Court*
> *Of* Prouidence, *of* Right:
> *Are these the bounds y'haue giuen,*
> *Th'Vntranspassable barres,*
> *That limit pride so short?*
> *Is greatnesse of this sort,*
> *That greatnesse greatnes marres,*
> *And wrackes it selfe, selfe driuen*
> *On rockes of her owne might?*
> *Doth order order so*
> *Disorders ouerthrow?*

(ll. 1842-55)

Unlike the Chorus of Egyptians in *Antonius*, its counterpart in *Cleopatra* seems in the main a vehicle for the interpretation which the author wishes to impose upon the pattern of events. And unlike Garnier, who leaves us wavering between opposed views on fate and human responsibility, Daniel, by reconciling all apparent contradictions and reiterating a coherent and systematic view of human history, allows no room for such uncertainty in the minds of his readers.

In *Antony and Cleopatra* Shakespeare shows none of Garnier's concern with the conflicting beliefs in Fate and man's transgressions as the causes of the *De Casibus* tragedy of the lovers, and is even further removed from Daniel's systematic view of history, which reconciles these beliefs. Like all Shakespeare's greatest and noblest characters, Antony occasionally speaks in conventional terms of Fate (3.13.169; 4.14.135), of the stars (3.13.145), of Fortune (3.11.74-5; 4.4.4; 4.12.19) as guiding men's affairs. Cleopatra rails against 'the false huswife Fortune' (4.15.44) whose servant Caesar is (5.2.3.). The latter views himself as a minister of Divine Justice (3.6.87-9), believes in necessity and destiny operating in the affairs of men (3.6.82-5), and speaks of their 'unreconciliable' stars which divided him from Antony (5.1.46-8). But all this does not make the play a 'tragedy of fate', any more than *Hamlet, Othello, Lear,* and *Macbeth* are such tragedies, in spite of the fatalistic utterances of some of their main characters. The soothsayer in the second scene of the play foresees and foretells the future, just as do the witches in *Macbeth,* but in neither play are we made to feel that predestination accompanies prescience, that the freedom of choice of the protagonists is in any way impaired. It is Cleopatra's irresistible fascination that controls Antony, not, we are made to feel, destiny or the stars. Where Plutarch tells us that at Actium Antony made his disastrous decisions 'for it was predestined that the government of all the world should fall into Octavius Caesar's hands',[1] Shakespeare makes them issue naturally from his character: his stringent code of Honour makes him feel obliged to fight by sea because Caesar 'dares us to't' (3.7.29).[2] Nor, when Antony is most in need of comfort, after his defeat at Actium, does anyone tell him that it was the will of the Gods, or Fortune's doing, as Lucilius tells Antonius in Garnier's play. The fault is squarely placed upon Antony, both by others and himself. 'Had our general / Been what he knew himself, it had gone well', is Canidius's comment (3.10. 26-7). 'Antony only, that would make his will / Lord of his reason' is responsible for his defeat, according to Enobarbus (3.13.3-4). Nor are we made to take the omens in the second half of the play, the departure of the god Hercules (4.3), the nesting of swallows in Cleopatra's sails (4.12.3-4), as pointing to the workings of destiny. Like the soothsayer's predictions, they merely prognosticate future events, but in no way shape them. Neither can I agree with Bradley that 'Caesar is felt to be the Man of Destiny, the agent of forces against which the interventions of an individual would avail nothing'.[3] This is how he sees himself and how Plutarch presents him, but it is

---

[1] *Shakespeare's Plutarch*, vol. 2, p. 89.

[2] There is no suggestion of this in any of Shakespeare's sources. Plutarch remarks that 'for Cleopatra's sake he would needs have this battle tried by sea' (*op. cit.,* p. 97).

[3] *Oxford Lectures on Poetry*, p. 290.

not, I think, how Shakespeare makes us view the matter. Error and human frailty are shown to be the cause of Antony's defeat, not the workings of destiny. Indeed, as we shall see, a part of Antony's tragic suffering depends for its intensity on his recognition of his own authorship of his destruction.

As for the human flaws that bring about the fall of Princes, the two chief, pride and the love of pleasure, are much stressed in both Garnier's and Daniel's plays. In *Antonius* both Caesar and Agrippa make a great deal of Antony's *hubris*, Agrippa comparing him to the Giants who warred against the Gods and were punished for their presumption.

> *For no one thing the Gods can lesse abide*
> *In dedes of men, then Arrogance and Pride.*
> *And still the proud, which too much takes in hand,*
> *Shall fowlest fall, where best he thinks to stand.*

(ll. 1412-15)

Caesar enforces this by referring to Plutarch's two chief examples of Antony's *hubris*, the one occurring

> When his two children, *Cleopatras* bratts,
> To *Phoebe* and her brother he compar'd,
> *Latonas* race, causing them to be call'd
> The Sunne and Moone

(ll. 1422-5)

the other when

> *Lydia* to her, and *Siria* he gaue,
> *Cyprus* of golde, *Arabia* rich of smelles,
> And to his children more, *Cilicia*,
> Parths, Medes, Armenia, Phaenicia:
> The kings of kings proclaiming them to be,
> By his owne worde, as by a sound decree.

(ll. 1432-7)

Love of pleasure as the chief cause of his downfall is adduced by Antonius himself, seconded by Lucilius:

> *Pleasure*, nought else, the plague of this our life,
> Our life which still a thousand plagues pursue,
> Alone hath me this strange disastre spunne,
> Falne from a souldior to a Chamberer,
> Careles of vertue, careles of all praise.

(ll. 1150-4)

And in Caesar's comment on his death the two flaws are made jointly responsible for Antony's downfall:

> I cannot but his tearfull chaunce lament,
> Although not I, but his owne pride the cause,
> And unchaste loue of this *Aegyptian*.

> (ll. 1693-5)

Hubris as the cause of the *De Casibus* tragedy also bulks large in Daniel's play. Where Garnier, anxious as always to keep Cleopatra free from blame, confined it to Antony, omitting any reference to Plutarch's account of how 'she did not only wear at that time (but at all other times else when she came abroad) the apparel of the goddess Isis, and so gave audience unto all her subjects, as a new Isis',[1] Daniel stresses Cleopatra's *hubris* in her former, unregenerate state, making her exclaim:

> Am I the woman whose inuentiue pride
> Adorn'd like *Isis* skorn'd mortalitie?
> Ist I would haue my frailtie so beli'd
> That flatterie could perswade I was not I?

> (ll. 402-5)

And Arius, the Philosopher, joining *hubris* with the love of pleasure, extends it to the whole Egyptian people.

> Who should not see we should be what we are,
> When pride and ryot grew to such abounding?
> When dissolute impietie possest
> Th'vnrespectiue mindes of prince and people,
> When insolent securitie found rest
> In wanton thoughts, with lust, and ease made feeble.

> (ll. 830-5)

In the second Chorus of Egyptians the concept of *hubris* is joined with that of *ate* (the blind infatuation that is consequent upon *hubris* in Aeschylean tragedy and thereafter) and *nemesis*, 'daughter of iustice, most seuere'.

> *Oh how the powers of heauen doe play*
> *With trauailed mortality:*
> *And doth their weakenesse still betray,*
> *In their best prosperitie:*
> *When beeing lifted vp so hie,*

[1] *Op. cit.*, p. 87.

> *They looke beyond themselues so farre,*
> *That to themselues they take no care;*
> *Whilst swift confusion downe doth lay,*
> *Their late prowd mounting vanity:*
> *Bringing their glory to decay,*
> *And with the ruine of their fall,*
> *Extinguish people, state and all.*
>
> (ll. 738-49)

And the concept of *ate* is even more explicitly formulated in the last Chorus:

> *We in our councels must be blinded,*
> *and not see what doth import vs:*
> *And oftentimes the thing least minded,*
> *is the thing that most must hurt vs.*
>
> (ll. 1480-3)

In comparison with Garnier, Daniel, or even Plutarch, who dwells a good deal on Antony's pride and 'insolency',[1] Shakespeare makes much less of this as the cause of his downfall. Because of the 'build-up' given to Antony throughout the play, which culminates in Cleopatra's description of him to Dolabella, much that would strike one as hubristic in the mouth of any one else, such as

> I will piece
> Her opulent throne with kingdoms
>
> (1.5.45-6)

or

> I, that with my sword
> Quarter'd the world, and o'er green Neptune's back
> With ships made cities
>
> (4.14.57-9)

seems merely fitting when it comes from him, and it is only through a hostile critic, like Caesar, in his report of Antony's division of his Empire (3.6.1 ff.), or through Antony himself when in temporary revulsion against Cleopatra, that we are made aware of his *hubris*. In that speech by Antony we are also given the best definition of what the Greeks understood by *ate* to be found anywhere in Shakespeare:

> But when we in our viciousness grow hard—
> O misery on't!—the wise gods seel our eyes,

---

[1] *Op. cit.*, pp. 15 (gloss), 16, 31, 56, 86.

In our own filth drop our clear judgments, make us
Adore our errors, laugh at's while we strut
To our confusion.

(3.13.111-15)

So much for the 'formal' way of looking at the tragedy. But
the *De Casibus* tragedy, whether caused by Fate and Fortune
or by *hubris* and the love of pleasure, is, as always in Shakespeare, only of importance in so far as it contributes to the
tragic suffering experienced by the main characters, and it is
to this aspect of the play considered as a tragedy that we must
now turn.

In our consideration of Tragedy in Chapter I we saw that
the two experiences which Shakespeare seems to have felt to
be tragic above all others, and one or both of which are undergone by all his tragic heroes, are (*a*) the realization of the loss,
through one's own blind folly, of a person or object especially
precious to one; and (*b*) a sense of disillusion with that person
or object, of desertion or betrayal by it. The second of these
bulks fairly large in our play, though not as large as in *Hamlet*,
Othello, or *Lear*. The first occurs, but plays only a very subordinate part in Antony's tragic suffering.

The tragic experience of disillusion with the person precious
to him above all others, the conviction of being deserted and
betrayed by her at the very moment when he stands most in
need of her loyalty and affection, comes to Antony twice in the
second half of the play: first in the scene with Thyreus (3.13),
when he suspects that Cleopatra is abandoning him to gain
Caesar's favour (for the hand-kissing seems only the ostensible
reason for Antony's outburst, as his 'To flatter Caesar, would
you mingle eyes / With one that ties his points?' and his 'Cold-
hearted toward me?' [3.13.156-8] also suggests). And the
experience of abandonment and betrayal recurs in the following act, now exacerbated by the loss of all his hopes of recover-
ing his worldly fortunes as the result of Cleopatra's supposed
act of treachery.

Betray'd I am.
O this false soul of Egypt! this grave charm—
Whose eye beck'd forth my wars and call'd them home,

Whose bosom was my crownet, my chief end—
Like a right gypsy hath at fast and loose
Beguil'd me to the very heart of loss.

(4.12.24-9)

And the same tragic experience is expressed even more poig-
nantly upon Antony's next appearance in his words to Eros:

Here I am Antony;
Yet cannot hold this visible shape, my knave.
I made these wars for Egypt; and the Queen—
Whose heart I thought I had, for she had mine,
Which, whilst it was mine, had annex'd unto't
A million moe, now lost—she, Eros, has
Pack'd cards with Caesar, and false-play'd my glory
Unto an enemy's triumph.

(4.14.13-20)

This is another way in which Shakespeare suggests the inter-
dependence and oneness of the two lovers. When Cleopatra
appears no longer to be what she seemed, Antony too cannot
'hold this visible shape', and a sense of utter loss of identity
ensues.

It is significant that in Shakespeare's treatment of Cleopatra's
parallel experience of disillusion, abandonment, and betrayal,
when hearing of Antony's marriage to Octavia (2.5), tragedy
is kept at bay, for Shakespeare does not wish it to enter at this
early stage, and he therefore makes what is almost a comic
scene of it.

The tragic experience of the loss, through one's own blind
action, of what is most precious to one is not undergone by
Cleopatra and comes to Antony in only one scene: after the
battle of Actium, when he is 'unqualitied with very shame'
(Iras's description of the experience [3.11.44] indicates that it,
too, involves the loss of a sense of identity on Antony's part) at
the thought of his flight.

Hark! the land bids me tread no more upon't;
It is asham'd to bear me. . . .
I have offended reputation—
A most unnoble swerving. . . .
O, whither hast thou led me, Egypt? See

177

How I convey my shame out of thine eyes
By looking back what I have left behind
'Stroy'd in dishonour.

(3.11.1-2, 49-50, 51-4)

It is the loss of his Honour, his reputation as a soldier, that
torments him, not the loss of his Empire, which also issued from
his flight. Indeed, the loss of Empire, though self-induced, and
not blamable on others, is never made to appear a source of
tragic suffering for Antony. It is the imagined loss of Cleopatra
and the real loss of his Honour which alone torments him. This
is another way in which Shakespeare diminishes the value of
Empire and exalts the values of Love and Honour in the play.

By contrast, Antonius in Garnier's play is very much tormented by the thought of the loss of his worldly fortunes, as well
as his military glory.

The ceasles thought of my felicitie
Plunges me more in this aduersitie.
For nothing so a man in ill torments,
As who to him his good state represents.
This makes my rack, my anguish, and my woe
Equall unto the hellish passions growe,
When I to minde my happie puisance call
Which erst I had by warlike conquest wonne,
And that good fortune which me neuer left,
Which hard disastre now hath me bereft.

(ll. 934-43)

There is no sense of the 'World Well Lost' here![1] But Antonius
shares with Shakespeare's Antony the experience of believing
himself betrayed and deserted by the woman who is above all
precious to him and for whom he has sacrificed all his worldly
fortunes. A little earlier in the same scene he confesses to
Lucilius,

---

[1] Only once in the play is there an expression of this attitude: when
Antonius exclaims,

Take *Caesar* conquest, take my goods, take he
Th'onor to be Lord of the earth alone,
My Sonnes, my life bent headlong to mishapps:
No force, so not my *Cleopatra* take.

(ll. 918-21)

178

> Yet nought afflicts me, nothing killes me so,
> As that I so my *Cleopatra* see
> Practize with *Caesar*, and to him transport
> My flame, her loue, more deare than life to me.
>
> (ll. 878-81)

The experience is much the same as that of Shakespeare's
Antony, and is expressed at great length in Antonius's opening
soliloquy. But it is unlikely to affect us deeply when vented in
such language as this:

> Yet, yet, which is of grief extreamest grief,
> Which is yet of mischiefe highest mischiefe,
> It's *Cleopatra* alas! alas it's she,
> It's she augments the torment of thy paine,
> Betraies thy loue, thy life (alas!) betraies,
> Caesar to please, whose grace she seekes to gaine:
> With thought her Crowne to saue, and fortune make
> Onely thy foe, which comon ought haue beene.
> If her I alwaies lou'd, and the first flame
> Of her heart-killing loue shall burn me last:
> Justly complaine I she disloyall is,
> Nor constant is, euen as I constant am.
>
> (ll. 131-42)

Cleopatra's tragic suffering is treated more briefly in Garnier's
play. At the beginning her greatest grief stems from having lost
Antonius's love, 'More deare than Scepter, children, freedome,
light' (l. 410), through his false suspicions of her constancy, and
from being thus deprived of the sole comfort left to her, that of
his companionship in the grave, and in the underworld.

> So I in shady plaines shall plaine alone,
> Not (as I hop'd) companion of thy mone,
> O height of griefe!
>
> (ll. 415-17)

And later, after Antonius's death, she is tormented above all by
the thought of having been 'the plague and poison' of all those
dearest to her,

> The crowne haue lost my ancestors me left,
> This Realme I haue to straungers subiect made,
> And robd my children of their heritage.
> Yet this is nought (alas!) vnto the price

Of you, deare husband, whome my snares entrap'd:
Of you, whome I haue plagu'd, whom I haue made
With bloudie hand a guest of mouldie Tombe:
Of you, whome I destroid, of you, deare Lord,
Whome I of Empire, honor, life haue spoil'd.

(ll. 1805-13)

In Daniel's play our attention is focussed on Cleopatra's suffering. Daniel tells us nothing (in Dircetus's report of his last hours, ll. 189-291) of Antony's tragic experience, caused by the loss of Honour and Empire, and by the supposed loss of Cleopatra's love when he believes himself abandoned and betrayed by her. The first Chorus dwells on 'the hell of minde' endured by the sinner who has plunged others into wretchedness.

> *Behold what furies still*
> *Torment their tortur'd brest,*
> *Who by their doing ill,*
> *Haue wrought the worlds vnrest.*
> *Which when being most distrest,*
> *Yet more to vexe their sprite,*
> *The hideous face of sinne,*
> *(In formes they must detest)*
> *Stands euer in their sight.*
> *Their conscience still within*
> *Th'eternall larum is,*
> *That euer-barkin dog that cals vpon their misse.*

(ll. 312-23)

But in Cleopatra's soliloquies there is no sign that the 'ever-barking dog' of conscience is particularly troublesome to her, or that the hideous face of sin affrights her unduly. Though she repents of her transgressions, she does so with dignity and restraint.

> Defects I grant I had, but this was worst,
> That being the first to fall, I di'd not first.

(ll. 517-18)

Her anguish is caused chiefly by her parting from her son, Caesario (1. 1), and by the death of her lover, which precedes the opening of the play.

Garnier's drama is thus much closer to *Antony and Cleopatra* than Daniel's, both in its concentration on Antonius's tragic suffering and in its portrayal of the nature of that suffering, stemming above all from a sense of betrayal and desertion by the woman for whom he has sacrificed all his worldly fortunes. As in his previous tragedies, Shakespeare, as we have seen, stresses the experience of disillusion and abandonment, while the other main tragic experience in his plays, that caused by the self-induced loss of a precious person or object, is kept subordinate, for even Honour means less to Antony than the love of Cleopatra, while the loss of Empire passes him by as if it were a trifle.

In its 'formal' and 'experiential' aspects, then, *Antony and Cleopatra* follows the usual pattern of Shakespearian tragedy. It is in its 'affective' aspect, in the impact made by its last scene upon the emotions of the audience, that it deviates from that pattern, so that a number of critics have been reluctant to grant it the name of tragedy.

Both at Antony's death and, much more powerfully, at Cleopatra's, the audience is made to experience a sense of reconciliation. Antony's last speech,

> The miserable change now at my end
> Lament nor sorrow at; but please your thoughts
> In feeding them with those my former fortunes
> Wherein I liv'd the greatest prince o' th' world,
> The noblest; and do now not basely die,
> Not cowardly put off my helmet to
> My countryman—a Roman by a Roman
> Valiantly vanquished
>
> (4.15.51-58)

has a double purpose and effect. It is designed by Antony to produce in Cleopatra a feeling of acceptance and reconciliation. But it is also designed by Shakespeare to produce that feeling in the audience. And much the same effect upon us is created by Charmian's comment on Cleopatra's death, where again Shakespeare closely follows Plutarch in the North translation:

> It is well done, and fitting for a princess
> Descended of so many royal kings.
>
> (5.2.324-5)

And yet our total response to the two deaths is not the same. Mingled with a sense of reconciliation there is in our response to Antony's death a strong feeling of 'the pity of it!' and 'would it were otherwise!', which is the customary emotion of the audience at the end of a Shakespeare tragedy. At the death of Cleopatra this emotion seems to be entirely lacking. 'Triumph', 'exultation', 'wonder' are the words most commonly used by critics to describe the feelings evoked in them by the play's last scene. 'The death of Cleopatra, which closes the play, is greeted by the reader with sympathy and admiration, even with exultation at the thought that she has foiled Octavius'[1]; 'Her death . . . so far from arousing pity, fills us with exultation and delight'[2]; 'Her death is so glorious as to be a triumph'[3]; 'the final mood of *Antony and Cleopatra* is triumphant. The play ends with serenity, not with pain but with grandeur'.[4] It is the complete absence, at the close, of the feeling of 'would it were otherwise!', even of the feeling of 'the pity of it!' which marks off *Antony and Cleopatra* from all the preceding tragedies, and especially from *Hamlet*, *Othello*, and *Lear*.

But if such words as 'triumph', 'exultation', 'delight' really express our feelings at the close, if we experience wonder but no woe, if pity and terror are both lacking in our response, can we still speak of the play's ending as belonging to the realm of tragedy? Or must we agree with Professor Stauffer when he declares: 'In the sense that its protagonists finally create their own glowing worlds, the play is not the next-to-the-last of the tragedies, but the first and greatest of the dramatic romances'?[5] Even if we refuse to surrender to what Professor Danby has called the delusion of 'the Egypt-beyond-the-grave of Antony and Cleopatra in their autotoxic exaltations',[6] there remains enough of a sense of wonder, of exultation, and delight to make our emotional experience resemble more closely that at the end of *The Winter's Tale* than that at the end of *Othello* or *Lear*. Our willingness to class *Antony and Cleopatra* as a tragedy will, in the end, depend on the importance we allot to the 'affective' element in Shakespearian tragedy. For it is when we look chiefly at its 'affective' aspect that we may be inclined to deny

---

[1] A. C. Bradley, *Shakespearean Tragedy*, p. 84.

[2] Dover Wilson, *op. cit.*, p. xxxiii.

[3] F. P. Wilson, *Elizabethan and Jacobean* (1945), p. 125.

[4] H. S. Wilson, *op. cit.*, p. 177.

[5] *Op. cit.*, p. 247.   [6] *Op. cit.*, p. 145.

it the title of tragedy, and to group it with *Cymbeline* and *The Winter's Tale* (where tragic suffering is succeeded by a serene and harmonious close). But when we focus our attention on its 'experiential' and 'formal' aspects (Antony's tragic suffering coupled with the *De Casibus* tragedy) we have no hesitation in pronouncing it a Shakespearian tragedy and we recognize its kinship with such earlier plays as *Hamlet* and *Lear*.

Except for the impact of its ending, which separates it in this respect from Shakespeare's previous tragedies, *Antony and Cleopatra* stands not in such isolation from the plays that precede it as has sometimes been maintained. Professor Danby, for instance, remarks that 'Between *Antony and Cleopatra* and the plays that have gone before there is no obvious connection in theme or technique.'[1] I have tried in the course of this chapter to bring out some of these connections. In theme and structural pattern it is closely linked with *Henry IV*; as a problem play it belongs with *Julius Caesar* and *Measure for Measure*; the nature of the tragic experience undergone by its hero links it with many of Shakespeare's tragedies, especially *Hamlet*, *Othello*, and *Lear*.

Of the innovations in methods of character-portrayal, claimed for the play by Professor Danby, I can find no evidence. There is nothing new in our being 'forced by Shakespeare himself not to take comment at its face value', in the fact that 'Judgment knits itself back into character as it might do in Ibsen, and character issues from a mutable and ambiguous flux of things'.[2] Precisely the same is found, for instance, in *Julius Caesar* and *Henry IV*. But though not a pioneer in any field, *Antony and Cleopatra* develops and brings to perfection methods and techniques used with less consummate skill before. It is by far the greatest, as well as the most quintessential, of Shakespeare's Problem Plays.

---

[1] *Ibid.*, p. 128.   [2] *Ibid.*, p. 130-1.

CONCLUSION

'THE WEB of our life is of a mingled yarn, good and ill together.' This remark, made by the second Lord in *All's Well*
(4.3.64) with reference to Bertram, holds true of a large number
of Shakespeare's characters and their actions. Plays as early as
Richard II and as late as *Coriolanus* exemplify it. And the response
which these characters and their actions elicit in the minds of
the audience is, in consequence, similarly mingled. But in the
case of our three Problem Plays one's experience is of a different
nature. It is not so much that our response to the protagonists
and their main actions is mixed, because of our awareness of
the tissue of good and evil in them, as that it is uncertain and
divided. Actions which one side of our minds approves of and
accepts, another side opposes and rejects. And it is the same
with regard to the characters who perform these actions. What
is frequently said about Shakespeare's tragic heroes, that their
main flaws are closely allied to their great virtues, does not here
seem to apply. Rather it may be said that what to one side of
our minds appears as their main flaws, to another side appears
as their great virtues. This seems particularly true of Antony,
but also applies to Brutus and Isabel. The completeness with
which Antony sacrifices all other ties and claims upon him to
his love for Cleopatra, the unswerving rigour with which
Brutus and Isabel sacrifice all personal loyalties to what they
regard as their higher loyalties, have been considered by some
critics as their deep flaws, by others as their singular virtues.

The image which these presentations suggest is not the web
woven of 'a mingled yarn, good and ill together', but rather the
toy which the Elizabethans called a 'perspective', presenting
two quite different pictures, according to our angle of vision.

This double vision and the divided, problematic response
which it evokes in our minds is, as we have seen, created by
Shakespeare through different means in each of the three plays.
In *Antony and Cleopatra* it is done most simply and emphatically,
through the constant juxtaposition of opposed evaluations of

184

the same actions and events (the play belongs, in a sense, to the *débat* tradition in literature). In *Measure for Measure* Shakespeare more indirectly and covertly questions Isabel's actions, chiefly by means of a series of parallels and contrasts drawn implicitly between her and Angelo. In *Julius Caesar* the double vision and problematic response is created principally through the series of contradictory images of Caesar presented throughout the first part of the play.

Shakespeare has been accused of an inclination to dodge moral problems. It seems to me that he neither dodges them nor brings them in at all costs. In plays where they would have interfered with his main purposes and designs he avoids them. In *Hamlet*, for example, where the problematic presentation of the protagonist's task of revenge, even if it had not been made to account for his delay and thus destroyed its mystery, would inevitably have shifted the focus of our attention from matters on which Shakespeare wished it to rest: on psychological rather than on moral problems, on the emotional experiences and contrasting actions of a variety of characters.

But when it suits his purposes Shakespeare does not hesitate to introduce moral problems, even in situations where they are absent in his sources. This is especially true of our three Problem Plays. In *Antony and Cleopatra* and *Measure for Measure*, as we have seen, the problematic presentation of the protagonist's acts of choice is not found in any of the plays' sources, but is entirely of Shakespeare's devising. In *Julius Caesar* he turns what in his sources is a divided and sometimes self-contradictory response to Caesar into a problematic presentation of the entire conspiracy.

I have singled out these three as Shakespeare's Problem Plays, and have argued that the term, as most usefully defined, fits them better than any other plays in the canon. But an acceptance of this view does not carry with it the corollary that they are first and foremost problem plays. I think in *Antony and Cleopatra* the problematic presentation of the love-relationship really does predominate over all the play's other concerns. But in *Measure for Measure* the problematic presentation of Isabel's choice seems only part of a larger concern with the nature of true justice, which does not leave us uncertain or divided. And in *Julius Caesar* the problematic presentation of the conspiracy seems subordinate to the play's concern with Brutus's tragic experiences. As has been emphasized in the Introduction, the term 'problem play' must not be thought of as an exclusive category, to be distinguished from tragedies, comedies, and histories. It merely describes a particular way in which moral problems are presented, and a certain centrality allotted to them, that is found in these plays. The attribution of the term to *Julius Caesar* and *Antony and Cleopatra* should not interfere with our continued classification of them among Shakespeare's Tragedies, as well as among his Roman Plays, just as *Measure for Measure* is not the less one of Shakespeare's Middle Comedies for being also one of his Problem Plays.

I hope the preceding chapters have shown that, when used in this limited and narrowly defined way, the term has considerable usefulness and brings out certain fundamental and significant points of kinship between the three plays discussed in these pages.

APPENDIX

Should *All's Well, Measure for Measure,* and *Troilus and Cressida* be grouped together?

THE grouping together of these three plays is one of the legacies of Victorian Shakespeare criticism. It is found as early as 1877 in Dowden's 'Shakespeare Primer',[1] where he makes them form a separate group among the Later Comedies. And it would seem, indeed, that it was Dowden who was chiefly responsible for imposing it upon the minds of later generations, so that it has become an almost unquestioned dogma that these three plays are to be classed and studied together. Dowden distinguished between their pre-dominant characteristics: they are, he says, 'three comedies, one earnest [*All's Well*], another dark and severe [*Measure for Measure*], the last, bitter and ironical [*Troilus and Cressida*]'. Later critics have devised various blanket terms to cover all three. Raleigh called them 'the later and darker Comedies'[2]; E. K. Chambers 'the three bitter and cynical pseudo-comedies'[3]; W. W. Lawrence 'the Problem Comedies'[4]; Dover Wilson 'the bitter comedies'[5]; Charlton 'the Dark Comedies'[6]; A. P. Rossiter 'the tragi-comedies'.[7]

Two trends in recent criticism have worked against the continued acceptance of this grouping: one is the growing recognition that the Folio compilers were right in placing *Troilus and Cressida* among the tragedies[8]; the other is the increasingly widespread feeling that there is nothing cynical or bitter or exceptionally dark about *All's Well* and *Measure for Measure*. But if *Troilus and Cressida* is not a comedy, if *All's Well* and *Measure for Measure* are not cynical or bitter or dark, what remains to justify their being grouped together? Are there,

---

[1] Pp. 53 and 57. It is also found in the Preface to the third edition of his *Shakespeare: His Mind and Art* (1897).

[2] *Shakespeare* (1907), p. 162.

[3] *Encyclopaedia Britannica*, 11th edition (1910), vol. 24, p. 785.

[4] *Shakespeare's Problem Comedies* (1931).

[5] *The Essential Shakespeare* (1932), p. 119.

[6] *Shakespearian Comedy* (1938), ch. 8.

[7] *Angel with Horns* (1961), pp. 116 ff.

[8] See above, p. 61, n. 1. Cf. also Brian Morris, 'The Tragic Structure of *Troilus and Cressida*', *Sh. Q.*, vol. 10 (1959), pp. 481 ff.

perhaps, other qualities which they have in common and which set them off from the rest of the canon?

'It is remarkable', writes F. S. Boas, 'that most of the plays which with more or less warrant may be assigned to the last three years of Elizabeth's reign, contain painful studies of the weakness, levity, and unbridled passion of young men. This is especially the case with *All's Well that Ends Well*, *Measure for Measure*, *Troilus and Cressida*, and *Hamlet*.'[1] Is it really illuminating to lump together Hamlet, Bertram, Troilus, and the Claudio of *Measure for Measure* as 'studies of the weakness, levity, and unbridled passion of young men'? And has not the Claudio of *Much Ado* or Proteus or Romeo as much a right to be among them? 'All these dramas', he continues, 'introduce us into highly artificial societies, whose civilization is ripe unto rottenness.' As ripe unto rottenness, we might ask, as that of the Athens of *Timon* or the Alexandria of *Antony and Cleopatra*? And does it really apply to *All's Well*? It seems to fit neither the scenes at the French court nor those at Florence or Rousillon.

'The striking and distinctive characteristics which differentiate the problem plays from other work in comedy, and set them apart by themselves,' writes W. W. Lawrence, 'arise from preoccupation with the darker sides of life, and a deeper and more serious probing of its mysteries, particularly those of sex. Intrigues drawn from romantic fiction are analyzed with unsparing realism, even though romance may still sometimes have its way. It is the mood of the tragedies, without the ultimate tragic issue.'[2] But are not these remarks at least as applicable to *The Winter's Tale* and to *Cymbeline* as they are to *All's Well*?

Much the fullest discussion of the various characteristics which are said to unite the three plays is provided by E. M. W. Tillyard[3] and A. P. Rossiter.[4] Tillyard, we remember, returned to Boas's grouping, which adds *Hamlet* to the three. He finds two large qualities and several detailed characteristics which the four plays have in common. The large qualities are: a concern 'throughout with either religious dogma or abstract speculation or both . . . felt rather more for their own and rather less for the drama's sake, as if, in this form at least, they were new and urgent in Shakespeare's mind, demanding at this point statement and articulation rather than solution and absorption into other material' (p. 3). I do not myself feel that in *Measure for Measure* and *Hamlet* they are 'less

---

[1] *Shakspere and his Predecessors* (1896), p. 345.
[2] *Op. cit.*, pp. 206-7.
[3] *Shakespeare's Problem Plays* (1951), pp. 3-9.
[4] *Op. cit.*, pp. 115-28. There is so much that I admire and strongly agree with in both these books that I feel sorry to have to be at odds with them in this matter.

completely absorbed into the general substance of these plays' than in *Lear* and *Macbeth*, which are at least as much concerned with religious dogma or abstract speculation. Our opinion here will depend very much on how we interpret these plays, on what we take to be their main preoccupations, and hence seems too subjective and elusive a criterion. Even less satisfying is Tillyard's other large quality: 'an acute interest in observing and recording the details of human nature' (p. 5). More acute, one wonders, in *All's Well* than in *Henry IV*?

Among the more detailed characteristics which Tillyard mentions, the two main ones are: (1) 'In each play, but in different degrees of importance, recurs the theme "a young man gets a shock" ' (p. 6). But is that as much true of the Claudio of *Measure for Measure* as of the Claudio of *Much Ado*? (2) 'Shakespeare's interest . . . in the old and new generations and in old and new habits of thought' (p. 9). This, Tillyard admits, is found only in two of his four plays, *All's Well* and *Troilus and Cressida* (though Peter Alexander has since declared it to be an important theme in *Hamlet*[1].) But it is central to *Lear* and plays a considerable part in *Antony and Cleopatra* (in the contrast between Antony and Caesar).

A. P. Rossiter again drops *Hamlet* from the group (while insisting, however, that the themes which the three plays have in common 'all have some echo or parallel in *Hamlet*'). It is worth noting that his list of characteristics seems to have nothing in common with Dr. Tillyard's. He mentions five chief points:

1. 'They share a common evaluation of conventionally accepted "nobilities": noble heroes in *Troilus and Cressida* . . .; Authority-in-ermine in *Measure for Measure*; a gentleman of family in *All's Well*. All are deflated; and with the deflation there runs concurrently the critical devaluation of man at large. . . .' But all this is found to an even more marked degree in *Lear* and *Timon*.

2. 'Interpolated into the critical-analytical patterns we find "ideal" figures who check our prattle of "cynicism", "satire" or "misanthropy" . . .' Much the same could be said of *Lear* (Cordelia, Kent) and *Timon* (Flavius).

3. '. . . these plays involve us in discoveries, always of a bad reality beneath the fair appearances of things: revelations, painful in the extreme—and we are *made to feel the pain*—of the distressing, disintegrating possibilities of human meanness. . . .'All this, again, fits *Lear* and *Timon* at least as well.

4. 'All the Problem Plays are profoundly concerned with seeming and being: and this can cover both sex and human worth . . . they

---

[1] *Hamlet, Father and Son* (1953).

share a quality which can be called *maskedness*. . . . This maskedness brings doubt, mixed feelings, an "edgy" curiosity, a kind of fear.' This seems much truer of *Hamlet*, *Lear*, *Timon* than of *All's Well* or *Troilus and Cressida*.

5. 'For a final shot at the overall qualities of the Problem Plays, I throw out the term *shiftingness*. All the firm points of view or *points d'appui* fail one, or are felt to be fallible. . . . Hence the "problem"-quality, and the ease with which any critic who takes a firm line is cancelled out by another. . . . Like Donne's love-poems, these plays throw opposed or contrary views into the mind: only to leave the resulting equations without any settled or soothing solutions.' This seems much truer of *Julius Caesar*, *Antony and Cleopatra*, *Henry IV*, and *Coriolanus* than of *Troilus and Cressida*. Of *All's Well* it does not seem to me to be true at all.

Of groupings based not on a community of subject-matter, such as Shakespeare's Roman Plays or his English History Plays, but on the supposed community of more elusive characteristics, such as theme and mood, the least we can ask is that more of these characteristics should be found in each member of the group than in any play outside it. I do not think that the grouping we have been considering meets this demand. Most of Rossiter's points, for instance, seem to fit *Lear* and *Timon* quite as well as any, and better than some, of the plays in his group.

To anyone coming to the study of Shakespeare with a fresh and unsullied mind the grouping of *Troilus and Cressida* with the two comedies must seem very strange and arbitrary.[1] To him the elements that unite that play with *Antony and Cleopatra*, for instance, must seem far more important, numerous, and obvious than those that unite it with *Measure for Measure*. *All's Well*, similarly, must seem to him to have far more links with *Cymbeline*, for example, than with *Troilus and Cressida*. *All's Well* and *Measure for Measure* are, of course, strongly linked, chiefly through the device of the 'bed-trick' and the closely similar handling of the *dénouement* in Act V. But even if two plays were enough to constitute a group, I do not feel at all confident that they have more elements of importance in common with each other than with any remaining play in the canon.

A grouping can be of great value when it helps to bring out common characteristics which shed light on each of its members.

---

[1] This has also been emphasized by Brian Morris, who speaks of 'an increasing uneasiness, a sense that the plays differ from each other perhaps more than from others of Shakespeare's plays, a feeling that in some way they have been forcibly and unequally yoked together. It has proved, in fact, impossible to find, or even invent, a term which can adequately define and cover three plays so different in subject and so diverse in effect' (*op. cit.*, p. 482).

(One of the aims of this book has, indeed, been to introduce a grouping of this kind.) But it can also cause much harm by fencing plays off from their kindred, exaggerating the supposed similarities between those inside the pale, and their supposed differences from those outside it. The grouping we have been looking at seems to be very much of this harmful kind, and ought, I strongly feel, to be abandoned.

INDEX

The more important or extensive references are indicated by figures in bold type. The names of translators and editors have not normally been indexed.

Index